THE
SELECT

ALSO BY HOWARD GREENE

Scaling the Ivy Wall (1987), with Robert Minton

Beyond the Ivy Wall (1989), with Robert Minton

Scaling the Ivy Wall in the '90s (1994), with Robert Minton

THE
SELECT

REALITIES OF

LIFE AND LEARNING IN

AMERICA'S ELITE COLLEGES

**Based on a Groundbreaking Survey
of More Than 4,000 Undergraduates**

Howard R. Greene, M.A., M.Ed.

Cliff Street Books
An Imprint of HarperCollinsPublishers

HarperCollins books may be purchased for educational, business, or sales promotional use. For information please write: Special Markets Department, HarperCollins Publishers, Inc., 10 East 53rd Street, New York, NY 10022.

FIRST EDITION

Designed by Kris Tobiassen

Library of Congress Cataloging-in-Publication Data

Greene, Howard, 1937–
    The select : realities of life and learning in America's elite colleges / Howard Greene. —1st ed.
      p. cm.
    Includes bibliographical references.
    ISBN 0-06-017815-9
    1. College students—United States. 2. Universities and colleges—Social aspects—United States. 3. Elite (Social sciences)—United States. I. Title.
LA229.G75   1998
378.1'98—dc21   98-19306

---

98 99 00 01 02 ❖/RRD 10 9 8 7 6 5 4 3 2 1

CONTENTS]

ACKNOWLEDGMENTS]

Like all authors who believe consummately in their project, I am indebted to my editor, Diane Reverand, for her vision in recognizing the importance of this book. I also owe a debt of gratitude to the Target Management team—David Morgan, Joyce Healey, and Jim O'Connor—without whom I could not have carried off the extraordinary research that lies at the heart of *The Select*. In the patience and support category, I express my deepest appreciation to my wife, Laurie Sheldon Greene.

PREFACE]

The Twenty Flagship Colleges and Universities

Private Sector
1. Brown University
2. Columbia University
3. Cornell University
4. Dartmouth College
5. Duke University
6. Georgetown University
7. Harvard University
8. Johns Hopkins University
9. Massachusetts Institute of Technology
10. Northwestern University
11. Princeton University
12. Stanford University
13. University of Chicago
14. University of Pennsylvania
15. Wesleyan University

16. Williams College
17. Yale University

Public Sector
1. University of California–Berkeley
2. University of North Carolina–Chapel Hill
3. University of Wisconsin–Madison

Twenty-College Survey Methodology

Through a series of carefully designed surveys of students at the leading colleges and universities, I assembled a detailed, statistically balanced portrait of each surveyed campus. I was ably assisted by a professional research group, Target Management of Wilton, Connecticut. To refine the process to its highest degree, we conducted focus groups during the preliminary phase of the questionnaire design. The questions were constructed after a wide range of topics and questions were discussed on an individual basis with over 100 undergraduates at many of the elite colleges and universities that were included in the study. Six focus groups were conducted at three different undergraduate campuses, each attended by seniors, juniors, sophomores, and freshmen, both men and women and students of color and Asian Americans.

The focus groups confirmed the appropriateness of the topics and the issues I raised on the basis of my many years of professional work in the admissions counseling field and interviews with individual students. The respondents' open and candid discussions in these sessions also helped narrow the field of potential topics and provide the necessary vocabulary and phraseology to eliminate any ambiguities for the students who ultimately participated in the actual survey.

In addition, during the preliminary stages of the project, I discussed both the issues revealed in the focus groups and the proposed on-campus research materials with academicians at several universities to elicit their opinions and suggestions regarding both content and methodology.

The detailed questionnaire then developed at Target Management utilized open- and close-ended questions and asked students to assign numerical ratings to their reactions to certain statements or to the priority that a particular issue held in their lives. The on-campus surveys at the twenty specially selected colleges and universities were carried out in late spring 1996 to gain the advantage of the full academic year's experience of all four classes of students.

Target Management's personnel went into the field with each institution's demographic breakdown in hand, the goal being to obtain a representative sample on each campus. Each college's demographic profile was obtained from the U.S. Department of Education's National Center for Education Statistics. The figures appeared in NCES's most recent report, *Integrated Post-Secondary Education Data Systems—Fall Enrollment Survey.* The surveys were personally distributed and supervised by the field personnel but were self-administered. The researchers remained on site at all times and were available if students had any questions or comments about the survey. The questionnaires were distributed at deliberately chosen sites on each campus, thereby ensuring representation of each class, gender, and ethnic group and a variety of disciplines and personal interests. Only questionnaires that students completed entirely were used in compiling the final data to ensure the validity of the findings.

The demographic profile of the sample actually surveyed from each school closely matched each college's published profile, verifying the strong "hands-on" approach of Target Management's field personnel. As a final step before the tabulations were published, the data was weighted according to the colleges' actual demographics, as reported by the U.S. Department of Education. The statistical model and the data programming for the weighting process was completed by ICR of Media, Pennsylvania, one of the leading market research firms in the country, and verified by an independent company.

Methodology

I. FOCUS GROUPS

Facilitators

David Morgan, President of Target Management
Howard Greene, President, Educational Consulting
Centers

II. SELECTION OF SCHOOLS FOR THE STUDY (TOTAL 20)

A. Ivy League (8)

1. Brown
2. Columbia
3. Cornell
4. Dartmouth
5. Harvard
6. Princeton
7. Pennsylvania
8. Yale

B. Private Colleges and Universities (9)

1. Duke
2. Georgetown
3. Johns Hopkins
4. Massachusetts Institute of Technology
5. Northwestern
6. Stanford
7. University of Chicago
8. Wesleyan
9. Williams

C. Public Universities (3)

1. University of California–Berkeley
2. University of North Carolina–Chapel Hill
3. University of Wisconsin–Madison

III. DATA COLLECTION

A. Collection Methodology

1. The researchers had personal contact with the respondents by distributing the questionnaires one by one, and when finished, the respondents handed their questionnaires back to the researchers.
2. Questionnaires were distributed at various locations around a campus and at different times of the day to

ensure a representative sample of the undergraduate
student body.

3. The researchers, dates, times, and places of data
collection are on file for each school.

IV. DATA COMPILATION

A. Sorted Questionnaires

1. Removed incomplete questionnaires that had two or more
blank pages.
2. Removed questionnaires that did not have the
demographic information regarding sex and class
completed.

B. Weighting

1. Broken down by
   a) school, by gender, by class, by ethnic group
   b) class, by gender, by ethnic group
   c) ethnic group, by gender
2. Obtained fall 1994 enrollment data from the U.S.
Department of Education, NCES, supplied by U.S.
Department of Education employee Samuel Barbett.
Source: *Integrated Post-Secondary Education Data Systems–1994
Fall Enrollment Survey*
3. ICR consultants attached weights to the demographic
breakdowns for each school.
4. ICR sent weight values for each school for each banner
point to the tabulating firm, Bolding Tab Service of Coral
Springs, Florida.
5. Bolding Tabulation Service produced tabulations with
weights attached for comparative purposes.

V. COMPLETED QUESTIONNAIRES

A. Totals—Tabulated: 3,711

1. Total males: 1,763
   a. White males: 1,096

  b. Males of color: 224
  c. Asian American males: 371
  d. Refused to classify: 72
2. Total females: 1,948
  a. White females: 1,222
  b. Females of color: 241
  c. Asian American females: 42
  d. Refused to classify: 64

INTRODUCTION
GETTING PAST THE HALO EFFECT]

What Is the Halo Effect?

A potent force is at work in the educational marketplace, one that will profoundly affect the best and brightest of our youths and the future leadership of our nation: It is the perpetuation of an elite class of colleges. We are in a culture that makes no apologies for attaining prestige and commercial success and thus have come to venerate this handful of time-honored institutions. Their graduates, we believe, out of all proportion to reality, are ensured lifelong fortune and maybe even fame. And so we are vulnerable to that extraordinary dynamic I call the "Halo Effect."

My thirty-three-year career in education includes counseling students at Harvard, working as an admissions officer and student adviser at Princeton, and consulting on educational planning with students and parents around the world. I have witnessed firsthand the pervasive and potentially damaging influence of the Halo Effect, from large universities like Harvard, Yale, and Cornell, to more undergraduate-oriented colleges like Williams and Dartmouth.

Repeatedly, I've been confronted by the assurance that admission to these lofty schools guarantees academic success, social happiness, access to the top graduate schools, and lifelong positions of leadership in any chosen endeavor.

Whenever my professional staff and I counsel one of the thousands of college-bound students we've been advising over the years, we ask both the students and their parents to complete questionnaires, which, among other things, reveal their attitudes toward the importance of institutional prestige when choosing a college. In virtually every case, both the student and the parents stress that importance. Later, when we talk, most will elaborate on just how much weight this factor imposes on their college search. Parents and students can be so eager to bathe in the halo's glow that they're blind to the inevitable tarnished reality it carries with it—even those colleges perceived as the most elite institutions are not problem-free, nor are they the right choice for everyone.

The purpose of this book is to provide prospective students and their families with a reality check—to get past the halo and see these colleges in a clearer light. As you will learn from firsthand accounts of some of the most accomplished of today's students, the land of ivy-covered colleges is not the Garden of Eden. I believe it is in the interest of both prospective students and their parents to step past their own dazzlement and learn the truths—good, bad, and challenging—about life at twenty of the most haloed higher educational institutions in America.

The Lure of the Halo

Parents speak reverently of their aspirations for their children's future security and well-being. It is vital to their sons and daughters to gain entrance to an Ivy League or comparably prestigious institution and become part of what I call the Select. These parents can recite like a mantra the names of the elite colleges—some 35 out of more than 3,500 colleges in America—for which they are willing to put both their emotional and financial security on the line. And talented students concur. To partake of the Halo Effect has become the ultimate goal of thousands of our most outstanding young scholars.

As early as the 1950s, eminent Harvard sociologist David Reisman studied the college environment and its impact on the student and society, describing higher education as the most significant American vehicle for economic and social mobility. In the subsequent forty years, Reisman's findings have proved accurate: An increasing number of immigrants, first-generation college-bound students from a mosaic of colors and ethnic groups, and socioeconomically disadvantaged students of nonminority backgrounds are knocking on the doors of our esteemed colleges for that same reason. A poignant personal description of this historic pattern comes from James Freedman, president emeritus of Dartmouth College, in his book, *Idealism and Liberal Education*:

> For my parents, the choice of the college I would attend was of pre-eminent concern. They understood that academic achievement was the vehicle to a prominent station in American life.

A scholarship student, Freedman graduated from Harvard in 1957 and attended Yale Law School. He served as dean of the University of Pennsylvania Law School and president of the University of Iowa before he accepted his recent leadership position at Dartmouth. A great many contemporary families of diverse economic or cultural backgrounds today wouldn't take issue with Freedman's parents' thinking. They want to follow in his footsteps—if not in academe, then in business, law, medicine, or science.

The desire to be, or to parent, a Select student grows more urgent every year. Because of a combination of factors in our educational system and our society, a state of virtual frenzy to "land the halo" affects consumers of higher education today. These factors include

- a work world in which no one feels secure in his or her position
- the acceleration of technical, scientific, and literate knowledge required to succeed in an increasingly competitive global economy
- the soaring costs of a college degree, which puts greater emphasis on getting one's money's worth

- the rising high school population and graduation rates in America
- the growing middle and professional classes, who seek a prestigious education for their children, which exacerbates the competition for admission to elite colleges

The thinking among high school students and their families as I hear it in my educational consulting goes something like this: The competition for the shrinking number of major positions in the corporate world, the legal profession, and other high-profile professions continues to intensify. The same is true in science: The competition for places in the medical and engineering-technical professions and other high-paying positions also continues to escalate. Therefore, I believe it is crucial for me—or my child—to have the best credentials and contacts to gain any possible advantage, which means getting into the best possible college.

Students and their families remain convinced that a degree from a Select college greatly enhances the odds of getting accepted to a medical, business, law, or engineering school, where the entrance gates shrink annually. For example, 47,000 people apply to medical school every year, at a time when both the government and the medical profession want to decrease the number of trained doctors. For many applicants, disappointment will not be the exception, but the rule.

Competing to Be Among the Select

More and more top students are competing for a fixed number of elite college placements. They feel it is worth it, despite skyrocketing tuition and living costs (close to $30,000 for the 1997–98 academic year). Families, in fact, will cite an institution's reputation as a far more significant factor than the price of tuition in determining their choice of a college. And to attain this dream, they are willing to make financial sacrifices, including the assumption of heavy educational loans and long-term debt.

Let's focus clearly on the situation by considering these statistics. Out of nearly 12.5 million college undergraduates, merely 47,500 are enrolled in the eight Ivy League colleges, while another 40,000 attend the nine other elite private colleges included in this study. This means that annually less than 5% of the total college population enters the 25 to 30 most selective private colleges. Of the 1.8 million high school seniors who take the Scholastic Assessment Test (SAT) each year, only some 30,000 score over 700 on the verbal section. About one-third of these students are enrolled in the ten most selective colleges, and 43% of these highest scorers enroll in the 30 most competitive colleges.

Ten major colleges—the eight Ivies, Stanford, and the Massachusetts Institute of Technology (MIT)—enroll only 1% of all undergraduates, yet their student bodies represent over 30% of the highest scorers on the SAT and top high school academic achievers. In 1996, all the institutions included in this study reported median SAT scores for their entering classes in the 1400 range (combined verbal and math); 85% to 90% of their students stood in the top 10% of their high school classes. Dartmouth, for example, has enrolled in its class of 2000 a number of students who attained a perfect score of 1600 on the SAT, while two hundred others had a perfect verbal or math score. At the same time, Dartmouth's applicant pool has increased by 41% in the past four years.

Dartmouth is not alone in the rise of applications. In 1955, Harvard College announced for the first time in its history and "with great reluctance" that it would require a ten-dollar application fee, to cover the costs of screening 4,000 applicants. By contrast, Harvard received 18,000 applications for the class of 2000, which would be comprised only of 1,600 superbly qualified young men and women. Of the candidates, 2,900 were high school class valedictorians, and nearly 9,500 aspirants had combined SAT scores of 1400 or higher. Incidentally, the price of applying to an elite college is now sixty dollars.

Such standardized test results are doubly impressive, since they were achieved at a time when the results of high school college entrance exams are at an all-time low. Over 11% of the students who took the SAT in 1972 achieved a verbal score over 600; by the mid–80s, this number had dropped to under 7%, where it has remained. In fact, in 1994 the College Board was forced to change its scoring midpoint to 500 on the verbal and math SATs because the median score had dropped some 90 points. Parents increasingly will spend considerable sums and their children intensive hours of tutoring for the exams in the hope of qualifying for the elite colleges.

As recently as the early 1960s, the median SAT scores for students who were admitted to the Ivy League colleges was a combined 1100 range. At that time, the competition for admission and the level of selectivity were significantly less than today; then, an average of two out of every three applicants were accepted. For example, in 1960 Stanford received 6,500 applications for 1,550 places in its freshmen class (twice this number would normally be admitted to meet the targeted enrollment, since some students would decide to attend elsewhere). In the spring of 1996, Stanford was inundated with more than 15,000 applications for the same 3,100 places! Moreover, the candidates' qualifications, as measured by entrance test scores, class ranking, and advanced-level courses, were much higher. This pattern is found at all twenty of the selective colleges I have included in this book. The eight Ivies alone received over 120,000 applications for the class that will graduate in the year 2000. Only 24% of that highly talented group was offered admission. Applications to the other elite colleges in the study bring the total number of candidates seeking a Select place to more than 200,000.

Winner Take All?

A major segment of the brightest high school seniors is applying to the smallest and most exclusive sector of the world's largest higher education system every year. As the baby boomers' children come of age, the number of high school students seeking entrance to the top colleges will only increase, and competition for the limited number of places will get tougher. As far as anyone can tell, this rising demand will allow college costs to continue escalating—owing to the Halo Effect. More and more students will be competing for a limited resource. More and more will fail.

In their intriguing book, *The Winner Take All Society*, Robert Frank and Philip Cook, who teach at Cornell and Duke universities, respectively, describe what they see as the mentality by which our culture is driven. In a winner-take-all environment, a greater number of individuals compete for a small, constant number of prizes or rewards. Those who win, win big, while the rest of the competition falls further behind in status and financial success. A phenomenon in the economic marketplace has spread to the educational community, where a small number of colleges and universities are perceived as the ultimate prize—the perception being that they award the greatest status to the winner and thus the greatest chance to control one's destiny.

As *The Winner Take All Society* states:

> Students are remarkably sophisticated about these matters. If access to the top jobs depends more and more on educational credentials, we would expect them to do everything in their power to improve their credentials and indeed they have. Education's growing role as gatekeeper has given rise to increasingly intense competition for admission into the nation's leading colleges and universities. Whereas it was once common for the brightest high school students to attend state universities close to home, increasingly they matriculate at a small handful of the most selective private institutions of higher learning.

What is the significance of a college degree today? The U.S. Department of Labor, which follows the relationship between education and income, estimates that a college graduate with a bachelor's degree will earn $600,000 more than a high school graduate over a working lifetime. An advanced degree will bring an additional $800,000, while a professional graduate degree in law, medicine, or business will result in an additional $1.3 million.

If such numbers are exceeded by graduates of the elite colleges, who—I presume—have greater access to the best graduate schools and top career tracks, then these numbers rise even higher. In 1996 *Forbes* magazine[*] surveyed 800 of America's most highly paid chief executive officers with a median annual income of $1.5 million. Of this group, 174 completed their undergraduate studies at one of the twenty colleges included in this study. The undergraduate colleges

---

[*]"The People at the Top of Corporate America," *Forbes*, May 20, 1996, pp. 192–229.

with the greatest number of CEOs were Harvard, Cornell, Princeton, and Stanford. If we include those CEOs who received their professional graduate degrees from one of the twenty institutions, 45% of the nation's highest paid executives hold degrees from the select twenty. Since the public tends not to differentiate between undergraduate and graduate schools when noting the educational backgrounds of the rich and powerful, the intensity of the Halo Effect is consequently expanded.

America has a significantly broad and diverse number of colleges that provide excellent educational experience, but not the ultimate degree of prestige. Thanks to the Halo Effect, a disproportionate number of high school seniors apply to the Select. In this system, the weak get weaker, while the strong get stronger. Anyone engaged professionally in college counseling and admissions will attest to the growing split between the "haves" and the "have-nots" among the 3,500 colleges, public and private, in the United States. The greater number of have-nots struggle continuously to fill their placements, with standards for admission either static or evidencing a steady decline. Private colleges try with aggressive marketing and tuition discounting to attract the better students to their ranks.

The Rise of the "Cognitive Elite"

In *The Bell Curve*—a controversial study of differences in intelligence among different racial and ethnic groups and their significance for both the individual and society at large—Richard Herrnstein and Charles Murray describe the evolution of what they call a "cognitive elite," which has gained advancement and power in America because it obtained the best possible education. We may not agree with all Herrnstein and Murray's theories of intelligence, but we should note that the authors do reveal an increasingly prevalent truth: Education creates the American prime class. As the majority of high school graduates move on to higher education, class stratification, based on both the level and quality of education achieved, does become pronounced. Highly ambitious people don't believe in merely furthering their education after high school; they deem it crucial to attain the most prestigious degrees. The concentration of the brightest young adults in a small cluster of colleges has become a fact of life.

Getting a college education has become a goal for more and more Americans because of a number of factors: the G.I. Bill at the end of World War II; the Great Society legislation of the 1960s, which aimed to provide access to college to every motivated citizen; and the present emphasis on affirmative action and enhancing campus diversity. In 1995, more than 1.1 million individuals received bachelor's degrees—a rise of 15% in only five years. Although this extraordinary development seems in keeping with American democratic principles, more degrees can mean greater exclusivity and status in the marketplace for the small band of 20,000 people who graduate each year from the Select.

Here is a small sampling of the finely screened population that makes up the elite group: Of the ninety-five intellectually outstanding undergraduates who were awarded fellowships for graduate study in the humanities by the Woodrow Wilson National Fellowship Foundation in 1996, fifty-three attended one of seventeen elite colleges in our survey. Other prestigious awards, such as the Rhodes, Marshall, Reynolds, and Churchill scholarships, go to a disproportionate number of elite college alumni. A rising socioeconomic elitist class is the most glaring result of this concentrated movement toward the educational apex.

About *The Select*

How healthy is this relentless push toward the top? Is it good for an eighteen-year-old to embark on a course of cut-throat competition? What are the costs to the individual and the institution? Bill Bender, the first administrator at Harvard with the actual title of director of admissions, oversaw a period of extensive growth and selectivity in his school's admissions. He expressed his concern as early as 1960 "that Harvard could become such an intellectual hothouse that the unfortunate aspects of a self-conscious 'intellectualism' would become dominant and the precious, the brittle, and the neurotic take over." In other words, would being part of a superelite group in a rarefied atmosphere be beneficial for the healthy development of the ablest 18- to 22-year-olds, or would it provide a warped and narrow worldview, ill preparing them for life beyond academia?

This book aims to answer these questions. It is not a guide to becoming one of the Select; I have already written about the college entrance process in my book *Scaling the Ivy Wall in the '90s*. *The Select* takes high school students and their families inside the gates of the elite colleges to familiarize them with facts, attitudes, statistics, and stories about real life in twenty excellent institutions. These major campuses are the eight members of the so-called Ivy League—Brown, Columbia, Cornell, Dartmouth, Harvard, Pennsylvania, Princeton, and Yale—plus Duke, Georgetown, Johns Hopkins, MIT, Northwestern, Stanford, the University of Chicago, Wesleyan, and Williams, as well as three of the nation's preeminent public institutions: the universities of California at Berkeley, North Carolina at Chapel Hill, and Wisconsin at Madison.

These twenty represent the majority of the most selective undergraduate colleges in the country. They are the flagship schools. Their reputation is such that, together with another twenty or so esteemed colleges, they set the general standard for academic programs, campus environments, affirmative action, and financial aid.

I can anticipate grievances by some educators and loyal alumni of many other great colleges and universities because their institution was not included in this project. The simple explanation is that it was necessary to set a numerical limit to make the data and the in-depth student interviews manageable and comprehensive. Another cluster of twenty or more selective institutions with comparably talented student bodies could easily be substituted for those that have been included; perhaps they will be in the next phase of my continuing effort to take the pulse of each generation of collegians.

The survey that forms the centerpiece of *The Select* is based on my several hundred personal interviews with college students and the statistical analysis of 3,711 questionnaires completed on campus by present undergraduates. The result is a comprehensive picture of the academic and social realities lived by today's Select students—how they manage their academic workloads, socialize, deal with their financial burdens, cope with campus realities, and construct their emotional lives and how their characters, goals, and ambitions change over four years at an elite college. I believe strongly that the findings of this survey reflect the experiences of students at other elite institutions nationwide. Undergraduates are enduring intense academic pressures even as they struggle to negotiate the ever more complex social and political territory that is the campus of today. In a landmark study of undergraduates, based on a much broader spectrum of colleges and universities, Ernest Boyer, the former president of the Carnegie Foundation, reports on the "disturbing realities of student life" that threaten not only the fabric of higher learning but, indeed, may be undermining the sense of community in the United States as a whole. Boyer's study, *Campus Life: In Search of Community* (Princeton University Press, 1990) discusses the rising alcohol abuse, campus crime, breakdown of social civility, fragmentation of the student population, and "an unhealthy separation between in-class and out-of-class activities." These are issues that, as you will see, Select students are dealing with while carving out healthy and productive places in their own educational communities. The dynamics of contemporary college life may come as a shock, however, because of the Halo Effect created by the colleges' prestigious reputations. This is one of the themes of *The Select*.

These are the issues with which contemporary collegians are concerned:

- personal safety, both inside and outside the campus walls
- alcohol and drug abuse and their impact on the academic community
- the cost of attending college and policies toward scholarship holders
- financial stress brought on by educational loans, plus too many hours spent working to earn tuition
- the lack of a structured, directive curricular plan
- teachers caught up in their own career advancement, who, in many instances, espouse their own political agenda
- the intense academic workload and competition to excel among one's fellow students
- the pressure to prepare for professional graduate school

- the activism of a racial, ethnic, political, and social mix of students unimaginable twenty-five years ago
- living arrangements based on sexual, racial, and ethnic preferences

The high school students I counsel tell me repeatedly of their strong desire to attend a college with a diverse community of students and faculty, to enjoy greater personal freedom and exposure to all kinds of people and ideas. I find that the more intelligent and achievement-oriented students, in particular, make these their major criteria in choosing colleges. Nevertheless, many find a vastly different environment than they had anticipated when they arrive on campus and encounter a socially and intellectually complex social organism.

Charles Eliot, the innovative president of Harvard University in the early years of this century, proclaimed that if he was free to found a new university, he would first build a dormitory, then a library filled with books; only if money was remaining would he then hire a faculty and build classrooms. Eliot's point was that the most important part of a young adult's learning experience is living away from home and being exposed to a broad range of personal beliefs, attitudes, and backgrounds. Of course, even Eliot would be stunned by the extent of the varied attitudes and backgrounds in his formerly small, male, white, Christian, private-school-educated, New England–dominated institution. The most significant impact on a student's thinking and development during his or her undergraduate life is the peer group that he or she encounters. The factors that entice an outstanding student to choose a particular selective college—from the prestige factor to academic programs to special resources—turn out to be less critical to his or her development. The importance of the student body is made dramatically clear in the responses of the students I surveyed. If it is true that we are moving rapidly toward an intellectual elitist class that dominates our social, political, and economic organizations—and, certainly, there is ample evidence to support this view—then it is even more important for us to understand how students at the most selective colleges think and what they feel about their experiences. The reader is likely to be surprised by many of the concerns and reactions of these students.

I have two hopes for *The Select*. The first is that elite-college aspirants and their families will now be able to choose colleges based on facts, not exaggerated reputations. I also hope that the colleges themselves—from the faculty to administrators to alumni who have a say in the direction of their colleges—will see this book as a mirror. They can learn much from what their most important constituency—the cream of the student crop—have to say about how they live and learn on campus and the implications for their future role in society.

I am proud of the honesty these Select students exhibited when they answered my survey. The students showed an admirable willingness to share their personal reasons for enrolling in their chosen colleges, along with their worries, pain, joys, and hopes. Their responses make it clear that the majority care about service to their communities and personal fulfillment after graduation; they do not merely engage in what F. Scott Fitzgerald called "the fear of poverty and the worship of success," which he believed characterized his generation some eighty years ago. Certainly, paying for the high price of their education and attaining some level of security influences the students' direction in life, but the students also believe that they are embarking on an intellectual and spiritual quest. I admire that belief. Their forthrightness and intelligence are tributes both to them and to the institutions that chose to admit them. It is to this wonderful group of young men and women that I dedicate this effort.

ONE
The Select Speak Out:
THE MAJOR FINDINGS

Long after midnight the towers and spires of Princeton were visible, with here and there a late-burning light—and suddenly out of the clear darkness the sound of bells. As an endless dream it went on; the spirit of the past brooding over a new generation, the chosen youth from the muddled, unchastened world. . . . Here was a new generation, shouting the old cries, learning the old creeds, through a revery of long days and nights; destined finally to go out into that dirty gray turmoil to follow love and pride; a new generation dedicated more than the last to the fear of poverty and the worship of success. . . .

—F. SCOTT FITZGERALD, *THIS SIDE OF PARADISE* (1920)

The Truth About Elite Students

Few images in our culture evoke such an idealization of student life as a historic, ivy-laden, elite college campus. The young men and women who people it seem so fortunate, so free—liberated for the first time from parental controls and the home environment, amid a multifaceted and multitalented student body, primed to explore new intellectual and social terrain without the constraints of a career or family. How confident they must feel about their futures and the infinite opportunities that await them. What could distress these gifted students as they mature into physical vigor and impressive mental powers?

Like all myths that people create in their constant search for a new Jerusalem, there has never been a great deal of truth to the romanticizing of the college experience. In the era of F. Scott Fitzgerald and every decade since, Select students have wrestled with academic work, making friends, fitting into the community, paying tuition, and preparing for life after graduation. Nevertheless, it should be obvious to anyone who has even a minimal interest in the subject that extraordinary changes have taken place in America's colleges and universities over the past three decades that make earlier periods seem positively idyllic. What were once bastions of social elitism run by and for white, Protestant, upper- and middle-class men—with a smaller number of parallel institutions for women—have become micromodels of our society at large.

Once the most prestigious colleges in America were defined largely by the social composition of their student bodies. Today they earn their reputation for the selectivity of their admissions; the academic richness and demands of their curricula; the reputation of their faculty; and the range of ethnic, racial, socioeconomic, intellectual, social, and political attitudes represented in their student bodies and instructors. As a result, these elite campuses are complex places that offer Select students both opportunities and difficult challenges unlike any they have faced. This Dartmouth sophomore male spoke for elite-college students everywhere:

66 Coming to Dartmouth, I was confident that I would excel as I had in high school. There are so many things—academic, social, extracurricular—to try out that I feel as if I am still adjusting and have not found my comfortable niche yet. Due to Dartmouth's fast-moving academic atmosphere, I feel like I am always making important decisions and opening

(or closing) new options for myself. After four years here I am certain I will be very independent and well-rounded and ready to do something with my life, but for now I will go on struggling, testing, and trying new things. 🙶

This woman, on the verge of graduating from Stanford, saw much more than ivy and complacent, easy learning on the campus she called "the farm":

🙶 I have loved my time at Stanford. There are so many resources here that one cannot begin to fathom all of them. The past, the present, and future all merge somehow here on the Farm. I am glad my time is up, but I would sign up for this ride if I had to do it all over again. There is more to Stanford than pre-med, pre-law, and pre-business people. 🙶

Beginning in the late 1960s and accelerating into the 1990s, the policy of selective colleges has been to create a well-rounded class comprised of a full spectrum of student types and talents. A system of meritocracy—the Jeffersonian dream of opportunity based on talent and industry—supplanted the earlier eras of first a theocratic and then a social elite. Gone from the campus scene are a majority of socially adept, well-rounded individuals who did a number of things reasonably well. The more prestigious the institution, the more it has molded a student body of uniquely talented young men and women, each of whom was chosen from a large pool of exceptionally well-qualified candidates. These are the Select, the aristocracy of academic achievers.

The earlier breed of well-rounded multitalented college men and women has been supplanted by leaders in smaller spheres whose special interests and abilities have been honed to a fine edge. What was once a relatively sanguine transition from home to college residence has become, in many ways, a rude awakening. In my survey of the Select, the academic adventurers who choose to test their mettle in the arena of highly competitive and talented achievers told a story of accomplishment, difficulty, fulfillment, and challenge.

A Road with Challenges

When many of the students I interviewed handed back the questionnaires about their lives as Select college students, they said they were impressed with the breadth of the questions. Answering my queries, they felt a sense of having journeyed through the emotions and intellectual attitudes they developed toward their colleges. I was glad to have given them the chance to reflect on their odysseys. Even if they don't have a college consultant like me asking them questions, I hope all the Select students will give themselves the chance to reflect on their lives in college—and I hope that they all achieve the kind of equanimity exhibited by this young man, a senior at Duke University:

> College has been an excellent experience. I am glad I picked Duke, an academically underrated school, over Princeton and Penn. While I think the "work hard/play hard" days are over due to the administration, which wants to play down the power of the Greek system and other social functions, the school's wonderfully accessible faculty, and its school spirit, among other factors, will remain. My social life is excellent (lots of dating), and I feel I have learned what it is to enjoy academics.

One of the most widely read books on college campuses over a number of years has been psychiatrist M. Scott Peck's profound volume of self-identity and personal seeking, *The Road Less Traveled.* In a real sense, students at America's elite colleges have taken a road less traveled by the majority of young adults—and not just because they won admission to the country's most selective schools. It comes as little or no surprise that they should identify with some of the major life challenges that Peck identifies in his book: the loneliness, pain, depression, anxiety, fear of failure, and the shock of new experiences encountered by those who aim to live extraordinary lives. Every day, Select students confront startling and discomfiting concepts that can challenge their religious beliefs, intellectual precepts, sexual codes, and personal ethics—all the facets that make up the essence of a collegian's character and the nature of the accomplishments that led them to their elite colleges in the first place.

Consider the specific factors or stressors that are at the core of student life in a highly competitive college environment: tests, final exams, grades, time demands, selection of a major, decisions about graduate school and a career, the fostering of intimate relationships, financial worries and concerns over debt, holding a job, physical safety, sleep deprivation, parental expectations of success, and the often-unnerving pressure that students feel to conform to other students' behavior. At all twenty colleges featured in *The Select*—as well as hundreds of other demanding schools—students need smarts, adaptability, emotional intelligence and resilience, parental support, a good perspective, and a measure of luck if they are going to flourish.

Responding to my survey, a Princeton junior shared both his feeling of pride in his institution and his belief in what it takes to succeed in the elite school environment. I found that a great many Select students had similar feelings about their colleges.

> It is my opinion that Princeton is the best undergraduate institution in the U.S. People work extremely hard in every aspect of their lives here, which is why Princeton has the academic reputation, the excellent sports teams, and active life that it does. I sometimes feel burned out, but I also feel I am challenging myself in many ways and growing as a person.

I frankly like the tinge of hubris in the attitude of both of the Princeton and Duke students toward their respective schools. With the right attitude and a willingness to work, a student at any of the highly selective colleges can achieve the kind of satisfaction and multilevel engagement that these students display.

As I began to analyze the immense amount of data I collected from the more than 4,000 students who responded to my questionnaire, I saw several significant patterns emerge. This talented, selective pool of individuals shares virtually the same goals, ambitions, and reasons for enrolling in their respective institutions. At the same time, their specific attitudes and needs differed, depending on their sex, race, and socioeconomic background. These differences are compelling. What the students told me about their lives and education are concerns that colleges must respond to. And college students themselves need to be aware of them. So should their parents, to understand what is happening to their children. Prospective enrollees who can integrate the real experiences of actual students into their expectations about the lives they will lead among the Select are likely to cope more successfully with the many issues that await them.

The Prestige Factor in Practice

Prestige, name recognition, and specific academic programs are the driving forces that led these top high school students to enroll in the elite colleges I surveyed. Of the students I questioned, 72% indicated that prestige and name recognition influenced their decisions to choose their colleges, and 74% cited the availability of specific academic offerings.

In the introduction to this book, I discussed the potent role that repetition and prestige play in the selection of a college. Regarding academic programs, the thousands of Select high school students I have counseled declare, with varying degrees of confidence, the particular fields of academic concentration they intend to pursue. Even before they apply, they investigate the programs that may interest them at each college, whether it's the Woodrow Wilson School of Public Affairs at Princeton or the premed program at Johns Hopkins. However, once they actually enroll and are exposed to the extraordinary variety of disciplines that elite institutions offer, the majority of students change their interests and goals.

Ironically, only 18% of the students I surveyed cited reputation as an important element now that they are securely established on campus. During the evolution that occurs over four years of college, the external value assigned to a college has diminished for them.

Even if undergraduates don't care much about their schools' cachet, many high school students are still driven by the prestige factor. Today, they make important decisions regarding their choice of college less influenced by traditional advisers—namely guidance counselors, educators, and even their parents. In fact, only a small number of the college students I surveyed were influenced by guidance counselors or teachers, their families, or even their peers. Even if they were indirectly swayed by others' opinions, the majority believe that they chose their own colleges. Only the Asian American students gave meaningful weight to the overt influence of their parents and peers in choosing their colleges.

College-bound students often rely on the many printed guidebooks and magazines that rank colleges through various forms of data manipulation, some of them highly questionable. Many now use the Internet to accumulate more information than they can possibly assimilate. When I talk to parents, they frequently express anxiety and guilt over their lack of expertise regarding the college admissions process and confusion about how best to help their children make the appropriate choices. They, too, rely heavily on the same sources of information as do their sons and daughters, most of it weighted to reputation and image. As a result, both parents and students often rely on the name and recognition element of a college instead of focusing on other critical factors like affordability and the appropriateness of the college for the particular student.

Academics and Ambitions

Many alumni who attended college a generation ago have warm memories of an active campus filled with dating, athletic events, and rewarding extracurricular programs. The present attitude toward the importance of extracurricular offerings is quite different, however. Fewer than 16% of the students I surveyed chose their colleges for the social life, athletic teams, preprofessional societies, fraternities, or artistic programs. This finding is ironic, since the admissions committees took into account their outstanding talents and contributions outside the classroom.

The majority of the students I surveyed remarked on the heavy demands of academics, and for many, of on-campus employment—both of which can make virtually impossible their participation in the very things that helped make them attractive as applicants.

The fabled "gentleman C" student—enjoying campus life with minimal worries about who pays the tuition bill or what he must do to achieve a top grade point average for graduate school admission—is now merely a distant memory. When I arrived on the Princeton campus as an admissions officer in the 1960s, I encountered many young men (the university had not yet begun to admit women) who proudly described themselves as "Princeton Charlies," casual learners and serious social hounds. Why did they need to worry about grades when the connections they formed through athletic teams, eating clubs, and campus organizations—not to mention their Ivy League diplomas—would lead them to jobs in the business or industry of their choosing? Many Charlies were products of old-line prep schools, and quite a few were legacies—sons of alumni.

Then in the late 1960s, the baby-boom generation, with its huge number of competitive students, changed academics forever. The applicant pool doubled and then tripled, while the number of available spaces in the entering classes remained virtually the same. Women arrived to accelerate the intensity of the competition for entry. The elite colleges began actively seeking more of the public school graduates who had excelled in a larger and more independent environment. Thus began the intense race for college admissions and the profoundly competitive atmosphere on campus that we witness today. The present population boom has only exacerbated that competition.

A contemporary junior male at Princeton described a campus environment that earlier generations of devoted alumni would scarcely recognize:

> I think the workload is extremely intense, but you adjust to it over time. The social life leaves a lot to be desired. Everyone here thinks about only one person, me, myself, and I. People have big egos when it comes to academic issues and especially when thinking about future jobs.

Only a fourth of the collegians I surveyed cited the availability of intellectual opportunities as the best feature of their colleges. Yet in conversations with thousands of high school students over the years, I have heard such opportunities referred to as major sources of appeal. I find that undergraduates take the great resources of their colleges for granted, choosing to focus on the other concerns I report in this book.

A particular gripe of many students at less endowed institutions is the dearth of academic majors or course and faculty depth of many departments. This is certainly not the case with our cluster of well-financed elitist colleges. I cannot count how many times I heard Select students lament that they could not start their college careers over and take all the fabulous courses they missed.

The Asian American students and students of color revealed different experiences on several important issues, especially academics. The overall Asian American responses to what they like best about their colleges demonstrates the higher value they place on academic resources and scholastic intensity. I was also struck by the high level of expectations for academic success and preparation for graduate school that many of their families express. These expectations can explain Asian American students' distinctive responses to other campus issues. Several young Asian American men and women described to me the pressure they feel to do well in their studies. Consequently, they tend to focus more on the academic components of their colleges than on the social or extracurricular aspects. I am not comfortable with generalizations that lead to stereotyping an entire ethnic group, but the responses to the survey questions do point out some of these priorities.

I frequently advise parents that one of the most difficult points in the college journey for many students comes in the second year, when they have to choose an academic concentration. Sophomore year can be a particularly difficult time, even for individuals who cruised through the challenges of their freshman year. In the minds of many of the Select, choosing a major triggers a chain reaction of questions regarding their future careers. At this point in the academic journey, many students lose confidence because of their average or poor performance in the disciplines they had intended to pursue or simply because they are no longer interested in their original fields of study. Subsequently, they often feel vulnerable and directionless. A Harvard sophomore spoke for the majority of undergraduates at the elite colleges with this perception:

> Harvard is a great vehicle for those who seek to go on to law, business, or medical school or to pursue their passions in graduate school. It is somewhat awful for those who have not decided what they

want to pursue in college or after college life. There is intense pressure put upon one's interests and goals in both academic and extracurricular areas. 99

Students' worries vary over both time and gender. During their four years of college, the women's concern about making it in the outside world declined steadily. Only 39% (from an initial high of over 60%) of the senior-year women focused on this factor, while other issues became more important to them. For example, the social atmosphere and style of the college was extremely to very important to 64% of the women surveyed. The emphasis that a majority of women placed on achieving a balance between their academic and social lives was nicely expressed by this junior woman at Stanford:

66 I think Stanford is the perfect balance of work and fun and, most of all, is adaptable to everyone. The academic work is challenging but never cutthroat. There is an overall relaxed atmosphere. The social life is wonderful; it offers such a variety. 99

In the Select survey, almost half the students polled were concerned with preparing for graduate school. A greater number of minority students indicated that their prospects for getting into graduate school determined which of the elite colleges they chose to attend. In fact, the minority students most strongly expressed their concern for establishing top academic credentials to secure a future of economic and social independence. They perceived that society had discriminated against them in the past and would do so again.

Among Select students, the preoccupation with graduate school and careers can alter the very nature of their college experience. One Yale senior described what she saw as the attitude of the majority of her classmates:

66 People are sometimes too concerned with grades and further career to enjoy the company of other students. Yale is relatively intellectual, but most students are less concerned about learning for learning's sake than they are about graduate schools and their careers. 99

I see the preoccupation with postcollegiate ambitions as further testimony to the view that education is the best possible pathway to economic and social advancement. College admissions deans increasingly refer to prospective students and their parents as "consumers of education." More and more, the higher-education agenda of parents and their children has more to do with chances for admission to and preparation for graduate schools than with the inherent value of the collegiate experience. I share the apprehension of educators who see students using their liberal arts training more as a vocational stepping stone than an opportunity to explore the ideas and ideals that are the basis of the society in which they live and which they will lead.

College Life Among the Select

What is the most positive college element for the majority of students? By far it is their peer group, the people they live and learn with. More than a third of all the undergraduates told me that the best feature of their college was the other students. The dynamic of bright and talented individuals being drawn to one another makes for an environment that is socially and intellectually challenging, engaging, and fun.

Women responded positively to this factor at a higher rate than men of all backgrounds. However, their positive attitude declined from 48% in their freshman year to 32% by the spring of their senior year. Women seem to be especially prone to a high level of disenchantment and possibly lack of interest during the four years of college. They become increasingly less engaged in campus life during this period; their participation in campus activities declines steadily, signaling a change in their attitude toward their environment.

One senior presented a scenario of her journey through Harvard that was similar to the scenario of a great many other women I interviewed on a number of the elite campuses:

> We have unlimited resources available to us and excellent faculty and students as well. The only thing that diminishes the quality of edu-

cation here is the lack of support students receive, both academically and, to a lesser degree, socially. Harvard is the ideal institution for the person who has fully matured before attending college, one who knows what he or she wants to do in life and has all the answers figured out. If you don't know exactly where you are going, then you feel you are left to fend for yourself. You stumble through freshman and sophomore years, and maybe by junior year you will have learned from your mistakes and been able to take full advantage of all the social and academic opportunities available to you.

In my overall findings, Select women are more concerned than men about the ethos of their campus and the mix of social and academic opportunities and attitudes that characterize their environment. Yet men care about life outside the classroom as well: More than half the students indicated that the social atmosphere was a factor in choosing their colleges. Once on campus, the particular dynamics of the social scene become even more important to them.

There are other interesting differences between how men and women rate various factors of their college experience. Geographic location mattered to 54% of the women and 44% of the men. As you will hear from students in subsequent chapters, these are the factors that concern them:

- crime and safety, both on the campus and in the adjacent neighborhoods
- students' attitudes toward one another
- opportunities for a diverse social life
- the quality of living accommodations
- the quality and choice of food

The students of color placed a higher value on social and political activities than the other students. Many were engaged in community service and action groups while in high school. Responding to my questionnaire, several Hispanic and African American students described the pressure from others on campus to join various social or political groups that are involved in advancing their place in the community. They also talked about the weight of the expectations to succeed from their families and home communities and how it affects their relationships with their fellow undergraduates. This excerpt from *A Darker Shade of Crimson*, by Ruben Navarrette, Jr., gives a firsthand understanding of what it feels like to carry your entire community on your shoulders as a minority student at a place like Harvard.

> A shared ethnicity provided a link between [his Chicano San Joaquin Valley neighbors] and me, allowing them to share in my accomplishments. My father understood much better than me, claiming that those who would approach him in the years to come and routinely ask about my progress somehow "claimed a piece" of me. They owned a part of any success that I might enjoy, my father explained. Not until much later would I appreciate fully, and eventually even resent, the weight of their claims.

Diversity Among the Select

A dramatic difference between the nonminority and minority students is reflected in the importance of racial and ethnic diversity when deciding where to enroll. Only 14% of the nonminority undergraduates said that diversity was a concern for them, while 41% of the students of color and 35% of the Asian Americans indicated that this was an extremely or very important factor. In Chapter 5, I explore the fallout from this dichotomy—as reflected in the opinions of a number of students on sensitive issues like segregated housing, university-sponsored ethnic and racial organizations, and special-interest studies.

We can be certain that the tensions surrounding racial and ethnic differences will not disappear in the foreseeable future. Talented minority high school students, having heard about the many divisive, racially driven incidents occurring in recent years on college campuses, are compelled to weight the diversity factor more heavily than their white counterparts.

Paying for It

In the 1970s, one Ivy League president created a homespun formula for measuring the constantly rising tuition at the elite private colleges. He compared the cost of a year of college to the much higher price of a mid-sized Chevrolet—demonstrating that higher education was a relative bargain. This piece of sophistry was referred to for years throughout academic circles as a benchmark for measuring the cost-benefit ratio of a college education. Try using this formula today, when total annual college costs can exceed the price of a Mercedes-Benz.

The soaring expense of a four-year education at a high-quality college is a fact of life that is recognized by every parent of a college-bound child. The inexorable increases that average 5% to 8% annually after jumps of as much as 18% in the 1980s have most families reeling under the financial burden. A recent study by the government's General Accounting Office indicated that the cost of a private college education as a percentage of an average family's income has risen from 21% to 39% from 1991 to 1996. For public institutions, the study found a rise from 9% to 15% in the same period. It is no surprise that there has been a parallel increase in the volume of federal loans for higher education of 435%, with the average student loan growing from $518 to over $2,000 per year.

The affordability gap continues to accelerate. Present and future undergraduates are expected to shoulder a greater part of their educational expenses than did their predecessors. This Cornell freshman expressed the frustration and worry about finances shared by many of his fellow Select undergraduates:

> 66 The university really doesn't give a hoot about students who must finance their own education. I struggle with managing my own finances while I am denied help beyond the bare minimum because they assume that all students come from rich families. I am graduating, I finally made it, and I will not play any part in the college in the future. 99

This Stanford student, a female who is a junior, worried about the long-term implications of college costs:

66 I believe the "grade paranoia" is a direct result of the astronomic cost of attending college here. America's elite schools must become more affordable or this trend will continue and our students will become mere "résumé machines," lacking the holistic learning that is needed for quality contribution out in the real world. 99

In spite of their large endowments, the elite institutions sit at the top of the tuition ladder. For example, the total cost of tuition, room and board, and fees at all the Ivies exceeded $29,000 for the 1997–98 academic year. Yet the drawing power of these institutions is so great that only 38.5% of the students polled indicated that financial aid was an extremely or very important factor in choosing which college they would attend. Acting on the attraction of the Halo Effect and the positioning for future earnings, these students and their families willingly chose the highest-priced colleges over many other less expensive options. Many turned down merit-based grants that represented a free ticket to an excellent education. Later in this book, you will find out the impact on undergraduates of the financial constraints and realities of working to help pay their obligations.

As I anticipated, over half the students of color listed financial aid as an extremely important factor in choosing which college to attend. Major schools heavily recruit from minority groups, no matter what the financial needs of the students' families, as part of their concerted effort to build diverse campus populations. The elite colleges use their huge endowments to ensure that talented students of all socioeconomic backgrounds can have access to their institutions. As I surveyed the Select, I listened to a number of disadvantaged students bemoan the fact that their financial aid packages were unrealistic for meeting their actual expenses.

Consequently, to make ends meet, many have had to take out larger loans than they anticipated or work several jobs on and off campus. These students described the Catch–22 situation this creates for them: Their financial burdens mean they cannot find enough time and energy to study to get the grades to qualify for graduate school or to participate in enjoyable and beneficial activities.

Concern over money is shared by students of all backgrounds who are on financial aid. I wouldn't be surprised to see in the future an increase in the number of Select students who take a break from college to earn money and ease some of the financial pressure.

Love It, Hate It

What do students like least about their colleges? Regardless of their backgrounds and persuasion, they seem to share an antipathy toward the bureaucratic behavior of administrators. More than a fifth of the students on all twenty campuses expressed their frustration with the inaction or indifference of the deans and advisory staff. Only the quality of the weather and food came close to matching these negative feelings. Undergraduates want more accessibility to the professional people whom they view as being there to help them resolve their various issues, from academic advising to financial aid counsel to career and graduate school planning.

All other negative features of campus life mentioned in my survey drop off sharply in number and intensity. But there are many that, taken in the aggregate, reflect dissatisfaction in a large portion of each campus's student body. Topics referred to included the following:

- social cliques and the Greek system
- campus polarization based on ethnicity and race
- race, religion, gender, and academic politicization
- safety on and off campus
- sexual harassment and date rape
- class size
- accessibility of the faculty and the quality of teaching
- social life
- academic workload and stress
- personal and medical health resources

What college men and women like least or most doesn't necessarily correlate with the things they actually want changed on their campuses. Students being students, my survey revealed a number of conflicting opinions and attitudes. For example, food, housing, faculty–student ratio, and school location may not be their most cited initial concerns, but when asked what they would like to be different, these items rose to the top of their list. By focusing on relatively minor discomforts, Select students feel they can contend with the everyday reality of academic demands, personal stresses, and challenges to self-confidence. To a certain extent, these minor beefs mask real pain. Many students spoke openly of drug and alcohol abuse on campus, eating disorders, and physically aggressive behavior as severe problems permeating college life.

One of my most interesting findings is the Select students' wide range of opinions regarding their elite college's positive and negative attributes. Each student has his or her unique prism, created from a personal set of experiences, history, and interests. But such pluralistic opinions reflect the goal of the college or university itself: to seek a student body of talented, intelligent, and diverse individuals from many backgrounds. There is no longer a uniform culture at any elite school because of the broad-based student population.

In Chapters 2 and 4, on academic and social life on campus, you will find a summary for every institution of the students' likes and dislikes. The range of responses offers a great deal of insight into the characteristics of the elite colleges, as well as the types of students they tend to attract.

Conclusion

Although each student arrives at college with a personal history and agenda, all appear to have much to grapple with before they move into the larger society, with its even greater demands, conflicts, and challenges. There is every indication that over their four years of college, Select students will have their very characters forged and finished. They will emerge with values and attitudes to guide them in their eventual roles as spouse, parent, careerist, and community member.

In the succeeding chapters, the students I interviewed will tell you much about college life that is good and that is bad. Along the way, I will evaluate their responses and suggest changes that could result in a more fulfilling and more productive experience for a great many students.

I hope that you will read this book with an appreciation of both the differences and similarities among a group of outstanding colleges.

Listen to what these young men and women have to say matters most to them as they experience undergraduate life. If you are a high school student or parent, I encourage you to choose a college on the basis of the special features of an institution that will make the college experience a successful one. Rather than rely on hearsay, contrived college ranking, or even the Halo Effect, focus on your needs, abilities, values, and personality to make the right decision.

Importance of Factors in Choosing School

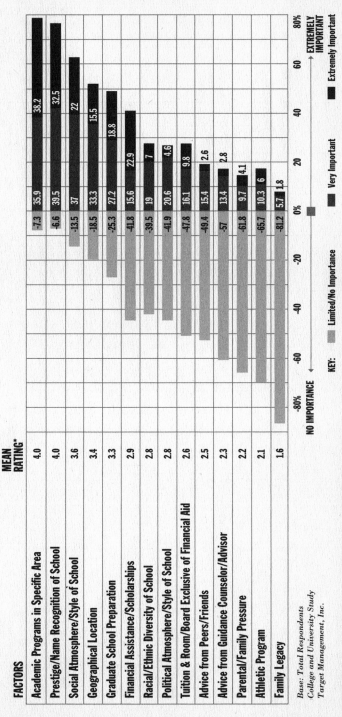

FACTORS	MEAN RATING*
Academic Programs in Specific Area	4.0
Prestige/Name Recognition of School	4.0
Social Atmosphere/Style of School	3.6
Geographical Location	3.4
Graduate School Preparation	3.3
Financial Assistance/Scholarships	2.9
Racial/Ethnic Diversity of School	2.8
Political Atmosphere/Style of School	2.8
Tuition & Room/Board Exclusive of Financial Aid	2.6
Advice from Peers/Friends	2.5
Advice from Guidance Counselor/Advisor	2.3
Parental/Family Pressure	2.2
Athletic Program	2.1
Family Legacy	1.6

Base: Total Respondents
College and University Study
Target Management, Inc.

*Ratings scale: 1= Of no importance, 2= Of limited importance, 3= Somewhat important, 4= Very important, 5= Extremely important

Importance of Factors in Choosing This School

(Total Ivy League)

FACTORS	MEAN RATING*	Limited/No Importance	Very Important	Extremely Important
Prestige/Name Recognition of School	4.1	-4.6	40.2	36.3
Academic Programs in Specific Area	4.0	7.6	37.3	37.5
Social Atmosphere/Style of School	3.6	-15.1	37.1	19.2
Graduate School Preparation	3.3	-25.0	25.8	20.7
Geographical Location	3.3	-19.7	32.0	13.6
Financial Assistance/Scholarships	2.9	-43.0	15.9	25.1
Racial/Ethnic Diversity of School	2.7	-43.3	18.5	6.8
Political Atmosphere/Style of School	2.5	-50.7	12.3	5.2
Tuition & Room/Board Exclusive of Financial Aid	2.4	-56.0	13.5	6.9
Advice from Peers/Friends	2.4	-53.0	14.2	2.8
Parental/Family Pressure	2.2	-63.0	10.0	5.1
Advice from Guidance Counselor/Advisor	2.2	-61.3	11.5	2.1
Athletic Program	2.0	-71.5	7.3	6.2
Family Legacy	1.4	-88.0	2.9	1.7

Axis: -100% NO IMPORTANCE ... -80 ... -60 ... -40 ... -20 ... 0% ... 20 ... 40 ... 60 ... 80 ... 100% EXTREMELY IMPORTANT

KEY: Limited/No Importance | Very Important | Extremely Important

College and University Study
Target Management, Inc.

*Ratings scale: 1= Of no importance, 2= Of limited importance, 3= Somewhat important, 4= Very important, 5= Extremely important

Importance of Prestige/Name Recognition as Factor in Choosing School

School	RANK*	Rating
MIT	2	4.5
Georgetown University	2	4.3
Johns Hopkins University	2	4.3
Cornell University	2	4.2
Duke University	1	4.2
Harvard University	1	4.2
Stanford University	1	4.2
U. of California—Berkeley	1	4.2
Columbia University	2	4.1
Princeton University	1	4.1
Yale University	1	4.1
Dartmouth College	1	4.0
Northwestern University	2	4.0
University of Pennsylvania	2	4.0
Brown University	3	3.8
University of Chicago	2	3.8
Williams College	1	3.8
U. of North Carolina—Chapel Hill	3	3.6
U. of Wisconsin—Madison	3	3.6
Wesleyan University	4	3.6

College and University Study
Target Management, Inc.

1 2 3 4 5
NO IMPORTANCE ← → EXTREMELY IMPORTANT

*Attribute's rank for each school among the fourteen rated attributes.

Two Things Like Most Now About School

(Total Ivy League vs. Dartmouth)

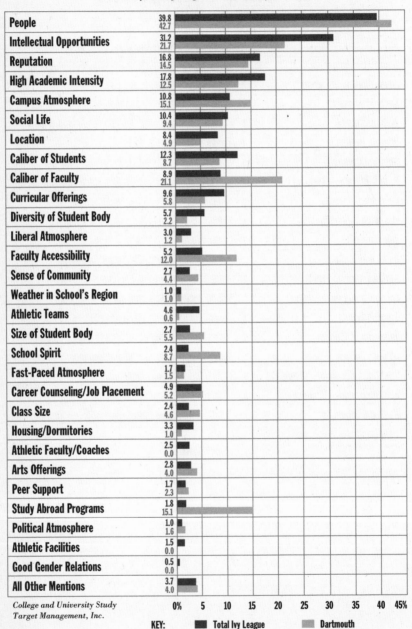

	Total Ivy League	Dartmouth
People	39.8	42.7
Intellectual Opportunities	31.2	21.7
Reputation	16.8	14.5
High Academic Intensity	17.8	12.5
Campus Atmosphere	10.8	15.1
Social Life	10.4	9.4
Location	8.4	4.9
Caliber of Students	12.3	8.7
Caliber of Faculty	8.9	21.1
Curricular Offerings	9.6	5.8
Diversity of Student Body	5.7	2.2
Liberal Atmosphere	3.0	1.2
Faculty Accessibility	5.2	12.0
Sense of Community	2.7	4.4
Weather in School's Region	1.0	1.0
Athletic Teams	4.6	0.6
Size of Student Body	2.7	5.5
School Spirit	2.4	8.7
Fast-Paced Atmosphere	1.7	1.5
Career Counseling/Job Placement	4.9	5.2
Class Size	2.4	4.6
Housing/Dormitories	3.3	1.0
Athletic Faculty/Coaches	2.5	0.0
Arts Offerings	2.8	4.0
Peer Support	1.7	2.3
Study Abroad Programs	1.8	15.1
Political Atmosphere	1.0	1.6
Athletic Facilities	1.5	0.0
Good Gender Relations	0.5	0.0
All Other Mentions	3.7	4.0

College and University Study
Target Management, Inc.

KEY: ■ Total Ivy League   ■ Dartmouth

Two Things Like Most Now About School

PART ONE

(Total Respondents vs. Ivy League vs. Yale)

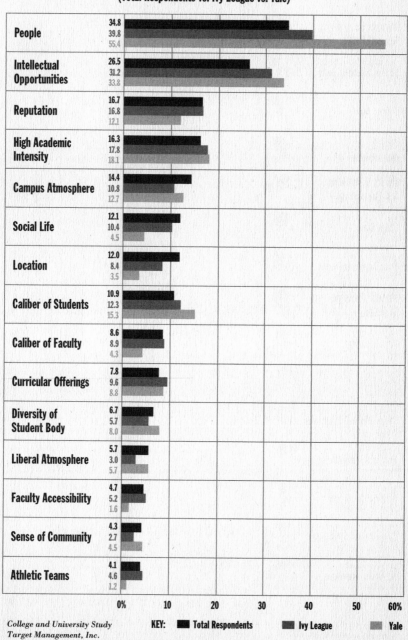

		Total Respondents	Ivy League	Yale
People		34.8	39.8	55.4
Intellectual Opportunities		26.5	31.2	33.8
Reputation		16.7	16.8	12.1
High Academic Intensity		16.3	17.8	18.1
Campus Atmosphere		14.4	10.8	12.7
Social Life		12.1	10.4	4.5
Location		12.0	8.4	3.5
Caliber of Students		10.9	12.3	15.3
Caliber of Faculty		8.6	8.9	4.3
Curricular Offerings		7.8	9.6	8.8
Diversity of Student Body		6.7	5.7	8.0
Liberal Atmosphere		5.7	3.0	5.7
Faculty Accessibility		4.7	5.2	1.6
Sense of Community		4.3	2.7	4.5
Athletic Teams		4.1	4.6	1.2

0%   10   20   30   40   50   60%

College and University Study
Target Management, Inc.

KEY: ■ Total Respondents   ■ Ivy League   ■ Yale

Two Things Like Most Now About School

PART TWO

(Total Respondents vs. Ivy League vs. Yale)

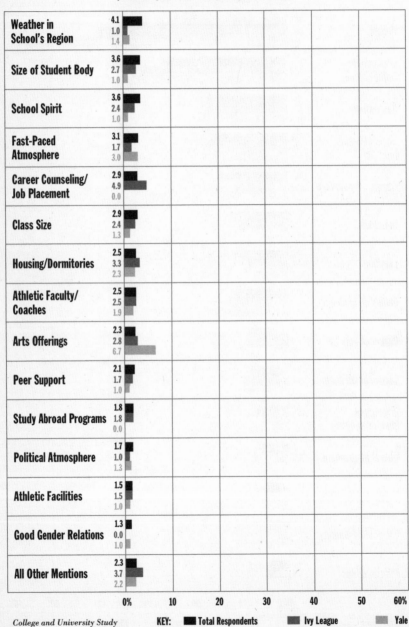

	0%	10	20	30	40	50	60%
Weather in School's Region	4.1 / 1.0 / 1.4						
Size of Student Body	3.6 / 2.7 / 1.0						
School Spirit	3.6 / 2.4 / 1.0						
Fast-Paced Atmosphere	3.1 / 1.7 / 3.0						
Career Counseling/ Job Placement	2.9 / 4.9 / 0.0						
Class Size	2.9 / 2.4 / 1.3						
Housing/Dormitories	2.5 / 3.3 / 2.3						
Athletic Faculty/ Coaches	2.5 / 2.5 / 1.9						
Arts Offerings	2.3 / 2.8 / 6.7						
Peer Support	2.1 / 1.7 / 1.0						
Study Abroad Programs	1.8 / 1.8 / 0.0						
Political Atmosphere	1.7 / 1.0 / 1.3						
Athletic Facilities	1.5 / 1.5 / 1.0						
Good Gender Relations	1.3 / 0.0 / 1.0						
All Other Mentions	2.3 / 3.7 / 2.2						

KEY: ■ Total Respondents ■ Ivy League ■ Yale

College and University Study Target Management, Inc.

Two Things Like Least Now About School

PART ONE

(Total Respondents vs. Ivy League vs. Yale)

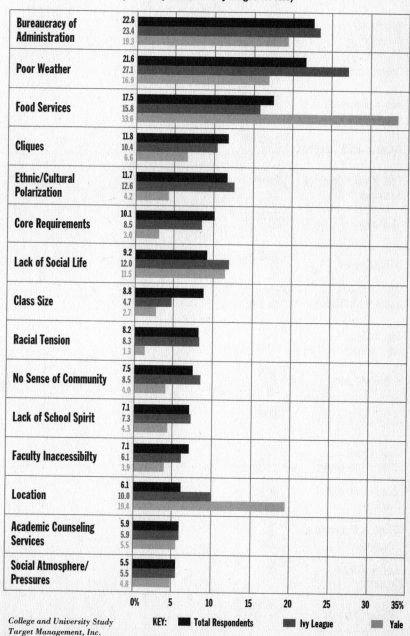

	Total Respondents	Ivy League	Yale
Bureaucracy of Administration	22.6	23.4	19.3
Poor Weather	21.6	27.1	16.9
Food Services	17.5	15.8	33.6
Cliques	11.8	10.4	6.6
Ethnic/Cultural Polarization	11.7	12.6	4.2
Core Requirements	10.1	8.5	3.0
Lack of Social Life	9.2	12.0	11.5
Class Size	8.8	4.7	2.7
Racial Tension	8.2	8.3	1.3
No Sense of Community	7.5	8.5	4.0
Lack of School Spirit	7.1	7.3	4.3
Faculty Inaccessibilty	7.1	6.1	3.9
Location	6.1	10.0	19.4
Academic Counseling Services	5.9	5.9	5.5
Social Atmosphere/ Pressures	5.5	5.5	4.8

KEY: Total Respondents   Ivy League   Yale

College and University Study
Target Management, Inc.

Two Things Like Least Now About School

PART TWO

(Total Respondents vs. Ivy League vs. Yale)

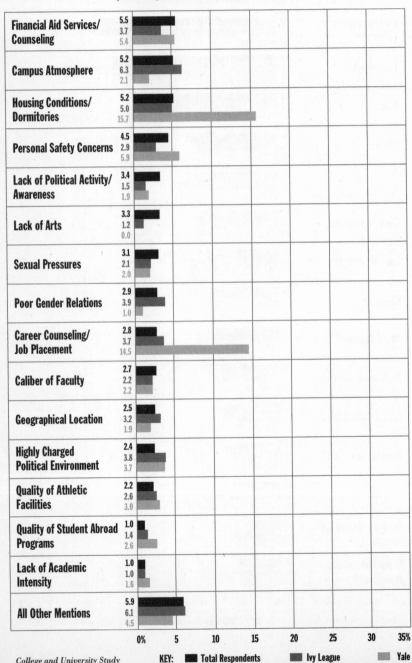

	Total Respondents	Ivy League	Yale
Financial Aid Services/ Counseling	5.5	3.7	5.4
Campus Atmosphere	5.2	6.3	2.1
Housing Conditions/ Dormitories	5.2	5.0	15.7
Personal Safety Concerns	4.5	2.9	5.9
Lack of Political Activity/ Awareness	3.4	1.5	1.9
Lack of Arts	3.3	1.2	0.0
Sexual Pressures	3.1	2.1	2.0
Poor Gender Relations	2.9	3.9	1.0
Career Counseling/ Job Placement	2.8	3.7	14.5
Caliber of Faculty	2.7	2.2	2.2
Geographical Location	2.5	3.2	1.9
Highly Charged Political Environment	2.4	3.8	3.7
Quality of Athletic Facilities	2.2	2.6	3.0
Quality of Student Abroad Programs	1.0	1.4	2.6
Lack of Academic Intensity	1.0	1.0	1.6
All Other Mentions	5.9	6.1	4.5

0%   5   10   15   20   25   30   35%

KEY: ■ Total Respondents   ■ Ivy League   ■ Yale

*College and University Study
Target Management, Inc.*

Dartmouth College

(Importance of Factors in Choosing This School)

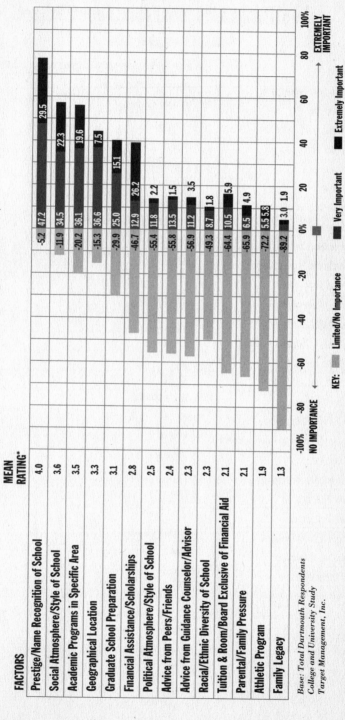

FACTORS	MEAN RATING*
Prestige/Name Recognition of School	4.0
Social Atmosphere/Style of School	3.6
Academic Programs in Specific Area	3.5
Geographical Location	3.3
Graduate School Preparation	3.1
Financial Assistance/Scholarships	2.8
Political Atmosphere/Style of School	2.5
Advice from Peers/Friends	2.4
Advice from Guidance Counselor/Advisor	2.3
Racial/Ethnic Diversity of School	2.3
Tuition & Room/Board Exclusive of Financial Aid	2.1
Parental/Family Pressure	2.1
Athletic Program	1.9
Family Legacy	1.3

KEY: ■ Limited/No Importance   ■ Very Important   ■ Extremely Important

Base: Total Dartmouth Respondents
College and University Study
Target Management, Inc.

*Ratings scale: 1= Of no importance, 2= Of limited importance, 3= Somewhat important, 4= Very important, 5= Extremely important

Two Things Like Most Now About School

(Dartmouth—Split by Gender)

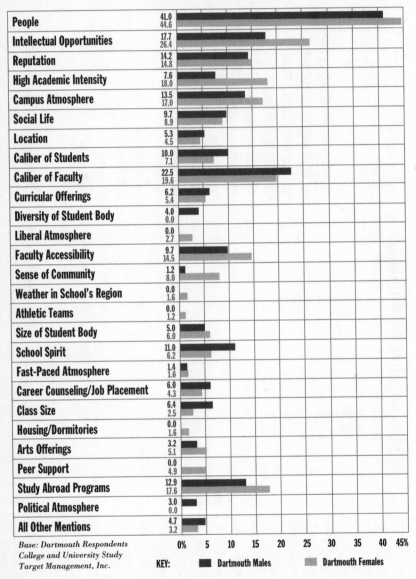

	Males	Females
People	41.0	44.6
Intellectual Opportunities	17.7	26.4
Reputation	14.2	14.8
High Academic Intensity	7.6	18.0
Campus Atmosphere	13.5	17.0
Social Life	9.7	8.9
Location	5.3	4.5
Caliber of Students	10.0	7.1
Caliber of Faculty	22.5	19.6
Curricular Offerings	6.2	5.4
Diversity of Student Body	4.0	0.0
Liberal Atmosphere	0.0	2.7
Faculty Accessibility	9.7	14.5
Sense of Community	1.2	8.0
Weather in School's Region	0.0	1.6
Athletic Teams	0.0	1.2
Size of Student Body	5.0	6.0
School Spirit	11.0	6.2
Fast-Paced Atmosphere	1.4	1.6
Career Counseling/Job Placement	6.0	4.3
Class Size	6.4	2.5
Housing/Dormitories	0.0	1.6
Arts Offerings	3.2	5.1
Peer Support	0.0	4.9
Study Abroad Programs	12.9	17.6
Political Atmosphere	3.0	0.0
All Other Mentions	4.7	3.2

Base: Dartmouth Respondents
College and University Study
Target Management, Inc.

0%   5   10   15   20   25   30   35   40   45%

KEY: ■ Dartmouth Males   ▨ Dartmouth Females

Importance of Factors in Choosing This School

(Dartmouth—Males)

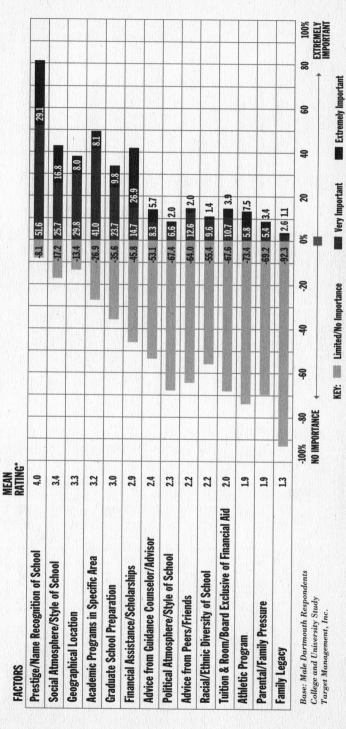

FACTORS	MEAN RATING*
Prestige/Name Recognition of School	4.0
Social Atmosphere/Style of School	3.4
Geographical Location	3.3
Academic Programs in Specific Area	3.2
Graduate School Preparation	3.0
Financial Assistance/Scholarships	2.9
Advice from Guidance Counselor/Advisor	2.4
Political Atmosphere/Style of School	2.3
Advice from Peers/Friends	2.2
Racial/Ethnic Diversity of School	2.2
Tuition & Room/Board Exclusive of Financial Aid	2.0
Athletic Program	1.9
Parental/Family Pressure	1.9
Family Legacy	1.3

KEY: ▪ Limited/No Importance   ▪ Very Important   ▪ Extremely Important

Base: Male Dartmouth Respondents
College and University Study
Target Management, Inc.

*Ratings scale: 1= Of no importance, 2= Of limited importance, 3= Somewhat important, 4= Very important, 5= Extremely important

Importance of Factors in Choosing This School

(Dartmouth—Females)

FACTORS	MEAN RATING*
Prestige/Name Recognition of School	4.0
Social Atmosphere/Style of School	3.9
Academic Programs in Specific Area	3.8
Geographical Location	3.4
Graduate School Preparation	3.4
Financial Assistance/Scholarships	2.8
Political Atmosphere/Style of School	2.7
Racial/Ethnic Diversity of School	2.5
Advice from Peers/Friends	2.5
Tuition & Room/Board Exclusive of Financial Aid	2.3
Parental/Family Pressure	2.3
Advice from Guidance Counselor/Advisor	2.2
Athletic Program	1.9
Family Legacy	1.4

Chart data (Limited/No Importance | Very Important | Extremely Important):
- Prestige/Name Recognition of School: -1.8 | 42.2 | 29.9
- Social Atmosphere/Style of School: -5.8 | 44.6 | 28.6
- Academic Programs in Specific Area: -12.5 | 30.5 | 32.7
- Geographical Location: -17.4 | 44.4 | 6.9
- Graduate School Preparation: -23.5 | 26.5 | 21.1
- Financial Assistance/Scholarships: -47.8 | 10.9 | 25.3
- Political Atmosphere/Style of School: -41.7 | 17.7 | 2.4
- Racial/Ethnic Diversity of School: -42.4 | 7.5 | 2.3
- Advice from Peers/Friends: -46.4 | 14.4 | 1.0
- Tuition & Room/Board Exclusive of Financial Aid: -60.7 | 10.1 | 8.2
- Parental/Family Pressure: -62.1 | 7.7 | 6.6
- Advice from Guidance Counselor/Advisor: -61.3 | 14.5 | 1.0
- Athletic Program: -70.8 | 5.1 | 3.9
- Family Legacy: -85.7 | 3.4 | 2.8

NO IMPORTANCE ← -100% -80 -60 -40 -20 0% 20 40 60 80 100% → EXTREMELY IMPORTANT

KEY: ■ Limited/No Importance ■ Very Important ■ Extremely Important

Base: Female Dartmouth Respondents
College and University Study
Target Management, Inc.

*Ratings scale: 1= Of no importance, 2= Of limited importance, 3= Somewhat important, 4= Very important, 5= Extremely important

TWO

The Academic Experience

My college education was no haphazard affair. My courses were all selected with a very definite aim in view, with a serious purpose in mind, no classes before eleven in the morning or after two-thirty in the afternoon, and nothing on Saturday at all. That was my slogan. On that rock was my education built.

—ROBERT BENCHLEY, "WHAT COLLEGE DID TO ME" (1927)

What do Select students think of academic life on elite college campuses? Their attitudes range from intensely engaged to angry and beleaguered. But nearly all of them agree on one thing: Their schoolwork is *hard*.

66 Mountain Dew is the fifth food group. Sleep is not mandatory. Eating is not mandatory. Worship the computer lab. Make sure to have outlets for stress. 99

—JOHNS HOPKINS SENIOR, MALE

66 Everyone here has a passion about something. People care about the school, learning, the world. Intellectually this place is fascinating, moral, and driven by a sense of searching. 99

—YALE SENIOR, FEMALE

66 I think the workload is extremely intense, but you adjust to it over time. The social life leaves a little to be desired. Everyone here thinks about only one person, me, myself, and I. People have big egos when it comes to academic issues and especially when thinking about future jobs. 99

—PRINCETON FRESHMAN

66 There is simply not enough time in a week to go to each and every class, eat, study, fulfill the academic requirements, and still be alive. I find myself hopelessly struggling to right my academic log. It is a virtual certainty that I will fail out after this semester and leave behind what could have been a wonderful experience. 99

—YALE FRESHWOMAN

66 It's very stressful here, and I have many thoughts of failure. I feel as though I may not be able to succeed here, and that frightens me. 99

—STANFORD FRESHWOMAN

I asked students to select two words or phrases from a list of nine that best describe their scholastic atmosphere. Their responses are a powerful statement of life in the academic fast lane. Of all the students, 90% checked a combination of these words:

- intense
- competitive
- cutthroat

To measure the level of personal stress in academic life, I asked students to choose from a 1 to 10 scale, with 1 representing tremendous stress. The mean for the total population was 3. Less than 3%

rated their personal stress level at 10, which would seem to indicate a relaxed attitude about college. Life for Select students may be fun and worthwhile, but it is profoundly challenging and has its costs, as this response of a junior at Harvard makes clear:

> ❝Harvard provides the means for academic expansion at the cost of a social life. While athletics and social events play a role in most students' lives, academics dominate your time. Harvard will give me an advantage as I enter the real world beyond education. I fear, however, that it promotes academics too strongly. As my roommate said, "we don't go to college the way my friends go to college."❞

Major Academic Concerns

Considering the population of high achievers at highly selective colleges, it's no surprise that the overall level of abilities and competitive spirit—together with the expectations of both faculty and family—create a highly intense learning environment; no matriculating student will have previously encountered such a critical mass of talented peers—a factor that is significant for all students and traumatic for some. Imagine yourself in an academic setting where the majority of your classmates have credentials like these actual recent high school graduates:

Liza: scored a perfect 1600 on the SAT, editor of two publications at her suburban private day school, captain of the school math team, performer with the School of American Ballet; speaks perfect French.

Andrew: a winner of the Westinghouse Science Competition, National Merit Scholar, winner of numerous national mathematics contests; holds a patent for an electronic measuring device.

Sally: all-state soccer player, class president of her large suburban high school, a National Merit semifinalist.

Alex: an émigré from Eastern Europe; class valedictorian of a large urban high school; a National Merit Scholar finalist;

principal clarinetist in the Juilliard School of Music's precollege program; member of the New York Youth Symphony; member of the school math team.

Jessica: scored a perfect 1600 on the SAT; a varsity fencer, editor of the school yearbook, performer in the school orchestra.

Jack: scored 1550 on the SAT and 800 on three achievement tests; the class valedictorian, a National Merit Scholar finalist, editor of the school newspaper.

When I asked the students questions about the nature of academic life, they used these descriptive terms, in order of frequency:

- challenging
- rigorous
- self-directive
- intense
- balanced between work and play
- well rounded
- broadening

The percentages of responses to all the questions can be reviewed in the graphs at the end of this chapter.

Women and men perceive their academic experiences differently. Although both genders showed a similar concern about their college workloads, a much higher percentage of women—almost half the group—described their academic environment as challenging and overall were more negative. While one-third of the first-year women described their college experience as broadening, only 14% of the seniors did. As I mentioned before, women seem to lose much of their interest and enthusiasm for the intellectual opportunities on their campuses. Perhaps this is why so many more women than men choose to study abroad each year: Beyond their greater interest in languages, they may be seeking relief from the academic atmosphere on their home campuses. Why shouldn't a larger number of men leave campus for alternative programs, given that a high proportion of them major in history, government, political science, and international relations?

To the credit of both the students and the colleges they attend, only a tiny number of the respondents described their college as "boring" or "narrow." While some students expressed surprise that academic demands were not as rigorous as they had expected, most were concerned with maintaining academic excellence in such a profoundly competitive environment. A male junior at Dartmouth put it this way:

> The only reason I would choose to come here again is because of the group of friends I have found here. The highly intense, competitive atmosphere could stand to change.

A loyal Columbia senior saw her school as right for certain people but not for others:

> Columbia is the best school in the country, but it requires a certain type of person (independent, committed to academics; individuals who love to study for its own sake) to truly appreciate this campus and what it has to offer.

When I asked what two words best describe the *overall* scholastic environment of their campus, students chose these adjectives, in this order:

- competitive
- intense
- fast paced
- enriching
- scholarly
- broadening
- energetic

Primary Academic Concerns of the Select

In the on-campus focus groups and my individual discussions with more than one hundred Select undergraduates, I asked the students to tell me their personal level of concern about a broad range of academic issues, from rampant preprofessionalism through faculty preparedness to their own philosophical outlooks. The findings are dramatic; they should be of interest not only to prospective Select students and their families but to educators on these campuses.

An overwhelming majority of students, 84%, indicated that the academic workload is their overriding worry. Only 1% stated that the workload didn't concern them. Unlike many other student concerns, the academic burden remains a constant throughout all four years of college—even as undergraduates become accustomed to academic demands and better adjusted to college life.

The impact of competition for grades can easily be understood when one considers the rise in grade point averages on the elite campuses. Stanford has reinstituted the F grade after realizing that A's and B's accounted for 93% of all grades handed out by the faculty. Dartmouth, Williams, and Duke are among the Select institutions readjusting their grading systems to reflect a differential by the difficulty of courses, as professors calibrate the grade distribution in their classes to reflect the difficulty of courses. At Harvard, 91% of the undergraduates achieve GPAs of B- or higher. Since 43% of the grades issued by the faculty are A or A-, the average grade for a Harvard student is elevated to a B+. The picture is the same at Princeton, which has historically been considered to be a tough-grading college: Of all the grades, the proportion of A's has reached 40%. Whereas the "Princeton Charlies" of the college world once were content with a C average, a B- is now considered a mediocre grade, with a B- average all but guaranteeing rejection from the major graduate schools. Students view this grade inflation as a signal that doing well is not good enough—that is, if they are ever to get accepted into the top graduate schools or to win the kind of fellowships and jobs that led them to enroll in elite colleges in the first place. They feel the pressure to attain A and A+ grades to stand out from the talented pack around them.

Other elements of academic life also preoccupy the Select—from the accessibility and communicativeness of the faculty to the quality of the library to building the emotional and psychological support they need to succeed academically and grow into confident and creative adults.

How Select Students Perceive Academic Pressure

One young man I counseled had been identified by an active Midwestern alumnus as an outstanding athlete and high school student. Recruited by the swimming coach at Princeton, he was ultimately admitted and enrolled. His original intention had been to attend his state university with a number of his high school friends and teammates. Being recruited to an Ivy League university, however, flattered him and his family, so he decided to go for it. About halfway through the spring term, I received an irate telephone call from this young man's father, who was about to withdraw his son from Princeton.

Having reviewed his first-term grades, I knew this student was doing reasonably well for someone at the beginning of his studies. When I asked the father what was the matter, he replied, "How could such a distinguished institution allow its pool to be closed by the health authorities for unsanitary conditions?" My thoughtful response was something like, "Are you mad?" I immediately called in the young swimmer to find out what the problem really was. It didn't take long for him to confide that he felt overwhelmed by the academic workload and painfully isolated from his classmates. He had not yet established a close friendship with anyone, and he was afraid he would fail academically. He was ashamed to share these worries with his parents, who perceived him as an all-American boy born to conquer the university world, so he invented the story about the condemned swimming pool. This young man had to learn how to reach out to others and to establish himself in his new setting—something he hadn't had to worry about in his high school and hometown.

Select students recognize that if they are going to meet their academic challenges, they have to establish high-quality friendships. Only through building strong relationships will they feel they have the emotional support to thrive not just socially but scholastically. During this survey, I heard student after student emphasize how important it was for them to find individuals with whom they could share their feelings. Close friends are crucial to success in college.

Many elite college students admit they would prefer to have less stress and a lighter academic workload, but insist that they would never give up the friends they have made. Graduates who haven't successfully bonded with others emerge less fulfilled by their college experience and tend not to become active alumni. My work as a counselor has convinced me that the urge today's students commonly feel to transfer from one college to another is the result of their failing to establish meaningful relationships on campus. The truth is that no matter what reservations about academic life a student may have, there is a strong correlation between the quality of community life and personal satisfaction. At the end of this book I have documented which of the colleges have the most satisfied student bodies.

How do students perceive one another with regard to their intellectual and academic priorities? When I asked the Select if their fellow students were primarily interested in learning, nearly two-thirds checked yes. When I phrased the question another way, asking whether their fellow students were interested primarily in attaining good grades, three-quarters also checked yes.

What do these findings imply? On the face of it, grades matter more than learning for its own sake. The anxiety-producing factors that dominate the campus environment—doing well and having future opportunities—create a conscious focus on grades. Many students openly expressed feeling conflict between getting good grades and learning. They worried about keeping a scholarship and about the expectations of and pressure from their families, as well as their own ambitions to get into the graduate school of their choice. Sometimes they had an emotional investment in being at the top of the class, as they had been in high school.

No matter what the extent of their support networks and perceptions of the learning environment, the students remained completely absorbed in coping with the academic issues on campus. These are the additional categories of concern they frequently cited:

- grade point average
- choice of major
- general stress
- postcollege plans: job placement and/or graduate school

Over half the students I surveyed were stressed about their grade point averages. Compared to the men, the women were more concerned about stress, their academic workloads, the quality of their friendships, and choosing a major. Curiously, they expressed less anxiety over their GPAs and plans for graduate school, but manifested much greater apprehension about post-college job placement. Several women described their disappointment and frustration over academic priorities on campus. A Georgetown senior's perception of the attitude on her campus was typical:

> The atmosphere is not intellectual, and students are more concerned about grades than learning. A less preprofessional student body would enrich the university greatly.

A female sophomore at Yale spoke to the same issue:

> People are sometimes too overly concerned with grades and future careers to enjoy the company of other students. Yale offers a relatively intellectual environment, but most students I know are less concerned about learning for learning's sake than for the sake of their careers, grad school prospects, or general success after school.

Select students have long been motivated by the drive to gain admission to graduate school. Many students discover early, however, that doing fairly well, but not well enough to distinguish themselves, can end their dream, as this sophomore woman at the University of Chicago recognized:

> Before coming to this school I expected my job opportunities and grad school choices to increase, yet I think they have actually decreased because of the competition.

As a college entrance counselor, I work constantly to get across to high school students and naive parents that they should not apply to elite colleges solely or primarily to gain an entrée to graduate school. Many high schoolers operate on that assumption, as the survey shows. Consequently, as college students, they must live with the stress of competing against other star students to achieve the necessary GPAs to accomplish the next step of their goals. Select students will ask me in plaintive tones if admissions officers at graduate schools take into account the high academic demands they have faced. The answer is: up to a point. Graduate schools and employers prefer to attract top performers in and out of the classroom from a broad range of good educational institutions. Why, they ask, should we offer places to Ivy League students in the lower half of their classes when there is so much talent to be found elsewhere?

College-bound students hear and read of the emphasis on academic work in the top institutions. Yet they cannot fully grasp what it means until they experience it themselves. One MIT sophomore described his learning environment rather passionately:

> Academic life is too rigorous at MIT. It does not leave its students with any room for personal growth, any extra time to become real people. Students are emotionally stunted, dorky people with little real ambition in life other than work. All work and no play makes Jack a dull boy, and I believe we are proving the case.

Some students do relish an intense intellectual environment. A senior at the University of Chicago expressed his high regard for his institution this way:

> The University of Chicago provides unique and singular opportunities to establish contact at various levels of academic society and a chance to participate in an intense and highly academic environment.

Many individuals appear to accept the pressures as they come and still find opportunities to have fun. One sophomore woman at Cornell described what life is like on many elite campuses:

> Although the workload is intense at times and stress levels are high, we know how to have fun and relax. During the week, Cornell is 99% academic, but on the weekends it becomes a party school. We study hard and party hard.

A junior male at Duke addressed frustrations that are common to many undergraduates:

❝ The students here are used to being the best, and they carry that into their intellectual and social lives. I think that many tend to get into their "I've got to get into med school" and "I've got to make sure that I am cooler than everyone else" modes and thus ignore more important issues (like community service). ❞

The Emotional Price of Academic Competitiveness

Roiling just below the surface of academic life is a layer of heated emotional factors that profoundly affect students' happiness and success. When I asked Select undergraduates to tell me what greatly concerns them besides academics, personal issues swiftly rose into view. A substantial number of students were caught up with such issues as these:

- personal safety
- physical-medical well-being
- alcohol abuse
- financial obligations
- living arrangements
- peer pressure
- political correctness
- racism
- suicide

I see many Select students perpetuating an unfortunate pattern: repressing personal needs and problems while concentrating on coping with academic requirements and expectations. No college campus is free of the problems of depression; persistent anxiety states; eating disorders; alcohol and drug abuse; suicide; and, in some extreme instances, even murder. Academic pressure is usually the primary contributing factor to any of these unhappy and sometimes tragic circumstances.

Stories of attempted or successful suicides by students abound on college campuses; their numbers are, fortunately, usually exaggerated. Yet enough incidents occur each year to stir grave concern among parents, students, and educators. The most publicized incident in the past several years occurred at Harvard, where a young woman, who cracked under the strain of her determination to do well enough to get accepted to medical school, killed herself and her roommate. Although most students cope successfully even with crushing academic pressures, there is always the potential for disaster when a young adult perceives her world as friendless and her future career in medicine lost because of an average performance in sophomore organic chemistry.

Highly selective colleges can wreak havoc on the self-esteem of the most confident. Having fostered communities of superstar students—and faculty who treat them accordingly—we need to pay careful and consistent attention to how students manage the demands their worlds lay upon them, as well as the further demands they lay on themselves.

Here is how one MIT freshwoman spoke to this issue:

> Life can be very difficult for the average student. The pool of students is very intelligent and therefore most students are prepared to be no longer the smartest. MIT crushes your self-esteem.

A Cornell junior who has worked hard to achieve her place in an Ivy League college told me:

> I do enjoy the academic side of life—the classes, the homework—but I do not like the way a person like me who works so hard, does things on time and never falls behind in class can still receive lower grades than those who cram, never attend class, and skip half the readings. It is not fair!

Her comment may sound familiar to many students and many college graduates who can remember the same frustrations.

A few students were angry, like this young man, a Harvard junior:

> School sucks! Too much stress, way too little sleep. Pressure and overextension makes me not a happy camper, but one year to go! I think I can make it. Then bye, bye Harvard and good riddance!

Another Harvard junior, this one a woman, wrote in a more balanced way about the fortitude required of Select students over four years of college, at Harvard and elsewhere.

66 We have unlimited resources available to us and excellent faculty and students as well. The only thing that diminishes the quality of education here is the lack of support both academically and (to a lesser degree) socially. Harvard is the ideal institution for the person who has fully matured before attending the college, one who knows what he/she wants to do in life and has all the answers figured out. If you don't have all of these stated qualities, then you feel as if you are left to fend for yourself. You stumble through freshman and sophomore years and, hopefully, by junior year you have learned from mistakes and have been able to take full advantage of all the opportunities available to you. 99

How the Faculty Fares

When I asked Select undergraduates if their expectations of their faculty had been met, they revealed a high level of regard and satisfaction. Whereas administrators were held in disrespect by large segments of the students, teachers emerged as the venerable center of the academic community. Here is the proportion of Select students I interviewed, who rated their faculty positively in different categories:

accessibility to students	73%
quality of teaching	71.5%
expertise in their disciplines	90%
personal relationships with students	60%
intellectual objectivity	78%
fairness	76.5%
academic counseling	49.5%
teaching geared to students' needs and interests	61.5%
course offerings	76%

Elite colleges and universities should be heartened by students' overall high level of satisfaction with their teachers. Although I have included students' comments that reflect criticism of parts of the educational process, the single greatest resource of the elite colleges—the faculty—was highly praised by this critical audience, who saw the faculty's role and limitations with a measure of realism, like this young man, a Cornell sophomore:

> Anything and everything in the world is on this campus—all you have to do is look. The faculty here will not come out and get you. They have no interest in that. But if you reach out to them and ask them based on a real intellectual interest, they will embrace you and help you immensely.

On all but three items—quality of teaching, personal relationships with students, and intellectual objectivity—the women demonstrated a significant decline in their positive view of faculty from the beginning to the end of their college experience. As they move from freshmen to seniors, women grow increasingly disenchanted, even as they continue to hold faculty in generally high esteem. If we can assume that teachers do not change dramatically in their knowledge or presentation of their subject over a four-year period, it follows that many young women of high ability and ambition feel something is missing from their learning experience. The comment of this sophomore woman at Yale seems poised between praise for the faculty and discontent with the atmosphere of the campus:

> I was surprised to see how truly devoted both the professors and students are to intellectual progression here. I was also surprised to discover how much drinking really went on here.

The students of color expressed a consistently lower level of satisfaction with their faculty. While overall they felt that their expectations had been met, their endorsement of their faculty was not as enthusiastic as the white students'. I interpret this difference to indicate that these students come to elite colleges with so much at stake for their futures and at such great personal sacrifice that their expectations of the faculty are simply greater.

I serve as a trustee of A Better Chance, an organization founded in the early 1960s to identify and recruit outstanding minority students to academically selective independent secondary schools, where they can prepare for the top colleges. After they've entered college, many of these ambitious young men and women tell me how much they value teachers as role models and mentors. Being disadvantaged represents a lot more than growing up in a low-income home; many students lack the educational resources and enrichment opportunities that more fortunate students take for granted. The term college administrators commonly use to identify this group, *nontraditional students,* really means that the students are the first in their families to attend college. Once they begin their higher education years, they tend to rely not just on their immediate families for guidance but on other adults. It is important that college administrators and faculty members make an extra effort to give them the engagement, challenge, and support they are seeking.

Two minority students in my survey evidenced the potential for frustration and anger that students of color can feel when their expectations for their college education fall short. One male sophomore at the University of Pennsylvania complained about teaching assistants:

> We're afflicted with poor teaching, with unqualified TAs teaching labs, while certain professors have not taught in years!

The second minority student, a male junior at the University of Chicago, had more general complaints:

> For the amount of money I pay and the prestige of this university, I expected to have all wonderful professors. About half of my professors have been good—this is simply not acceptable. And now they want to increase class size and continue to increase tuition.

In another set of questions, I asked students to indicate their use of campus resources. The majority—84%—replied that they took advantage of the academic faculty and, in the case of the research universities in the study, teaching assistants. Some complained that they were taught primarily by teaching assistants, while tenured professors stayed removed from undergraduate instruction. A Wesleyan freshwoman may have provided the most concise brief ever for changing the tenure system:

66 How could we make education better? Improve the tenure prac-
tices to retain the good and expel "beyond-their-prime" professors. 99

The central role teaching assistants play in the academic life of
undergraduates at all but the small liberal arts colleges sends a loud
message to university leaders: Be cognizant of the need to train graduate students in the art of teaching and advising students and help
those who have problems with communicating in English, while you
make sure that professors are engaged with their courses and students. That way, more undergraduates should be moved to write, as
this woman, a junior at Dartmouth, did:

66 I like Dartmouth better every day. Professors are extremely accessible. My best friend on campus is a woman professor. She is great! 99

A Brown freshwoman takes pride in what she believes is a significant difference between her college and the sister Ivies:

66 The relationship between the students and the faculty is excellent and the faculty seems to care about the students. Academically, the
school is extremely competitive, though in a different way from how its
Ivy League brethren are perceived to be; that is, there are no compulsive
pre-meds destroying chemical experiments for the sake of their GPAs.
The students and the faculty are supportive of each other. 99

Every school establishes its own educational culture between
teacher and student. No matter the college, every successful Select
student will forge a distinctive bond with at least a few professors
who will be central in forming the student's outlook on the collegiate
experience.

Campus Resources

It is not surprising that 97% of the Select students regarded the
school library as a major resource. An outstanding library is usually
not at the top of prospective college students' priority list, but once
enrolled, the students come to appreciate how critical the library is

to their education. This is an issue that needs greater articulation by high school advisers and college officials. The actual accessibility of library books, the comfort of the facility, levels of staff assistance, and the focus on having resources available for undergraduates all differentiate the libraries at elite institutions.

But books matter less than people, it appears. When I asked the students to rate campus resources of great value to their education, 72% listed their fellow students as more important than the library, laboratory, computer center, or academic faculty. Whatever the student's background, his or her peers mattered the most. Thus, 89% of my survey's respondents turn to their fellow undergraduates for counsel on academic and personal issues.

Two-thirds of the students said that programs that allow them to study abroad are of great value, both as an additional part of their schools' academic offerings and as a respite from campus life. Over half the students cited the science laboratories and computer center as central to their college routines. Asian Americans had a higher level of usage of these facilities, which reflects their pattern of greater concentration in science and technology studies. Both the Asian American students and students of color made greater use of tutorial and academic skills resources.

Dishonesty: Cheating and Plagiarism on Campus

All of us have heard stories about rampant academic cheating and plagiarism at schools nationwide. Even the students I interviewed who were at colleges with honor codes of academic behavior expressed a cynical attitude toward honesty on campus. I set out to learn what the best and brightest undergraduates experience in the area of ethics and how it affects them.

A significant proportion of the students on all the campuses I surveyed declared that cheating and plagiarism occur regularly. A dismal trend is evident in their responses: As the students progressed from the freshman to the senior year, their awareness of dishonesty increased dramatically, and undergraduates of all backgrounds and both sexes noted a rise in academic dishonesty over the course of their college careers.

In a corollary to this question, I asked the students about the frequency of academic cheating. The good news is that only 11% of all the respondents told me that cheating happened "frequently." The bad news? One half of all students said it happened "occasionally."

I posed questions based on these findings to my Select students.

- Why do students observe a greater frequency of cheating and plagiarism the longer they are in college?
- Do the faculty and administration recognize this behavior? If so, what action do they take?
- Why do so many intelligent individuals feel the need to cheat?
- Is there a direct correlation between the level of academic rigor and dishonest behavior?
- Is so much at stake in the minds of competitive students that cheating and plagiarism are acceptable?
- How will Select students conduct themselves in their personal and professional lives when they graduate? Will some or most rely on a code of behavior that incorporates dishonesty and getting ahead at all costs?

Of the students I interviewed, 29% told me that academic cheating had a direct effect on their class position or grades. We can react to this finding in several ways. First, a great many students—more than a quarter—believe that cheating has an impact on them. Yet a substantial portion of students feel unaffected by it—which means that the negative behavior of half their fellow students has not affected them directly. On the other hand, a larger proportion of unaffected students may not care to raise the issue of integrity. After all, there haven't been any student-led demonstrations protesting violations of their schools' honor codes.

How Select Students Judge Themselves Academically

A key component of the elite college experience is an individual student's intellectual self-image as compared to his or her peers. Given the academic environment that characterizes these campuses, I asked how good or bad, how confident or intimidated, each student felt about himself or herself. How would you rate yourself, I asked each student, compared to a majority of your classmates? Are you smarter, as smart, or not as smart? The results show several varying and important patterns.

Overall, the great majority of the students hold up rather well in judging themselves against their schoolmates. However, there are several marked differences in the self-evaluations of the men and women. A third of the men consider themselves to be smarter than the majority of their classmates, whereas only one-sixth of the women have a similar regard for their own abilities. First-year women demonstrate particular vulnerability, with only 13% rating themselves smarter than their classmates. There is, however, a positive progression in the women's self-evaluations over the four years. Women grow more self-assured over four years of college—but men do even more.

Over half the students view themselves as equal in ability to their classmates. There is an interesting twist here: 63% of the women rate themselves as smart over their four-year experience, while the number of men in this category drops from the freshman to the senior year.

Only a small percentage of the students perceive themselves to be less intelligent than their classmates, 14% overall. The four-year curve drops from 23% in the first year to 7.4% by the final year of college. This is a healthy sign. While the majority of students struggle with their academic workloads and worry about their performance and future prospects, their self-confidence appears to increase over time, and they recognize that they are as capable as most of their peers.

Academic Issues for Women

One young sophomore at Stanford shared her personal struggle as she responded to my survey. I know that a great many other students, especially women, can identify with her experience:

> A lot of life at college depends on what is inside yourself . . . last year I was very stressed and had not accepted the fact that at an institution like this it was not possible to remain at the top of the class. I sacrificed too much attempting to get straight A's. An eating disorder which

had been in remission returned. This year, however, I feel more relaxed, with life in perspective. Life at Stanford can be full and wonderful. 99

As the survey shows, Select women face even greater academic challenges than Select men. My findings in this regard are not likely to surprise most educators and psychologists. There is a great deal of literature that addresses young women's perception of themselves— both issues of self-confidence and competence and the external forces that influence their development. For example, approximately half the undergraduates at the private colleges I surveyed majored in the sciences. In high school, however, girls are grossly underrepresented in chemistry, physics, and mathematics classes. Virtually every academically talented high school girl I have counseled over the years has experienced the discomfort and, often, the intimidation of being a minority member in advanced-level courses in physical science and mathematics. The American Association of University Women (AAUW) found that only 29% of the high school girls, versus 52% of the high school boys, consider science as a career. I find that young men are better positioned to cope with the intensity of college curricula in these fields as a result. To cite only one of many findings on the socialization process that affects young women: In its study, *Shortchanging Girls, Shortchanging America,* the AAUW found that through the crucial developmental years of adolescence, girls lose their sense of confidence, maintain a poor self-image, and regard themselves as less talented than boys. Other studies have shown that women respond differently from men in the learning environment, place a greater value on collaborative efforts and more practical matters, are less theoretical and abstract in their intellectual functioning, take fewer risks, are less questioning and confrontational, and are more concerned with intimate relationships.

These factors and more are evidenced in the variances in the men's and women's responses in this survey. Several historic factors are at play here. The majority of elite private colleges were originally all-male institutions with a powerful culture. Institutions that have always been coeducational and those that began admitting women in the 1970s have a larger population of men in most instances and a decidedly smaller number of female tenured faculty. Carol Gilligan, of Harvard University, stated in her study *In a Different Voice* that young women are different from men "by nature" in a number of ways that cause them conflict in a predominantly male environment. The social and personal issues I report in Chapter 4 lend further credence to this interpretation. A 1994 survey of student satisfaction on the MIT campus highlighted some of these factors by virtue of MIT being a traditionally male, scientifically oriented institution:

A survey of seniors' attitudes towards their institution indicates that 73% of seniors in 1994 were satisfied with their overall undergraduate education. Four comparable elite research universities reported a 74% senior satisfaction rate. MIT called attention to the difference in the satisfaction rate of women who were less satisfied with their overall experience at MIT. Women referred more frequently than men to the academic pressure and competition as a negative factor in their experience. MIT women did not view themselves as having grown in self-confidence, self-esteem, and creativity. 42% of men and only 23% of women said that their self-esteem had improved over their four year experience. Several explanations were put forth by Educational Studies Working Group which conducted the study. One is that the smaller population of women on campus hinders women from participating more comfortably in and out of the classroom. Another is that the MIT culture undermines the self-esteem of a majority of students by virtue of the intensity of grading and competition.*

Our high schools and colleges have much to do to ensure that academically gifted women get as much, as happily, from elite colleges as men do.

Comparison of Elite Colleges on Academic Factors

My survey points up both great similarities and contrasts among the elite group of colleges and universities in this study. They differ in size, location, and the amount of emphasis they place on research and

---

*"Survey Reveals Student Satisfaction, But Many Results Differ by Gender," by Jennifer Lane, News Editor. Copyright 1995, 1996, *The Tech*. All rights reserved. This story was published on November 19, 1996; volume 116, number 60.

teaching. They have historically appealed to different kinds of students. While they are all committed to diversity in their student bodies, they vary in their wealth (known as endowments) and, consequently, their ability to offer financial support to needy, qualified students. The physical and human resources for learning and curricular and extracurricular offerings are either the same or differ from institution to institution.

Profound as these distinctions are, they can be ascertained easily by parents or prospective students, thanks to the abundant resource material available about elite colleges. What is of equal or even greater interest to prospective students and their families are issues of a less palpable nature, which are thus harder to measure. These are the qualities called social and academic tone, and they establish the ethos of a campus community.

What follows is a comparison of the students' perceptions and feelings on several of the significant dynamics of nineteen of the twenty institutions in the study (I omitted the University of North Carolina–Chapel Hill because of the limited number of responses). This comparison is included to underscore one of the themes of the study, namely, that a commonality of academic prestige and selective admissions standards does not necessarily translate into a common experience for undergraduates.

I asked each Select student to react positively or negatively to facets of academic life on his or her campus, indicating the one thing about it that came as the biggest surprise. Here are the two most frequently cited sets of responses for each college.

1. Brown University: level of academics are disappointing; not as high as hoped for
2. Columbia University: faculty are accessible and good; too many graduate students teaching
3. Cornell University: too competitive and cutthroat; a difficult, heavy workload
4. Dartmouth College: faculty accessible, friendly, enthusiastic; intense and challenging work
5. Duke University: faculty outstanding, distinguished, caring, accessible; too much emphasis on grades

6. Georgetown University: intense and challenging; faculty caring, interested, great
7. Harvard University: intense, challenging, stimulating environment; faculty removed, not good teachers
8. Johns Hopkins University: cutthroat and competitive atmosphere; challenging and intense
9. MIT: academics difficult and a hard workload; a noncompetitive attitude—students help one another
10. Northwestern University: a competitive environment; not hard, sometimes a boring workload
11. Princeton University: faculty accessible, caring, high quality; a positive competitive atmosphere
12. Stanford University: too many teaching assistants; faculty intimidating, poor social skills, disinterested; not as academic or difficult as expected
13. University of California–Berkeley: too much competition, cutthroat; a difficult, intense workload
14. University of Chicago: intense and rigorous; the core curriculum is a negative
15. University of Pennsylvania: too competitive and cutthroat; faculty helpful, friendly, and accessible
16. University of Wisconsin–Madison: faculty of high quality and accessible; yet many also declared the faculty inaccessible, distant, uncaring
17. Wesleyan University: faculty great, encourage expression and interaction; academics demanding and intense
18. Williams College: faculty good teachers, highly accessible; atmosphere noncompetitive and cooperative
19. Yale University: faculty accessible, devoted, caring; work not as hard as expected

Conclusion

Given the intense demands of academic competition, what is most impressive about Select students is their staying power. Every class over the past decade has averaged a 90% to 97% graduation rate, compared to the national college-completion rate of only two-fifths of the students within five years of entering college. These "achieving survivors," as one student described himself and his classmates, are most likely to realize success in the future outside college. Whether they will be happy and self-fulfilled is not so easily predicted. The final chapter of this study presents a number of interesting, even surprising, findings about the priorities for the future that Select students have set for themselves.

Aristotle's observation of the educational process speaks to the experience reported by many of the intrepid respondents: "In education we use pleasure and pain as rudders to steer their course." The vast amount of work demanded by the faculty and their level of expectations for their students leads to the stress, both emotional and physical, that most Select students experience. However, I found that for the majority, the ultimate reward of achievement and recognition was worth the pain.

Two Words/Phrases That Best Describe the Academic Environment

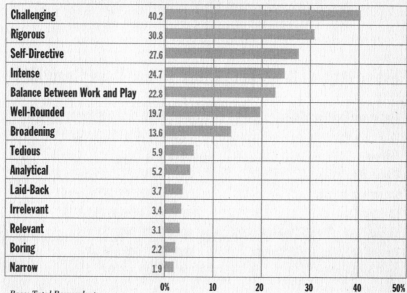

Challenging	40.2
Rigorous	30.8
Self-Directive	27.6
Intense	24.7
Balance Between Work and Play	22.8
Well-Rounded	19.7
Broadening	13.6
Tedious	5.9
Analytical	5.2
Laid-Back	3.7
Irrelevant	3.4
Relevant	3.1
Boring	2.2
Narrow	1.9

Base: Total Respondents
College and University Study
Target Management, Inc.

Two Words/Phrases That Best Describe the Academic Environment

(Split by School Type)

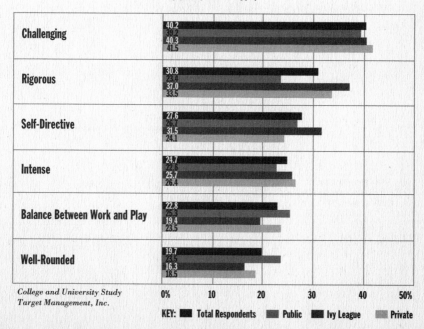

	Total Respondents	Public	Ivy League	Private
Challenging	40.2	39.2	40.3	41.5
Rigorous	30.8	27.2	37.0	33.5
Self-Directive	27.6	26.7	31.5	24.1
Intense	24.7	22.5	25.7	26.4
Balance Between Work and Play	22.8	25.3	19.4	23.5
Well-Rounded	19.7	23.5	16.3	18.5

College and University Study
Target Management, Inc.

KEY: ■ Total Respondents ■ Public ■ Ivy League ■ Private

Expectations Regarding Faculty That Have Been Met

	0%	20	40	60	80	100%
Expertise in Their Disciplines	89.6					
Intellectual Objectivity	77.8					
Fairness	76.5					
Course Offerings	75.7					
Accessibility to Students	73.0					
Quality of Teaching	71.5					
Teaching Geared Toward Student Needs/Interests	61.5					
Personal Relationships with Students	60.1					
Academic Counseling	49.5					

Base: Total Respondents
College and University Study
Target Management, Inc.

Awareness of Cheating or Plagiarism on Campus

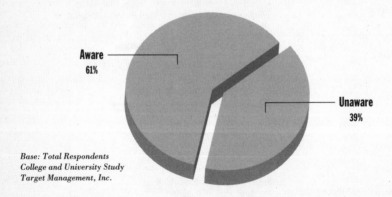

Aware
61%

Unaware
39%

Base: Total Respondents
College and University Study
Target Management, Inc.

Frequency of Cheating on Campus

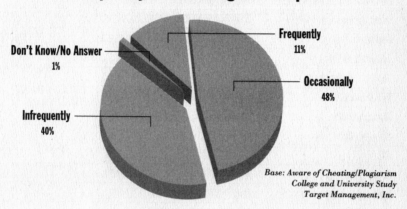

Frequently
11%

Don't Know/No Answer
1%

Occasionally
48%

Infrequently
40%

Base: Aware of Cheating/Plagiarism
College and University Study
Target Management, Inc.

Whether Cheating Has Affected
Respondent's Class Position or Grades

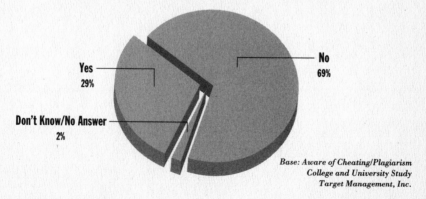

Yes
29%

No
69%

Don't Know/No Answer
2%

Base: Aware of Cheating/Plagiarism
College and University Study
Target Management, Inc.

Academic Stress Level on Campus

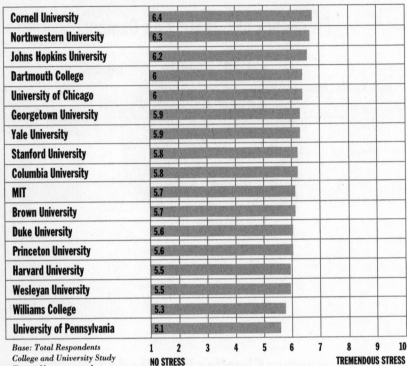

Cornell University	6.4								
Northwestern University	6.3								
Johns Hopkins University	6.2								
Dartmouth College	6								
University of Chicago	6								
Georgetown University	5.9								
Yale University	5.9								
Stanford University	5.8								
Columbia University	5.8								
MIT	5.7								
Brown University	5.7								
Duke University	5.6								
Princeton University	5.6								
Harvard University	5.5								
Wesleyan University	5.5								
Williams College	5.3								
University of Pennsylvania	5.1								

Base: Total Respondents
College and University Study
Target Management, Inc.

1   2   3   4   5   6   7   8   9   10
NO STRESS   **TREMENDOUS STRESS**

Two Words/Phrases That Best Describe the Overall Academic Environment

(Total Ivy League vs. Cornell)

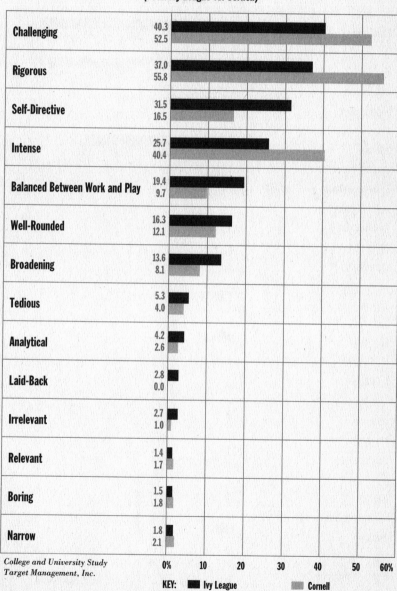

	Ivy League	Cornell
Challenging	40.3	52.5
Rigorous	37.0	55.8
Self-Directive	31.5	16.5
Intense	25.7	40.4
Balanced Between Work and Play	19.4	9.7
Well-Rounded	16.3	12.1
Broadening	13.6	8.1
Tedious	5.3	4.0
Analytical	4.2	2.6
Laid-Back	2.8	0.0
Irrelevant	2.7	1.0
Relevant	1.4	1.7
Boring	1.5	1.8
Narrow	1.8	2.1

*College and University Study
Target Management, Inc.*

0% 10 20 30 40 50 60%

KEY: Ivy League   Cornell

Two Words/Phrases That Best Describe the Overall Academic Environment

(Cornell—Split by Gender)

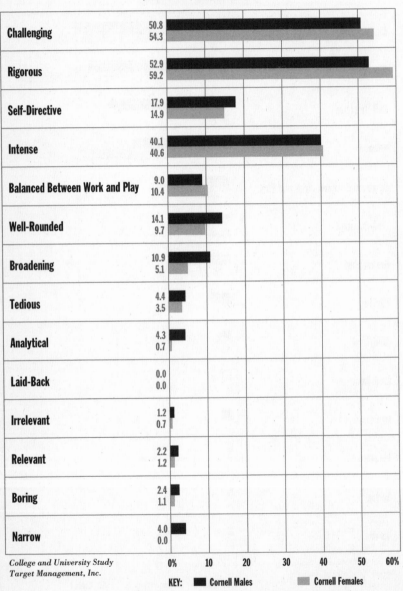

	Males	Females
Challenging	50.8	54.3
Rigorous	52.9	59.2
Self-Directive	17.9	14.9
Intense	40.1	40.6
Balanced Between Work and Play	9.0	10.4
Well-Rounded	14.1	9.7
Broadening	10.9	5.1
Tedious	4.4	3.5
Analytical	4.3	0.7
Laid-Back	0.0	0.0
Irrelevant	1.2	0.7
Relevant	2.2	1.2
Boring	2.4	1.1
Narrow	4.0	0.0

College and University Study
Target Management, Inc.

0%   10   20   30   40   50   60%

KEY: ■ Cornell Males   ▨ Cornell Females

Two Words/Phrases That Best Describe the Academic Environment

(PART ONE)

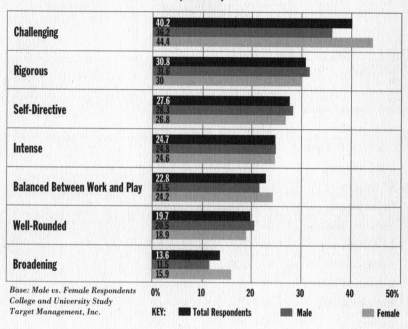

	Total Respondents	Male	Female
Challenging	40.2	36.2	44.4
Rigorous	30.8	31.6	30
Self-Directive	27.6	28.3	26.8
Intense	24.7	24.8	24.6
Balanced Between Work and Play	22.8	21.5	24.2
Well-Rounded	19.7	20.5	18.9
Broadening	13.6	11.5	15.9

Base: Male vs. Female Respondents
College and University Study
Target Management, Inc.

KEY: Total Respondents   Male   Female

(PART TWO)

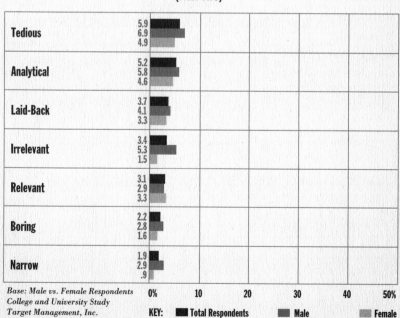

	Total Respondents	Male	Female
Tedious	5.9	6.9	4.9
Analytical	5.2	5.8	4.6
Laid-Back	3.7	4.1	3.3
Irrelevant	3.4	5.3	1.5
Relevant	3.1	2.9	3.3
Boring	2.2	2.8	1.6
Narrow	1.9	2.9	.9

Base: Male vs. Female Respondents
College and University Study
Target Management, Inc.

KEY: Total Respondents   Male   Female

% of Students Saying Behavior of Classmates Is Cutthroat

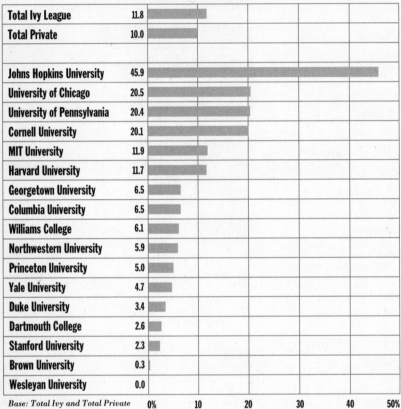

		0%	10	20	30	40	50%
Total Ivy League	11.8						
Total Private	10.0						
Johns Hopkins University	45.9						
University of Chicago	20.5						
University of Pennsylvania	20.4						
Cornell University	20.1						
MIT University	11.9						
Harvard University	11.7						
Georgetown University	6.5						
Columbia University	6.5						
Williams College	6.1						
Northwestern University	5.9						
Princeton University	5.0						
Yale University	4.7						
Duke University	3.4						
Dartmouth College	2.6						
Stanford University	2.3						
Brown University	0.3						
Wesleyan University	0.0						

Base: Total Ivy and Total Private
College and University Study
Target Management, Inc.

% of Students Aware of Cheating or Plagiarism Who Said It Had Directly Affected Their Class Position or Grades

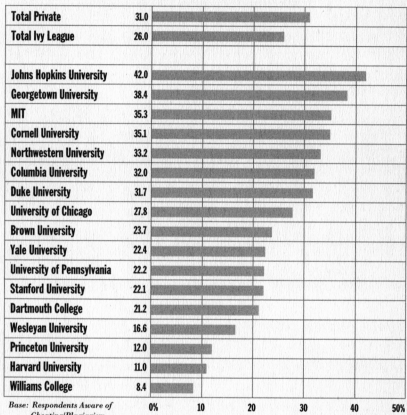

Total Private	31.0	
Total Ivy League	26.0	
Johns Hopkins University	42.0	
Georgetown University	38.4	
MIT	35.3	
Cornell University	35.1	
Northwestern University	33.2	
Columbia University	32.0	
Duke University	31.7	
University of Chicago	27.8	
Brown University	23.7	
Yale University	22.4	
University of Pennsylvania	22.2	
Stanford University	22.1	
Dartmouth College	21.2	
Wesleyan University	16.6	
Princeton University	12.0	
Harvard University	11.0	
Williams College	8.4	

0%   10   20   30   40   50%

Base: Respondents Aware of Cheating/Plagiarism
College and University Study
Target Management, Inc.

THREE
The Cost of an Elite Education

Sky-High Costs

After successfully completing the hurdles to cross the finish line ahead of thousands of other talented competitors, Select students are presented with a staggering bill: more than $29,000 a year. The expense of college tuition and room and board has outpaced inflation and doubled in the past fifteen years in both public and private colleges. As recently as 1982, Harvard and its fellow elite institutions cost a student $10,000. While the average tuition at America's private colleges is $10,671, the Ivies and other selective institutions now average more than $22,000 a year. Brown now has the dubious distinction of charging the highest tuition of any elite school: $23,124. Dartmouth, MIT, and Yale follow closely behind.

In response to the spiral of increases that have occurred over the past decade, Harvard limited its tuition increase for the 1996–97 school year to 4.8%—the smallest hike since 1969. Still, Harvard's restraint was mostly a gesture; its endowment exceeds $8 billion, and the rise in the cost of living in that year was almost flat. Tuition, room, and board at Harvard cost a full-paying student $29,895. To compensate for this hefty charge, Harvard grants slightly more than 52% of its undergraduates financial aid. Both the cost and the percentage of students who receive financial assistance are similar in the other private institutions I surveyed for *The Select*.

Princeton's trustees voted to limit its increase in tuition by 4.6% for the 1996–97 academic year after reviewing with considerable concern the double-digit annual increases of the 1980s. In the same deliberations, the trustees voted to continue Princeton's commitment to need-blind admission—a policy of admitting students without consideration of their financial need. As one of fewer than ten colleges left that can remain committed to this policy because of its huge endowment (some of the other elite institutions that have the funds and the commitment to need-blind admission include Dartmouth, Harvard, Stanford, Williams, and Yale), Princeton found it had a shortfall in its financial aid budget of $1 million for the 1996–97 school year. To fulfill the goals of its commendable policy, it and other institutions have had to increase the burden of loans and on-campus job expectations a student is expected to bear. Students who might have worked ten hours a week in 1979 are now required to work as many as twenty hours.

It has become a conundrum: As tuition and room and board fees continue to escalate each year at a rate well beyond the cost of living index, colleges have to award more financial aid to more students, which means that to compensate, they have to increase their tuition in succeeding years. The federal government's failure to keep pace with funding higher education's needs only adds to that urgency. The seventeen private colleges in my survey provide financial aid to 40% to 60% of their undergraduates. Those with great endowments are struggling to strike a balance between, on the one hand, their goal of diversifying each entering class by using financial aid and, on the other hand, remaining solvent. Without periodic fundraising campaigns—campaigns that are increasing in duration and frequency— this policy will disappear quickly.

It is not uncommon to hear students and parents who are not in need of financial aid complain that their hard-earned dollars are paying for those who receive "handouts." That is an ugly attitude, in my opinion, but one often triggered by college administrators, who rationalize that the rising tuition is a result of recruiting more "nontraditional students" to help meet the goal of diversifying their student bodies.

As an admissions officer at Princeton in the late 1960s, I would hesitate before quoting to a parent the total cost of a year of study at the university. After all, $3,200 for room, board, tuition, and fees was a huge sum compared to the $2,100 Dartmouth had exacted from me only six years earlier! I share the concern of a Yale undergraduate in my survey:

> I am afraid that if Yale's tuition continues to increase at a rate well above the inflation rate, it will price itself out of the market. Yale will attract a weaker student body because only those extremely rich or those on full scholarship will be able to attend.

And yet there are innumerable stories of how far an individual will go to enroll in an expensive and elite university, no matter the financial and psychic cost. Here is a startling example, much covered in the national media, which is excerpted below from *The Chronicle of Higher Education*:

> When 18-year-old Camber Barrett left his mother's house four days before he took the Scholastic Assessment Test, he resigned himself to live on the streets—and study in the subway trains running between Brooklyn and Manhattan. Mr. Barrett made the subway his study hall because it was the quietest place he knew. . . . Mr. Barrett, a Jamaican immigrant, says: "I never thought I'd get all this attention. I didn't want publicity or money—I just wanted a scholarship because I knew I couldn't pay for college, and sitting on the subway for four days and three nights was the only way I knew how to do it." He waited tables at a Manhattan restaurant until 4 A.M. Then he would ride the train and do his homework. In June, Mr. Barrett graduated from Thomas Jefferson High School in Brooklyn, where he was the student-body president and class valedictorian. He received a full scholarship to Cornell University, where he plans to enroll this fall and prepare for medical school. "Failing would have meant losing out on all my ambitions, and I'd have ended up in the

gutter somewhere, so I didn't think about it too much because it was too scary," he says. "Cornell is definitely going to be the biggest hurdle I've had to face yet."

Because of students like Camber Barrett—as well as parents and prospective Select students at all income levels—America's elite schools will retain the allure required to charge what the market will bear. Nationally, under 10% of 15 million undergraduates pay over $12,000 a year in tuition. But the most elite schools can charge twice that amount because of the drawing power of their names and prestige. Why else would half the students who enroll in the elite colleges take on such financial burdens when they would easily have qualified for significant academic scholarships at any of the other excellent colleges, both public and private, that try to woo them? The Halo Effect is, indeed, a powerful force for many families.

Select students are troubled that they are asked to finance their education with an increasing reliance on loans and campus jobs. In 1992 the federal government revised the Higher Education Act to make borrowing for college and graduate school much easier. Since then, both the ratio of loans to grants and the amount of loans to students have increased dramatically. Today, 6.5 million undergraduates take out government loans to the tune of $24 billion. From 1990 to the beginning of the 1996–97 academic year, college students and their families had borrowed $100 billion. The rate of borrowing is accelerating as the cost of college continues to grow at a greater pace than most families' disposal income. The elite colleges have to include these government-sponsored loan funds in their aid packages to almost all of their students; there is no other way to close the gap between the total costs and the resources available to over half the admitted students. With more responsibility for paying for their education being passed on to students, getting their money's worth and paying off their debts have become major campus issues. The bitterness in the words of this Brown undergraduate is, I am certain, common among those paying for their education by work, loans, and family sacrifice:

66The people here are extremely sheltered—that makes it rather unpleasant for someone who doesn't live off of Daddy's money, someone who actually has contact with the pressures of the real world. The classes are wonderful academic opportunities, but not for the money. 💬💬

How Students Pay for Their Education

In my survey, I explored how the Select students felt about college costs. Half the nonminority participants in the survey, and 63% of the students of color, were receiving financial assistance from their respective colleges. The students' responses reflect a number of interesting patterns. Gender, race, and age all influenced how each student felt about the cost of college. For a third to almost half the respondents, depending on their socioeconomic background, financial aid was a factor in choosing which school to attend. Only a quarter to a third of these students indicated that the cost of tuition, room, and board was a crucial factor in choosing which colleges they initially *applied* to. Though their concerns were real, paying for college was less of a deciding factor than the reasons the students mentioned most frequently, namely, prestige and name recognition, academic programs, and preparation for graduate school. Getting into an elite school mattered more than worrying about how to pay for it.

What happens, however, once students are *enrolled* reflects an important shift in their concerns. Asked what components of college life had a direct negative effect on them, 40% of the students cited financial responsibilities. For 54% of the students of color, financial matters were a major concern. A third of the women and students of color reported that having to hold a job had a direct negative effect on them. More men than women indicated that financial responsibilities had no direct negative effect on them.

I was intrigued, but not surprised, to find that women worry more about the cost of their education and the need to hold a job. It is possible, even probable, that more men are awarded larger outright grants in their financial aid packages because they are recruited athletes. This situation may well change in the coming years because the eight Ivy League colleges have audited themselves to ensure that they are playing fair with one another and not awarding unusually large financial aid packages to recruited athletes, while providing less aid for nonathletes. Historically, the Ivies have agreed on a policy of awarding all students financial assistance only on the basis of demonstrated need. Each college can determine, however, the components of its aid package, which means that a star athlete could be assigned a large grant, rather than a loan, to meet the overall need amount. In 1991 the U.S. Department of Justice brought a suit against the eight Ivies and fifteen other highly selective colleges to bar their annual discussions of financial aid candidates. According to the Justice Department, these discussions were a form of collusion that were intended to lower the amount of financial awards. The new, self-imposed auditing may well have been caused by the large differences in the amounts or makeup of the aid packages awarded to athletes.

Other gender factors also affect how students pay for their higher education. Men are more likely to accumulate greater earnings during the summer breaks by doing physical seasonal work that women tend not to seek. More men than women use the greater portion of their earnings to pay direct college costs. At many of these colleges, women tend to spend more money on personal items and better-quality, safer housing. Last, women's greater financial concerns may arise because they are planning for careers in fields that may not be as high paying as the traditional careers men tend to choose. Thus, female graduates would have more trouble paying off college loans. Many college students have addressed this issue with me as they discuss potential career tracks.

As further evidence of the burden that many Select students shoulder to pay for their education, I found a disturbing pattern reflected in the survey group: Over their four years of school, an ever-greater number of students have paying jobs. For women, the percentage who work goes from 42% of freshwomen to 70% of seniors. For men, the increase is from 35% to 56%. What is happening here? Many students find that the cost of getting an education is greater than they had anticipated; many also have had their families allocate the greater portion of their resources to the first year or two of college costs. Moreover, as the shape of the economy has changed in the 1990s, the families of Select students have often directly felt the impact of corporate downsizing and parental job loss—thus creating a new category of legitimate need-based applicants among students already in college. In recent years, college financial aid directors have experienced a dramatic increase in the number of enrolled students requesting reviews of their financial situation. All these factors combine to expand the pool of undergraduates who are working; worrying about money; and, consequently, feeling greater stress.

The Psychic Cost of College Expenses

Financial costs can become the last straw that finally damages a student's overall well-being, especially expenses unanticipated before enrollment. Not covered in a student's $30,000 tuition, room, and board are major add-on expenses like these:

- books for required reading in each course
- science materials for specific courses
- fees for student services
- entrance and social dues for private clubs, fraternities, and sororities
- travel to and from school
- food beyond the basic meal plan
- clothing and other basic necessities
- entertainment and dating
- housing, if a student lives off campus
- computer equipment and programs

A federally subsidized work-study program provides campus employment, administered by the individual colleges, for 700,000 students annually. The average income it provides, about $1,100, does not go far in meeting the expenses that students are faced with. From speaking with undergraduates, I know that many scholarship recipients are working more than the regulation twenty hours a week at their assigned campus jobs. It is not atypical for students to take on two or three jobs at one time to make up for the shortfall in their expenses. Many talk of falling asleep at their desks or in class because of their overloaded work schedules. One Yale woman expressed the plight of many of her peers throughout the elite colleges:

> 66 Unfortunately, my financial obligations prevent me from partici-
> pating in sports and some other activities as well as studying as much
> as I need to. 99

Students complain about the gap between their financial aid packages and their obligations. How determined to fill the gap are some
students? A group of enterprising undergraduates at Brown
University and other colleges have joined the ranks of professional
strippers. With the opportunity to earn as much as $1,000 a week,
these young women have no qualms about their off-campus employment and face down the criticism of their peers.

To understand the impact that the loan portion of a financial aid
package has on students, consider the average amount of debt for
which Select 1996 graduates were responsible: from $11,650 at
Harvard to over $17,500 at Brown, Columbia, and Pennsylvania. In
comparison, the national average of indebtedness for graduates of
private colleges in the same year was nearly $11,000. These figures
do not take into account loans from other sources that students and
their families may have incurred. Increasingly, parents are taking out
educational loans from banks and credit unions and putting second
mortgages on their homes as they struggle to help meet their children's college expenses. How can these financial burdens not add
extra stress to overtaxed Select students?

The overwhelming cost of elite colleges affects more than just students' wallets. It affects their choices. Many of our potential future
leaders are inevitably influenced in their career decisions and commitments by academic indebtedness; my many conversations with undergraduates and recent graduates have confirmed the influence that their
finances play in choosing careers. Once they have tallied the debts
they will have to repay, a number of talented young adults are aban-
doning earlier plans to enter education, the public sector, social service, and other lower-paying careers. These decisions have serious
implications for the community as well as the individuals. Generations
of students have taken seriously the summons of John Harvard to enter
college "to grow in wisdom, depart to serve better thy country and thy
kind." I worry that their financial burdens will allow fewer of the present and future generations of elite college graduates to heed that call.

Is the Select Education Worth the Cost?

The atmosphere on elite campuses may be changing in direct relation to the rising costs, as this Stanford student claimed:

> I believe the "grade paranoia" is a direct result of the astronomic cost of attending college here. America's elite schools must become more affordable or this trend will continue and our students will become mere "résumé machines," lacking the holistic learning that is needed for quality contribution out in the real world.

I asked the Select students in my survey to rate their colleges in terms of value received for money spent on tuition, room, and board. On the academic side, more than half the men and women of all backgrounds felt they were receiving excellent or very good value for the money they and their families spent. One quarter judged the value satisfactory. This junior male at Georgetown would be in the remaining quarter:

> I truly believe they are more concerned here with tuition for the college than the convenience of the students, and I am convinced this attitude will hurt the college financially in the future.

These responses can be interpreted as either positive or negative. What is wrong with a 61% overall satisfaction rate? Given the normal critical nature of adolescents and young adults, isn't this a pretty good ratio? Yet if these are the most competitive colleges in the land, why shouldn't 100% of the students feel they are getting their money's worth? Other questions in the survey clarified the findings as the students evaluated such defining issues as the quality of teaching, their relation to the curriculum, the size of classes, the accessibility of famous or even merely tenured faculty, the levels of competition and stress, and the effect of ambitions and preoccupation with grades and admission to graduate school. Certainly 100% of the students arrive on campus assuming they'll get their money's worth—why else would they pay such high tuition and incur great long-term financial obligations? Another Georgetown student answered this question with brutal practicality:

66 I feel I could receive the same education at a cheaper college, but the name of Georgetown will help in the future. 99

This freshwoman at Brown would agree:

66 They expect you to pay too much money . . . it's not worth $30,000 a year. I am very disappointed with the school. 99

The Price and Perils of Room and Board

When I asked about the value they received for room and board, only a quarter of the Select students thought they received excellent or very good value. A little more than a third said they received satisfactory to average value. Almost a third of the students thought they were receiving poor value for the costs incurred. Young adults are no different from anyone else in enjoying the creature comforts of food, privacy, and pleasant surroundings. The effect of these factors can be considerable, especially on young people who are away from home for a lengthy period, often for the first time, under various levels of stress and anxiety. A Cornell senior put it this way:

66 Along with the outrageous tuition costs and room/board costs, the school puts nickel-and-dime costs on everything. Even the meal plan is costing me an arm and a leg. For all this money I don't think I am getting any better an education than at a state school. The only thing my money is buying is "the name" of the school and its reputation. 99

Some undergraduates feel that they receive the short end of the stick compared to various interest groups on campus. A University of Pennsylvania student made this observation:

66 I feel that the benefits derived from the high tuition we pay are not evenly spread out among the undergraduates. A lot of the sports teams use a considerable amount of money to go off to tournaments or to maintain the expensive sports complexes. 99

Anyone who has attended college can sympathize with the near-universal disdain for campus food. Is there a generation of collegians who has not experienced platter banging or food fights in the Commons, brought on by hostility to the day's menu—when today's chicken Parmesan patties are dubbed "elephant scabs" and the Friday entrée gets redubbed "Weekly Menu in Review"? Although such complaints are real, this fierce dissatisfaction with the cuisine and other living conditions is often an outlet for the stress of work: the critical comments and the less-than-perfect grade on a paper returned that morning, the homesickness, the love lost over the weekend, and the dashed hopes of making a team or getting the lead in the theater group's new play.

What strikes me is that quality-of-life issues seem so much more central to contemporary students. The students' dependence on basic creature comforts and their sense of financial value have greatly intensified. So many more students are working to help pay for their education and maintenance. So many more varied ethnic and cultural groups sorely miss the foods they have grown up with. Comfort food is a notion that many young people embrace, since they recognize its role in their emotional well-being. The following randomly selected comments from a large pool of responses provide a flavor of the attitudes on the various campuses about the quality of the essentials of food and shelter:

> The quality of food is good but the diversity does not satisfy. Many Asian and Hispanic minorities who are used to eating spicy foods are left with bland turkey, mashed potatoes, pizzas, hamburger, salads or some weak imitation of ethnic foods.
> —UNIVERSITY OF CHICAGO JUNIOR, MALE

> The first-year dining plan is atrocious—you have to eat in a dining hall that serves below-par prison-grade food.
> —COLUMBIA SOPHOMORE, MALE

> The food sucks! I have an ulcer.
> —COLUMBIA JUNIOR, FEMALE

  ❝The way the college spends its students' parents' money is ridiculous, especially the food services and mandatory housing.❞

—BROWN SOPHOMORE, FEMALE

  ❝The food is really great—the meal plan, however, is really expensive and may not be affordable for many students. The housing situation is really bad because after freshman year people have to move off campus—few dorm spaces are available. This is extremely expensive and doesn't do much to give the school a feeling of community.❞

—CORNELL SOPHOMORE, MALE

As the last comment suggests, there is a powerfully important quality-of-life concern for many undergraduates at the elite colleges: housing. All these schools have historically been residential undergraduate colleges, committed to the philosophical advantages inherent in a community of young scholars living together. However, the increased popularity of these colleges, even in the face of their high costs, has led to higher admission yields than college administrators anticipated. The result is a swelling demand for housing facilities. On a number of campuses, such as Yale and the University of Pennsylvania, a legacy of poor dormitory maintenance, owing to financial constraints and deferred repairs, has resulted in severely inadequate living spaces. More students are living off campus for a second set of reasons: The rent is cheaper, and they can cook their own food. In just about every Select institution, except for the small-town schools like Dartmouth and Williams, there is a growing movement toward off-campus living. This phenomenon must exert a significant negative effect on the cohesiveness and collegiality of campus life.

The rising costs of room and board plague both Select students and their colleges. The Stanford administrators' spring 1996 review of the university's student meal plan revealed that it was one of the most expensive such programs in the nation. In comparison to its neighbor, the University of California–Berkeley, which charges $1,675 for nineteen meals per week, Stanford undergraduates are obligated to pay $3,692 for the same number of meals. Stanford

claimed its high costs were due to the nature of the residential college system; its food service personnel run 35 different dining rooms
on campus. This is a classic example of how educational policy,
which can make eminently good sense, may have serious financial
ramifications for students who have to pay for it.

In the early 1930s, Yale lavished money and artistic detail on
building its residential colleges, which were central to its educational philosophy—that smaller clusters of student scholars and faculty should be living, eating, and discoursing with one another. In
recent years, however, the combination of an expensive and inflexi-
ble meal plan, high board costs, and cramped living spaces that pre-
clude privacy has led many Yalies to move out. A month-long series
of strikes by maintenance, custodial, and dining hall workers in 1996
forced students to forage for their own food and clean their own living
quarters. This situation did not endear the university and its expensive residential situation to many students. More and more Yale students have moved off campus, where they feel they are in control of
their personal well-being. This is a new and discouraging social pattern at a venerable institution that believes in the social and intellectual values that are created through the residential colleges.

More students than anticipated enrolled at Princeton in fall 1995,
forcing the university to rent a number of trailers from the ironically
named After Disaster Housing Corporation to house thirty-five
sophomores. Living in mobile shelters was not quite what the students and their parents had in mind when they originally considered
enrolling at this most beautiful of American gothic campuses. The
university had to offer a $1,000 reduction in the standard room and
board costs to encourage volunteers to sign up for the trailers.
Demonstrating the spark of humor for which undergraduates, thank-
fully, are still famous, plastic pink flamingos appeared outside the
trailer doors. The Princeton administrators took a more conservative
course in the next admissions cycle to prevent a repeat of "the trailer
epoch."

Brown experienced a similar problem, brought about by its bur-
geoning popularity. Ninety more candidates accepted the school's
offer of admission than anticipated in spring 1996. Brown spent the
summer hastily converting a number of its dormitories' student

lounges into rooms to accommodate the overflow. The happiest students turned out to be sophomores who were allowed to move off campus to alleviate the housing crisis.

What Price Prestige?

It is not within the purview of this book to explore the myriad reasons an elite education costs so much today. However, my survey of Select students corroborates the belief that they and their parents have reason to explore a number of key financial issues about the schools they are considering or attending:

- For what is their tuition money spent?
- What are the credentials of those who teach? Are they professors or graduate students?
- How many actual class days are on the academic calendar?
- What are the actual costs for students' out-of-pocket necessities?
- What are the quality and level of safety of on-campus living?
- Does the college offer housing guarantee and, if so, for how many terms?
- What is the cost of meal plans, and what do the plans cover?
- What is the availability and cost, if any, of services, such as academic and career counseling?
- Does the college provide financial counseling on scholarship, work study programs, loans, and the terms of repayment plans?

In other chapters I examine more about Select students' attitudes toward their respective institutions and whether they would choose to attend if given a second chance; although the vast majority would enroll all over again, *all would first get answers to the questions just listed.*

I am not 100% convinced that tickets of admission to elite institutions should automatically be grabbed by students who will face great stress because of the debt they will incur. Financial burdens can have a profound effect on college students' performance and future options in life. I raise this issue as a challenge to all those who are engaged in the college-selection process, from counselors to admissions officers to parents and students. As a college admissions counselor, I have guided dozens of talented young men and women who need some degree of financial assistance to excellent state universities and less expensive private colleges. I know they will be able to achieve a successful balance of academic work, social life, and contribution to their community because they are under less pressure financially. What price prestige? It is, I am sorry to say, too high for many unknowing individuals who cannot see beyond the glitter of the Halo Effect.

The Price Tag of a Prestigious Education
1997–98 Tuition, Room, and Board

Private Colleges	Tuition and Fees	Room and Board	Rounded Total
Brown University	$23,124	$6,776	$29,900
Columbia University	22,650	7,332	30,000
Cornell University	21,914	7,110	29,000
Dartmouth College	23,035	6,590	29,600
Duke University	22,179	6,830	29,000
Georgetown University	21,405	8,092	29,500
Harvard University	21,900	6,995	29,000
Johns Hopkins University	21,700	7,355	29,100
Massachusetts Institute of Technology	23,100	6,550	29,700
Northwestern University	18,144	6,054	24,500
Princeton University	22,920	6,515	29,500
Stanford University	21,300	7,560	28,900
University of Chicago	22,671	7,604	30,300
University of Pennsylvania	22,250	7,280	29,500
Wesleyan University	22,980	7,760	30,700
Williams College	22,995	6,355	29,400
Yale University	23,100	6,850	30,000

Public Universities	Tuition and Fees	Room/Board	Rounded Total
University of California– Berkeley			
(In state)	$4,354	$7,657	$12,000
(Out of state)	13,338	7,657	21,000
University of North Carolina–Chapel Hill			
(In state)	2,183	4,760	7,000
(Out of state)	10,715	4,760	15,500
University of Wisconsin– Madison			
(In state)	3,180	4,860	8,000
(Out of state)	10,750	4,860	15,600

Personal expenses, books, and supplies should be added to college costs. They currently range from approximately $1,700 to as high as $2,700.

(Figures reported by the College Board in its annual survey of its member institutions.)

Items of Primary Concern to Student Life

	%
Academic Workload	84.2
Friends/Quality of Friendships	72.5
Grade Point Average	56.5
Choice of Major	48.8
Romantic Relationship	45.2
General Stress	44.1
Post-College Job Placement	41.7
Graduate School Plans	39.7
School and Living Expenses	35.0
Living Arrangements	32.6
Personal Safety on Campus	9.9
Political Correctness Issues	7.4
Peer Pressure	6.3
Physical/Medical Problem	5.2
Psychological Problem	4.8
Alcohol Abuse	4.0
Suicide	1.8

Base: Total Respondents
College and University Study
Target Management, Inc.

0% 10 20 30 40 50 60 70 80 90%

Items of Secondary Concern to Student Life

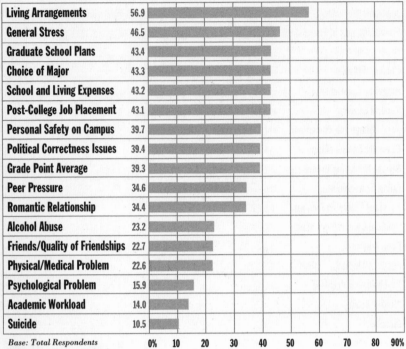

Living Arrangements	56.9
General Stress	46.5
Graduate School Plans	43.4
Choice of Major	43.3
School and Living Expenses	43.2
Post-College Job Placement	43.1
Personal Safety on Campus	39.7
Political Correctness Issues	39.4
Grade Point Average	39.3
Peer Pressure	34.6
Romantic Relationship	34.4
Alcohol Abuse	23.2
Friends/Quality of Friendships	22.7
Physical/Medical Problem	22.6
Psychological Problem	15.9
Academic Workload	14.0
Suicide	10.5

0% 10 20 30 40 50 60 70 80 90%

Base: Total Respondents
College and University Study
Target Management, Inc.

Items of No Concern to Student Life

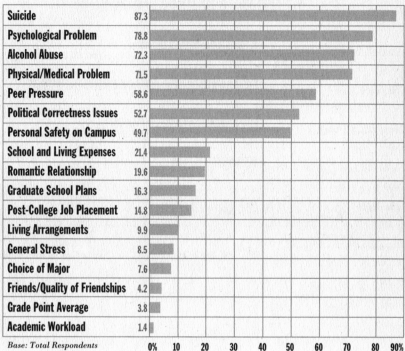

Suicide	87.3										
Psychological Problem	78.8										
Alcohol Abuse	72.3										
Physical/Medical Problem	71.5										
Peer Pressure	58.6										
Political Correctness Issues	52.7										
Personal Safety on Campus	49.7										
School and Living Expenses	21.4										
Romantic Relationship	19.6										
Graduate School Plans	16.3										
Post-College Job Placement	14.8										
Living Arrangements	9.9										
General Stress	8.5										
Choice of Major	7.6										
Friends/Quality of Friendships	4.2										
Grade Point Average	3.8										
Academic Workload	1.4										

Base: Total Respondents
College and University Study
Target Management, Inc.

0% 10 20 30 40 50 60 70 80 90%

Value Received for Money Spent
on Tuition and Room/Board

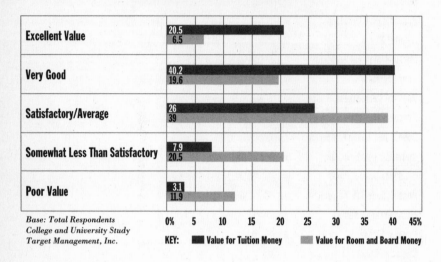

Excellent Value — 20.5 / 6.5

Very Good — 40.2 / 19.6

Satisfactory/Average — 26 / 39

Somewhat Less Than Satisfactory — 7.9 / 20.5

Poor Value — 3.1 / 11.9

0% 5 10 15 20 25 30 35 40 45%

Base: Total Respondents
College and University Study
Target Management, Inc.

KEY: ■ Value for Tuition Money   ■ Value for Room and Board Money

Future Value of School's Education

(Total Ivy League)

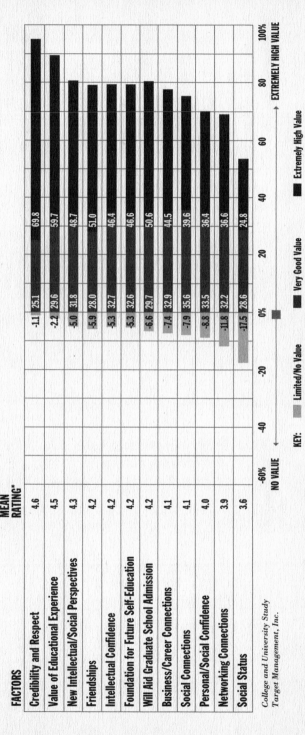

FACTORS	MEAN RATING*			
Credibility and Respect	4.6	-1.1	25.1	69.8
Value of Educational Experience	4.5	-2.2	29.6	59.7
New Intellectual/Social Perspectives	4.3	-5.0	31.8	48.7
Friendships	4.2	-5.9	28.0	51.0
Intellectual Confidence	4.2	-5.3	32.7	46.4
Foundation for Future Self-Education	4.2	-5.3	32.6	46.6
Will Aid Graduate School Admission	4.2	-6.6	29.7	50.6
Business/Career Connections	4.1	-7.4	32.9	44.5
Social Connections	4.1	-7.9	35.6	39.6
Personal/Social Confidence	4.0	-8.8	33.5	36.4
Networking Connections	3.9	-11.8	32.2	36.6
Social Status	3.6	-17.5	28.6	24.8

-60%   -40   -20   0%   20   40   60   80   100%

NO VALUE ← → EXTREMELY HIGH VALUE

KEY: ▨ Limited/No Value   ▨ Very Good Value   ■ Extremely High Value

College and University Study
Target Management, Inc.

*Ratings scale: 1= Of no value, 2= Of limited value, 3= Somewhat a value, 4= Very good value, 5= Extremely high value

Future Value of School's Education

(Total—Harvard)

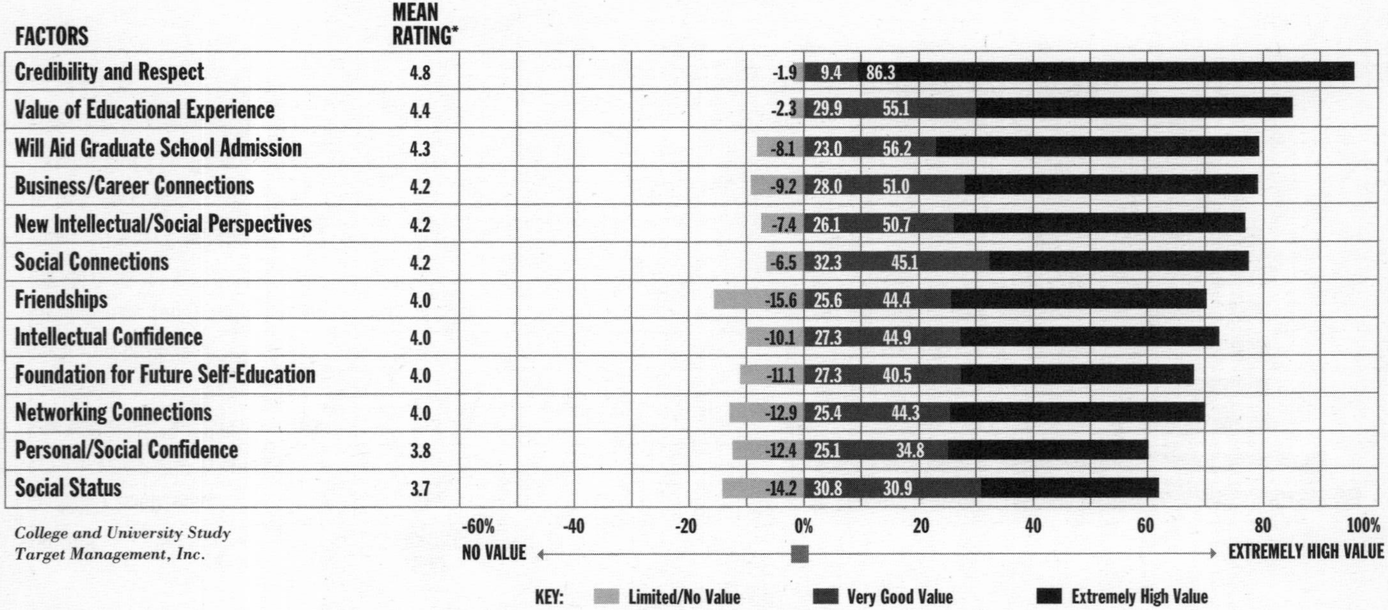
FACTORS
MEAN RATING*
Credibility and Respect 4.8 -1.9 9.4 86.3
Value of Educational Experience 4.4 -2.3 29.9 55.1
Will Aid Graduate School Admission 4.3 -8.1 23.0 56.2
Business/Career Connections 4.2 -9.2 28.0 51.0
New Intellectual/Social Perspectives 4.2 -7.4 26.1 50.7
Social Connections 4.2 -6.5 32.3 45.1
Friendships 4.0 -15.6 25.6 44.4
Intellectual Confidence 4.0 -10.1 27.3 44.9
Foundation for Future Self-Education 4.0 -11.1 27.3 40.5
Networking Connections 4.0 -12.9 25.4 44.3
Personal/Social Confidence 3.8 -12.4 25.1 34.8
Social Status 3.7 -14.2 30.8 30.9
-60% -40 -20 0% 20 40 60 80 100%
NO VALUE
EXTREMELY HIGH VALUE
College and University Study
Target Management, Inc.
KEY:
Limited/No Value
Very Good Value
Extremely High Value

*Ratings scale: 1= Of no value, 2= Of limited value, 3= Somewhat of a value, 4= Very good value, 5= Extremely high value

Future Value of School's Education

(Harvard—Males)

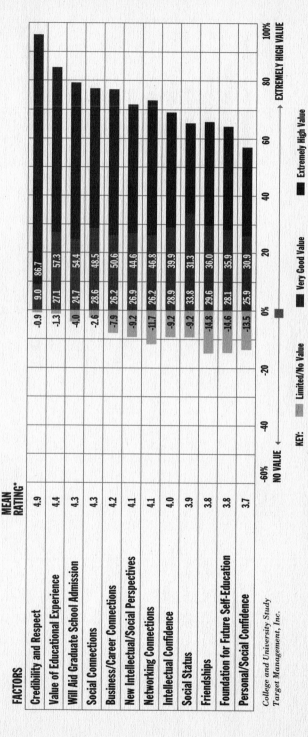

FACTORS	MEAN RATING*	NO VALUE	Limited/No Value	0%	Very Good Value	Extremely High Value
Credibility and Respect	4.9		-0.9	9.0	86.7	
Value of Educational Experience	4.4		-1.3	27.1	57.3	
Will Aid Graduate School Admission	4.3		-4.0	24.7	54.4	
Social Connections	4.3		-2.6	28.6	48.5	
Business/Career Connections	4.2		-7.9	26.2	50.6	
New Intellectual/Social Perspectives	4.1		-9.2	26.9	44.6	
Networking Connections	4.1		-11.7	26.2	46.8	
Intellectual Confidence	4.0		-9.2	28.9	39.9	
Social Status	3.9		-9.2	33.8	31.3	
Friendships	3.8		-14.8	29.6	36.0	
Foundation for Future Self-Education	3.8		-14.6	28.1	35.9	
Personal/Social Confidence	3.7		-13.5	25.9	30.9	

-60% -40 -20 0% 20 40 60 80 100%

NO VALUE ←   → EXTREMELY HIGH VALUE

College and University Study
Target Management, Inc.

KEY: ■ Limited/No Value   ■ Very Good Value   ■ Extremely High Value

*Ratings scale: 1= Of no value, 2= Of limited value, 3= Somewhat of a value, 4= Very good value, 5= Extremely high value

Future Value of School's Education

(Harvard—Females)

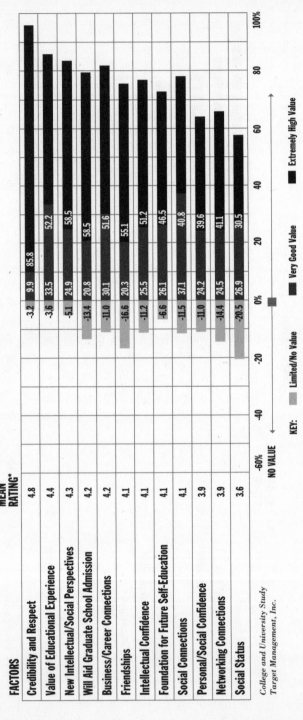

FACTORS	MEAN RATING*			
Credibility and Respect	4.8	-3.2	9.9	85.8
Value of Educational Experience	4.4	-3.6	33.5	52.2
New Intellectual/Social Perspectives	4.3	-5.1	24.9	58.5
Will Aid Graduate School Admission	4.2	-13.4	20.8	58.5
Business/Career Connections	4.2	-11.0	30.1	51.6
Friendships	4.1	-16.6	20.3	55.1
Intellectual Confidence	4.1	-11.2	25.5	51.2
Foundation for Future Self-Education	4.1	-6.6	26.1	46.5
Social Connections	4.1	-11.5	37.1	40.8
Personal/Social Confidence	3.9	-11.0	24.2	39.6
Networking Connections	3.9	-14.4	24.5	41.1
Social Status	3.6	-20.5	26.9	30.5

KEY: Limited/No Value   Very Good Value   Extremely High Value

College and University Study Target Management, Inc.

*Ratings scale: 1= Of no value, 2= Of limited value, 3= Somewhat of a value, 4= Very good value, 5= Extremely high value

Students Who Receive
Financial Assistance From School

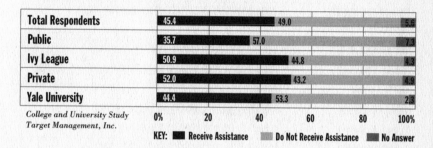

Total Respondents	45.4	49.0	5.6
Public	35.7	57.0	7.3
Ivy League	50.9	44.8	4.3
Private	52.0	43.2	4.9
Yale University	44.4	53.3	2.3

College and University Study
Target Management, Inc.

0%   20   40   60   80   100%

KEY: ■ Receive Assistance   ▨ Do Not Receive Assistance   ■ No Answer

Students Who Work at Paying Job
During the School Year

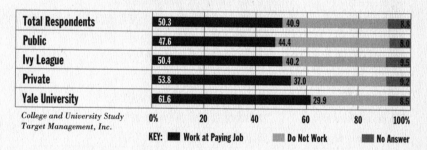

Total Respondents	50.3	40.9	8.8
Public	47.6	44.4	8.0
Ivy League	50.4	40.2	9.5
Private	53.8	37.0	9.2
Yale University	61.6	29.9	8.5

College and University Study
Target Management, Inc.

0%   20   40   60   80   100%

KEY: ■ Work at Paying Job   ▨ Do Not Work   ■ No Answer

% of Students Who Work and Use Salary
to Defray Cost of Tuition/Room & Board

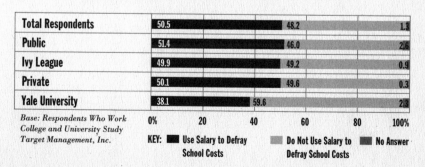

Total Respondents	50.5	48.2	1.3
Public	51.4	46.0	2.6
Ivy League	49.9	49.2	0.9
Private	50.1	49.6	0.3
Yale University	38.1	59.6	2.3

Base: Respondents Who Work
College and University Study
Target Management, Inc.

0%   20   40   60   80   100%

KEY: ■ Use Salary to Defray   ▨ Do Not Use Salary to   ■ No Answer
     School Costs   Defray School Costs

Value Received for Money Spent on Tuition

(Summary of Top Two Ratings, "Extremely High"/"Very Good Value")

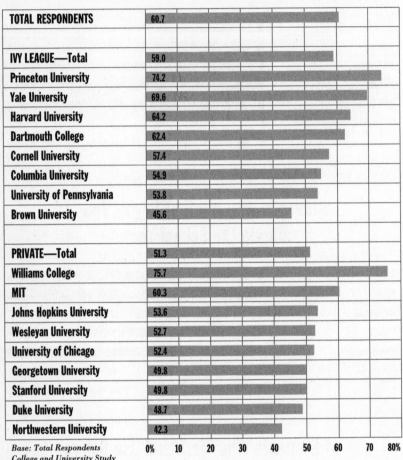

	0%	10	20	30	40	50	60	70	80%
TOTAL RESPONDENTS	60.7								
IVY LEAGUE—Total	59.0								
Princeton University	74.2								
Yale University	69.6								
Harvard University	64.2								
Dartmouth College	62.4								
Cornell University	57.4								
Columbia University	54.9								
University of Pennsylvania	53.8								
Brown University	45.6								
PRIVATE—Total	51.3								
Williams College	75.7								
MIT	60.3								
Johns Hopkins University	53.6								
Wesleyan University	52.7								
University of Chicago	52.4								
Georgetown University	49.8								
Stanford University	49.8								
Duke University	48.7								
Northwestern University	42.3								

Base: Total Respondents
College and University Study
Target Management, Inc.

Value Received for Money Spent on Room & Board

(Summary of Top Two Ratings, "Extremely High"/"Very Good Value")

TOTAL RESPONDENTS	26.2
IVY LEAGUE—Total	30.4
Harvard University	50.6
Dartmouth College	38.3
Cornell University	32.5
Columbia University	30.8
Princeton University	27.1
University of Pennsylvania	26.6
Brown University	22.6
Yale University	13.9
PRIVATE—Total	23.7
Williams College	58.3
MIT	39.1
Johns Hopkins University	27.8
Wesleyan University	24.8
Duke University	24.7
Stanford University	20.0
Georgetown University	19.4
University of Chicago	15.2
Northwestern University	13.1

0%   10   20   30   40   50   60   70   80%

Base: Total Respondents
College and University Study
Target Management, Inc.

Value Received for Money Spent on Tuition

(Summary of Bottom Two Ratings, "Less Than Satisfactory"/"Poor")

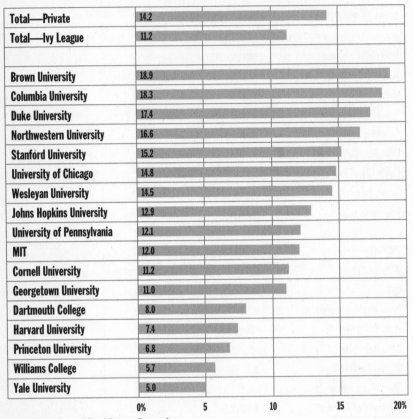

	0%	5	10	15	20%
Total—Private	14.2				
Total—Ivy League	11.2				
Brown University	18.9				
Columbia University	18.3				
Duke University	17.4				
Northwestern University	16.6				
Stanford University	15.2				
University of Chicago	14.8				
Wesleyan University	14.5				
Johns Hopkins University	12.9				
University of Pennsylvania	12.1				
MIT	12.0				
Cornell University	11.2				
Georgetown University	11.0				
Dartmouth College	8.0				
Harvard University	7.4				
Princeton University	6.8				
Williams College	5.7				
Yale University	5.0				

Base: Total Ivy and Total Private Respondents
College and University Study
Target Management, Inc.

FOUR

Is This All There Is?
SOCIAL LIFE ON CAMPUS

The Social Challenge for Select Students

As I organized and reviewed the reams of data from my survey and
the hundreds of anecdotal statements that students had shared with
me, I could not get out of my head several lines from the Beatles'
"Eleanor Rigby": "All the lonely people, where do they all come
from?" As they seek to connect socially with others on campus, many
Select students experience a great deal of sadness, isolation, loneliness, disappointment, yearning, and even anger; in their social lives,
they face the same sort of intense challenges as they do in the classroom.

No matter how intent on academic success, every Select student
wants to make close friends, date people of equal mind and spirit,
have fun at parties, participate in some way in campus happenings,
and maybe even join a fraternity or sorority or special-interest group.
Select students worked hard and sacrificed a lot to get into an elite
school. A great many have told me that once they enroll in college,

they hope they can finally "get a life." For the majority of these highly focused individuals, high school was an either-or choice between a lousy social life and academic success. Once in college, they assume that their future classmates will be just as eager as they to establish the elusive harmony between the life of the mind and the social scene.

In ways that Select students may never anticipate, the balance between "getting a life" and succeeding in the classroom can be very hard to achieve. This young man at Princeton expressed the feelings that many new students experience in the dog days of freshman year:

> 66 For a freshman, life at Princeton can be rough. You pretty much have to make a clear choice between academics and social life, and as a freshman male, you're going to have a tough time. 99

Another freshman, this one at Harvard, had already developed a more helpful philosophical attitude toward the social environment:

> 66 Harvard is academically intense, and sometimes that can be isolating socially. But minimal effort will produce legions of similarly lonely yet terrific individuals to hang with. The people make the place. 99

And this woman junior from Stanford saw the stress that arises between the talents of the students and the demands of the academic environment:

> 66 The people here are amazing. I think the atmosphere stifles and withers their hopes for the future. At the same time, it creates strength. I love and hate it here. 99

In the responses to the part of my survey dealing with social experiences, I found several striking differences between the men and women—and among the different racial and ethnic groups—about what affects them negatively and positively. What these Select students told me, particularly about the negative aspects of the social scene, needs to be taken seriously, not just by prospective Select students and their parents, but by college leaders as well. Sad to say, the social atmosphere at elite colleges can have a deleterious effect on a sizable portion of the student body.

The Social Atmosphere for Select Students

As I mentioned earlier, over 70% of the survey respondents told me that prestige, name recognition, and academic programs were the most significant factors they considered in choosing which colleges to apply to. Once they arrived at their elite campuses, however, social concerns played a larger role than they'd imagined in how they generally felt about school. When I asked what things they liked best about their colleges now that they were on campus, they cited two major elements:

- the people   35%
- intellectual opportunities   27%

When they were asked what they liked *least* about their colleges, Select students most often mentioned

- the bureaucracy of the administration   23%
- poor weather   22%
- food services   18%

Cold weather and bad food may be intractable problems, but the administrators, the students thought, established much of the quality-of-life elements for the campus. One Stanford sophomore delivered what is the worst possible opprobrium in the minds of collegians, it seems, by comparing many of her peers to the university administrators:

> Little did I know that the majority of the students here would be as uptight as the tie-doffing, slick-haired, ulcer-afflicted administrators who run the school!

The quality of the food at school had a greater negative impact on first-year students, almost one-third of them—further testimony to the role the basic amenities play in the psychological lives of undergraduates. Given that virtually all freshmen are required to participate in their college's meal plan, the quality of the food and the setting in which it is served takes on a significance that affects their states of mind.

When I asked the survey students to choose the two words or phrases that best describe the social environment on their campuses, they chose many positive terms and several worrisomely negative ones. College life for these students was more frequently from a long list of options:

full of choices	26%
diverse	24%
friendly	29%
relaxed	15%
exciting	15%
polarized	15%
superficial	15%

The women respondents took a different direction from the men over the course of their college careers. Compared to freshwomen, 13% fewer senior women agreed that campus life was "full of choices." Is this a sign of women's accelerating disaffection with their campus communities and disappointment in themselves or a positive sign of their maturation and eagerness to move into the larger world?

More senior men than senior women perceived their campuses as "less friendly." Is this a sign of the competition that men, in particular, seem to feel about admission to graduate school, fellowships, and job offers? (The senior women generally seemed less driven at this point by these factors.) This senior man at Yale felt that way:

> A large majority of undergraduates are arrogant, snobbish, irresponsible, and spoiled. Many of them can be described as materialistic brats. Many women gravitate to more affluent guys; many women are prejudicial toward guys of lower income.

This senior woman at Brown would agree with him:

> Unfortunately, Brown is not safe from the horrible features of every-day society—cheating, dishonesty, greed, racism, theft, competition.

These students represented a significant number of college students, but the majority would challenge such a negative view of the social climate—not just at Yale and Brown but at elite schools in general. Students of different experiences and temperaments have different reactions to similar social environments. This Yale student challenged his classmate's opinion:

> Yale is a fantastically overwhelming place. It takes a year or so to find your niche. It's a fast-paced, busy, and stressful place, and the balancing of classes and social activities is difficult, but overall the school is exhilarating.

And this senior's feelings about Brown echoed those of the majority of his fellow students:

> Brown offers excellent academic and social opportunities while remaining unbelievably low-pressured and cooperative.

I next asked the students to describe the overall milieu of their campuses. Their responses were diverse, contradictory, honest, and compelling.

- *Competitive* was the word cited by 28% of the respondents, with an upward trend in the junior and senior years for men and women.
- *Friendly* was the next most frequent choice, of 20% of the students.

Here are the other descriptive terms that clustered together:

- intense
- fast-paced

- enriching
- scholarly
- broadening
- energetic

When it comes to mingling with others outside the classroom, Select students offer—and demand—a lot from each other. This woman at Yale, a junior, spoke about the environment not only at her own school but at many elite schools nationwide:

> I think Yale is an all-or-nothing environment. People are either studying and that's all or partying and that's all. I think they have a hard time doing either in a nonintense way.

Negative Aspects of Campus Life

You might think that today's students would complain about the same elements of collegiate social life that irked their predecessors: the Greek system, relating to other students, and finding a date. These concerns are constant, but students have major new worries too. When I asked them to identify the factors that had a direct negative impact on their lives, the top contenders were these:

financial responsibilities	40%
cohabitation of others in one's living space	40%
dating	25%
family expectations and pressures	25%
alcohol consumption	17%
influence of sororities, fraternities, and eating clubs	12%
racism	11%

Over four years of college, men worry about the same things in a fairly constant way. For women, however, the picture grows progressively more dreary. Of the respondents to my survey, 28% of the freshwomen and 36% of the senior women had negative feelings about the dating scene on campus. I think that these responses are related to young women's maturity. Women, even more than men, are concerned with issues not just of romantic connection but of character. A greater percentage of senior women, over one-third, feel burdened by how much is socially expected of them. I queried a group of junior and senior women on three campuses about this issue. Overall, they told me they felt compelled to justify the costs of their elite education by successfully moving on to the next stage of their lives. They were pressured by high expectation not only from their families but from feminism itself; they were very aware that they had been primed for visible and proactive positions in the larger society, in which sex roles remain in flux. Much depends upon a student's fortitude and self-confidence in meeting the challenge of a selective college. A Berkeley sophomore woman viewed the experience this way:

> UC–Berkeley's truly a unique institution in the way it combines such high academic rigor with social opportunities and experiences. I feel very privileged to be attending this university.

The stress of having to hold down a paying job is also perceived as greater by women than men. Only 19% of the men felt excessively burdened by work, whereas a third of the women were troubled by their employment responsibilities. As I noted in Chapter 3, on the costs of an elite education, in many cases women receive less financial aid, especially outright grant money, than do men and, consequently, feel more intense financial pressures. My survey also showed that more women work to pay for their personal expenses and create a life somewhat apart from traditional campus activities. But women may also perceive their work obligations differently and feel more oppressed by them. Elite colleges should further explore students' work issues and how the two sexes relate to them.

When I asked the Select students what negative factors of college social life affected them indirectly—that is, whether they had a personal negative experience and thought it exemplified social issues affecting the entire community—even more students affirmed they had a great deal to be concerned about. The issues that affected the community the most intensely were these:

alcohol consumption	36%
racism	35%
campus safety	35%
safety in the local community	30%
eating disorders	27%
drug usage	26%
cheating, plagiarism	26%
family expectations and pressures	23%
sexism, sexual harassment	22%
cohabitation of others in one's living space	21%
campus causes	21%
sororities, fraternities, and eating clubs	20%
dating	19%
holding a paying job	18%
date and acquaintance rape	17%
physical abuse in a relationship	10%

These responses show that serious American social issues can occur with even greater force in the hothouse environments of elite colleges. Although most individuals are concerned directly about financial responsibilities and academic performance, many indirect negative components are also at play within the close community of student living. Women are frequently the victims of the various forms of negative behavior related to physical safety and well-being—more engaged than men with the impact of alcohol abuse, the preservation of physical safety, racism, eating disorders, sexual harassment, date and acquaintance rape, and physical abuse from a partner. The survey provides clear evidence of the legitimate anxiety women live with in elite colleges. All this must come as a shock to a young woman who arrives at college with an entirely different image of life inside the ivy tower.

Not that men are entirely free from the negative elements of life on campus; both sexes offered critiques of the social issues that define much of their undergraduate experience, from the dangers of drinking to the insidious effects of racism and sexist behaviors. A junior man at Duke commented on the drinking scene he's experienced in college, which is common to the majority of the elite colleges:

66 Too many alcoholics, too many immature people doing negative things, too judgmental, too much gossip. 99

Another Duke student, this one a sophomore woman, believed that serious issues on campus can go unrecognized:

66 The average Duke student is concerned only with grades and social standing. If you look hard, you can find people who care about racism, sexism, homophobia, poverty, but you have to look. 99

A sophomore at Berkeley saw similar issues on his campus:

66 The social scene is very polarized: by race, the Greek system, church organizations, and various other exclusive groups. 99

Some students thought that social paralysis is endemic to their campuses, as did this young man, a junior at Johns Hopkins:

66 People at this school have a highly apathetic approach to social life. In order for Hopkins to establish itself as the premier non-Ivy, it needs strong improvement in the area of the arts and more student participation and school spirit. Hopkins is full of potential—the reservoir simply needs to be tapped and managed correctly. 99

This man, a junior at the University of Chicago, saw similar problems on his campus:

66 I am basically here to serve my four years and move on. While here, I've been disappointed with the social life, mostly due to the inaction of the students, not the university. Whatever is not right with the school lies in the hands of those paying to be here. 99

A woman at Princeton saw the same issues on her campus after four years there:

66 I dislike the fact that people are so self-absorbed. At times academics are too intense and people do nothing but study. We need more bal-

anced people who can relax more and enjoy one another's company. They need to be more aware of the needs of people around them at school. 🙶🙶

Students' attitudes toward social issues can vary greatly, depending on the circumstances of their campuses. While many at a diverse school like Berkeley are affected by numerous issues related to identity-based socializing, at the University of Wisconsin–Madison, some students—like this junior female—are concerned about the lack of social diversity:

🙶🙶 This school needs more diversity. It's too white. 🙶🙶

And this senior woman, also at Wisconsin, would agree:

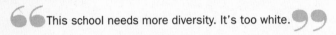 🙶🙶 Wisconsin is too conservative, very homogeneous, with a very conservative Board of Regents. Even the Asian students here are conservative. There is a lack of people of color. 🙶🙶

Many students remain immune to negative aspects of life on campus or manage to resolve the issues that their circumstances present to them. For example, only 35% of the men and 25% of the women indicated that financial responsibilities are not an issue for them. As for alcohol consumption, 46% of the men and 37% of the women claimed they have not been directly affected by it in any negative way. Cohabitation of others in their room was of no concern to 50% of the men and 40% of the women. Having to hold a job had no negative effect on 60% of the men and 51% of the women.

Yet significantly, the negative effect of many aspects of college life distresses a quarter to a half of all students on the elite campuses. While Select students attempt to meet their academic responsibilities, "a host of furies are on the loose," as one undergraduate woman at an Ivy League college described the challenge.

The Dating Scene

Select students, like young people everywhere, are preoccupied with finding intimate connections and even romance with other people.

Discovering true love or even getting a date has never been easy on the elite campuses. Before the formerly all-male Select schools began to admit women, it could be difficult to impossible to find on-campus romance. Students at the all-male colleges imported women from other campuses for weekend parties, which didn't exactly make for regular or easygoing relations between the sexes. And when the all-male elite schools admitted women in the 1960s, interaction between men and women was often dicey. Men could resent the presence of talented and assertive women in the classroom; underclassmen could feel intimidated by the presence of women a few years older and wiser than they. Women, a minority at many newly coeducational schools, were at once venerated and scorned by their male classmates. That situation continues today at many schools, as men continue to outnumber women.

In the past thirty years, social mores between the genders have evolved nationwide; college students, in the vanguard of the transformation, have been thrown into even greater turmoil. Today, men and women must make up the rules as they go along. Gay men and lesbians face similar issues, along with concerns about defining their own sexuality in a closed and oftentimes perilous environment. Combine the inevitable vagaries of youthful sex and love with the pressures of elite academia, and you have an inevitably volatile environment.

One University of Chicago male junior reacted to these concerns in a serious but casual way:

> ❝People here definitely need to learn how to kick back more. A true story . . . at a party my first year, I heard two students getting drunk and talking about theoretical physics. I think people here have to separate their classroom life from their social life.❞

The Select students use a number of strategies to negotiate the uncertain terrain of dating and romance. They are extremely aware of the negative factors I've just discussed: Alcohol abuse, sexually transmitted diseases, and date and acquaintance rape are key concerns. Some students take refuge in an intense focus on their academic work and activities, leaving little time and perhaps expressing little desire to get seriously involved in relationships. Others have more conventional doubts that are manifest in shyness and worry over potential rejection. One Stanford woman, a junior, thought that these feelings were representative of larger issues on her campus and others:

> 66 The students at Stanford are some of the smartest people I have ever met. However, I find that a lot of them are socially dysfunctional. They don't know how to interact socially. A good half of the people here have never even gone out with a member of the opposite sex! 99

A Princeton sophomore articulated the feeling of many of her fellow undergraduates that she may not measure up in the competitive social milieu of her campus:

> 66 The people who say the social life is limited have not looked for other things. Sometimes I feel like there's a lot of pressure to stand out and not be just another average person. 99

And her fellow Princeton sophomore expressed dissatisfaction from the male point of view, which many of his fellow Select undergraduates would echo:

> 66 Everything here is too structured. People seldom do anything too spontaneous socially, except when drunk! Dating is a disaster. 99

Overall, the search for intimacy is much harder on today's undergraduates than it was for a previous generation. Some grow frustrated about connecting with other people, either as partners or friends, like this Columbia junior who described an attitude not uncommon among many of her contemporaries:

> 66 I can't say I experience a huge feeling of connectedness to the college or my peers. I have acquired a distaste for the superficial, materialistic attitude of many of my fellow students. 99

This Williams male sophomore took dating itself more lightly but with seriousness:

> Williams College: the most expensive form of birth control known to man. Superficial or serious, any kind of intimate relationships are found out and discussed openly on campus. There are not many social opportunities on campus. Videos and beer dominate.

This Duke freshman had another version of the same complaint:

> The dating scene is horrible. Too many girls prefer to stay in their rooms and study. I would like to see a more friendly and concerned student body.

One promising matchmaker among students didn't even exist a decade ago: electronic communication. Computer technology may have a heart after all. The revolution it has brought about in education extends beyond the classroom, library, and labs to encompass social life on many campuses today. Computer dating and communications in general among undergraduates have become a way of life for many; they also provide a hint of the standards of social interaction by which undergraduates at the elite colleges behave. Examples abound.

A popular form of blind dating on the Princeton campus, once known for the popularity of its formal proms and club parties, is the Computer-Dating Dance, which is sponsored by the Inter-College Council. The program matches freshmen and sophomore men and women who have indicated by computer their personal interests and tastes, including sexual orientation. About 80% of the students participate in the program annually. Other creative forms of blind dating have been tried, including a takeoff on "The Newlyweds." These efforts reflect the reluctance and self-consciousness of students regarding pairing off and maintaining intimate relationships.

Students at Brown also participate in a computer-based date-matching program called HUGS (Helping Undergraduates to Socialize). Campus sponsors cite the failure of student dances to attract many participants and the fact that most students are too intense and individualistic to engage in old-fashioned dating rituals. At Dartmouth, long renowned for its use of technology in teaching and communicating between faculty and students, the choice of social interaction for many students is E-mail, or blitzmail as it is known on the Hanover campus. Students stay in contact with their friends by blitzing one another virtually around the clock. This has become a popular means—some believe too much so—of staying connected to close friends and seeking new acquaintances or possible dates.

Beyond computer E-mail and ice-breaking gimmicks, many students want more college-sponsored social activities to improve their social lives and their intimate connections of all kinds. Students in the 1960s wanted administrators to butt out of their personal lives; today's students want the colleges to make the introductions.

How Students View One Another

I asked the Select students to describe the attributes of their fellow students that exceeded, met, or failed to meet their expectations. A third of the students were disappointed in the level of school spirit. Over a quarter felt that most students meet their expectations in terms of class participation, political activity and awareness, and degree of independent thinking.

What components of the community exceeded their expectations? The Select students answered with meaningful response rates in four areas, two of them academic and two social:

- academic ability (a third of all students)
- intellectualism (close to a third of all students)
- friendliness (one-quarter of all students)
- social composition (one-fifth of all students)

I like the upbeat attitude of a Columbia junior who focused more on the positive elements of her college. Many of the students we interviewed have the same feelings about their colleges and peers:

> Columbia is an incredible place for students who have broad interests and strong personal identities. It provides an environment that is at the same time fun, exciting, diverse, challenging, intellectual, and somehow still homey.

A Wisconsin sophomore, a woman, had a similar overall outlook:

> 66 This is a great school; the community and the atmosphere make for a top learning environment. The profs are excellent, and the friends I have met will last forever. It was great to go to college in a different part of the country. 99

There is a bell curve in the overall responses to campus social and academic expectations. On both tails of the curve are individuals who are highly pleased or displeased by their collegiate experience. The large majority, naturally, have more temperate, mixed attitudes that are based on their individual issues.

Social Stress and Select Undergraduates

As the last of the inquiries in the social side of my questionnaire, I asked the students to rate, on a scale of 1 to 10, their personal level of stress as it pertains to their social lives—with 1 the lowest indicator of stress and 10 an indication of extreme stress. The findings are not highly dramatic. A tiny fraction of students rated their stress level 10, one-fifth rated it 5, and less than a tenth rated it 1. The mean for the total population is between 5 and 6. By comparison, the mean for academic stress is between 6 and 7, with a much higher percentage of students in the 8, 9, and 10 range. It is clear that students have concerns and strong opinions about the social lives of their colleges, but are not functioning at the same levels of intensity around this issue as they do around academics.

To underscore the pervasiveness of stress and anxiety on college campuses today, I want to summarize the findings of the major professional organizations who work directly with college-age students. These organizations represent campus counselors, psychologists, psychiatrists, and officials of the National Institutes of Health. The bad news from them is that each year over 23 million people will suffer from anxiety disorders that show up as panic attacks, depression, or alcohol or drug abuse to alleviate those symptoms. These disorders frequently appear in late adolescence or early adulthood, just when students are exposed to the demands and rigors of college life.

The issues we've heard about from the Select are reflective of this problem.

How Select Students Feel About Campus Activities

What are the activities of importance to students on the elite campuses today? The tradition of athletic competition as a mainstay of collegiate life is still alive, but it is certainly not as vigorous a unifier as it once was. As I expected, I found significant variance in athletic fandom among colleges, since several elite schools continue to field teams in highly competitive leagues—Stanford, Duke, Northwestern, and the state universities included in the study. Here are several activities that the students rated very important:

- One-half the respondents rated men's varsity athletics as consequential for them.
- One-third rated women's athletics as very important.
- Slightly more than one-fifth of the male and female students rated intramurals as very important, reflecting the large interest in physical activity at a less competitive level that takes up less time.
- The school newspaper was cited by 62% of all the students as very important. The women attached greater importance to this activity, with 69% of the women, compared to 56% of the men, valuing it.
- Fraternities and sororities are very important to a third of all the students.

The Greek system that exists on the majority of campuses is an undergraduate bone of contention. I heard strong opinions for and against its existence, voiced by students of all backgrounds. For many, the Greek organizations or other sorts of campus fraternity activities are a vital part of the social scene; for others, they are perceived as sexist, snobbish, racist, and anti-intellectual bastions. When I asked how they would improve their campuses, many students recommended that the Greek system be eliminated or its social role diminished.

Other campus activities that the students rated somewhat highly included student government (24% men, 38% women), where the greater value placed on it by women could portend the development of future female political leaders; drama (20% men, 28% women); and marching band (22% men, 30% women). All the performing arts were rated fairly to very important by more women than men.

The advancements that have been made in enrolling a more diverse population of Select students are reflected in the many ethnic, racial, and cultural organizations to be found on the elite campuses. Over a third of the students of all backgrounds regarded such groups as a very important social outlet. More women perceived that involvement in an identity social group is an important activity. Such organizations can have a vital role for many. An African American sophomore at Northwestern said she felt something missing socially for her:

> I wish I had asked more questions about the social opportunities for minority students before I came here. This is a great academic institution, but my personal life can leave me feeling isolated and frustrated, even with the offerings of black campus groups.

I predict that as the elite colleges continue their policy of assembling a broad mix of students, an increasing number of undergraduates will seek active engagement in and identify with racial, ethnic, and cultural organizations. For many people, such social bodies offer both a traditional social vehicle and a haven in the face of racism, discrimination, and isolation. Nontraditional students, as they are often referred to, seek the comfort and companionship of their peers with similar interests and concerns. This situation has set off considerable debate on virtually all campuses as to whether the goal of integrating a diverse student population is being fulfilled—a controversy I explore in the next chapter, about the many faces and issues of diversity on campus.

A large number of students indicated that virtually all the typical extracurricular organizations on campus are of some importance to them. Thus, it appears that the majority of the respondents are engaged in one or more activities at a level of commitment that is comfortable for them; finding a balance between academic work and play; and, what is most important, making close friends. As the century ends, a new campus social pattern is emerging, with traditional dating activities being replaced by extracurricular activities that build and sustain friendships and may even help a student find a companion for a Saturday night.

The Social Atmosphere at Specific Schools

In Chapter 2 you read a summary of students' responses, either positive or negative, regarding academic factors on their particular campuses that came as a surprise to them. The students' broad spectrum of opinions is even greater on the topic of social issues; particular negative components vary to a large degree among the colleges in the survey. The more campus-bound, traditional colleges reflect a higher frequency of negative references to alcohol, racism, and fraternities. On other, more so-called liberal campuses, the students seem more bothered by drugs, political activism, and pressure to conform.

On the basis of the Select students' written responses on the survey, what follows are two revealing comparisons, by college, of the levels of social stress students experience and the most surprising aspects of the social scene. Again, take careful note of how different Select students regard their colleges on this key subject. The answers may surprise you, even as they surprised some of the Select students themselves.

A popular game among Select students is to stereotype the student bodies at their peer institutions. While most of this typecasting is simply good-natured rivalry, such pigeonholing can actually affect some students' views of themselves. It definitely influences how prospective students view various colleges. One of the most entertaining parts of assembling the findings of this survey was to see some of these stereotypes turned on their heads. MIT is a case in point. The commonly held image of this great research university as an antisocial technical institute is far from the prevailing sentiment on campus. The MIT students declared, more frequently than students at all the other Select institutions, they have positive social lives. One female junior noted with pleasure and surprise:

“MIT is one of the most diverse places I've ever been, not only socially but academically. When I first came here, I expected to be among extremely smart but socially inept people. I have found out how wrong my assumptions were. Every person I come across is impressive academically as well as socially. I wouldn't go anywhere else.”

I urge the reader to study these summaries on two levels: first to gain an appreciation of the myriad differences among these great institutions and second to grasp the negative factors that affect the Select students. I have listed the two categories most frequently mentioned by students on each campus.

1. Brown University: lack of a social life, very limited activities; absence of dating with an emphasis on group social life
2. Columbia University: too much emphasis on drugs and alcohol; too many cliques and too much segregation by groups
3. Cornell University: too much emphasis on drugs and alcohol; dominance of the Greek system
4. Dartmouth College: dominance of the Greek system; too much alcohol
5. Duke University: importance of alcohol to social life; dominance of the Greek system
6. Georgetown University: emphasis on alcohol; a diverse social life and good parties
7. Harvard University: lack of a social life; too much alcohol and drugs
8. Johns Hopkins University: no social life; too many cliques and segregation by groups
9. MIT: a diverse, active social life; too much alcohol
10. Northwestern University: a limited social life; dominance of the Greek system
11. Princeton University: dominance of alcohol; lack of social options
12. Stanford University: friendliness and tolerance of student body; a limited social life, lack of dating
13. University of California–Berkeley: polarization, racism; friendliness, openness of campus

14. University of Chicago: a limited social life; need to create own social fun
15. University of Pennsylvania: abuse of alcohol and its influence on social life; dominance of fraternities
16. University of Wisconsin–Madison: dominance of alcohol; a great variety of activities
17. Wesleyan University: social cliques, a polarized and segregated student body; openness, campuswide tolerance
18. Williams College: dominance of alcohol and its abuse; the lack of dating
19. Yale University: a diverse, active social life; yet limited social options perceived by many students

Conclusion

What should prospective students make of the many positive and negative features of the social scene at elite colleges? Simply put, each will need to determine what he or she most wants to gain from being undergraduates. Students must understand that they will be confronted with a range of new and daunting challenges and experiences and should ask themselves what they're seeking. Just as important, each student will have to choose the college that suits his or her particular style, value system, and personality. I urge all prospective students to turn a deaf ear to those who would steer them to the "right name," rather than to the right college because they will have to live with the consequences of their choices.

From my many years of counseling students and dealing directly with the selective institutions and their administrators, I can say confidently that the trends and dynamics that now characterize these campuses will become even more intensified. While the population of high school graduates increases dramatically, the number of available spaces in the competitive colleges will not expand. Competition for admission will become thornier and thornier—for all the reasons detailed in the introduction to this book. At the same time, the commitment of elite institutions to "an aristocracy of talent based on a meritocracy of opportunity"—the driving force in selecting a class of entering students—will continue.

Thus, the forces at work that present-day students describe here will continue for a long time. The number of students of color from nontraditional backgrounds, of students with more varied political and sexual orientations, along with more women and minorities competing for the opportunities and advantages traditionally enjoyed by men, will make their presence ever more felt in the groves of academia. Beyond the requisite level of high intelligence, Select students in the elite colleges will need to have the poise and spirit of understanding and open-mindedness to adapt and flourish.

Two Words/Phrases That Best Describe the Social Atmosphere

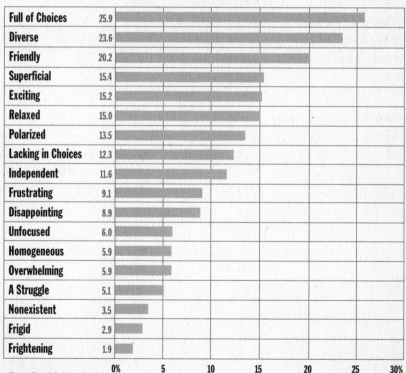

Full of Choices	25.9	
Diverse	23.6	
Friendly	20.2	
Superficial	15.4	
Exciting	15.2	
Relaxed	15.0	
Polarized	13.5	
Lacking in Choices	12.3	
Independent	11.6	
Frustrating	9.1	
Disappointing	8.9	
Unfocused	6.0	
Homogeneous	5.9	
Overwhelming	5.9	
A Struggle	5.1	
Nonexistent	3.5	
Frigid	2.9	
Frightening	1.9	

0%   5   10   15   20   25   30%

Base: Total Respondents
College and University Study
Target Management, Inc.

Social Stress Level on Campus

	1	2	3	4	5	6	7	8	9	10
Cornell University				4.2						
Georgetown University				4.2						
Northwestern University				4.2						
Harvard University				4.1						
Yale University				4.1						
Duke University				4.1						
University of NC–Chapel Hill				4.1						
Dartmouth College				4						
Wesleyan University				4						
Johns Hopkins University				3.9						
Stanford University				3.8						
University of California–Berkeley				3.8						
Princeton University				3.6						
University of Chicago				3.6						
Williams College				3.6						
Columbia University				3.5						
MIT				3.5						
Brown University				3.4						
University of Wisconsin–Madison				3.4						
University of Pennsylvania				3.3						

Base: Total Respondents
College and University Study   **NO STRESS**   **TREMENDOUS STRESS**
Target Management, Inc.

Two Words/Phrases That Best Describe the Overall Campus Environment

(PART ONE)

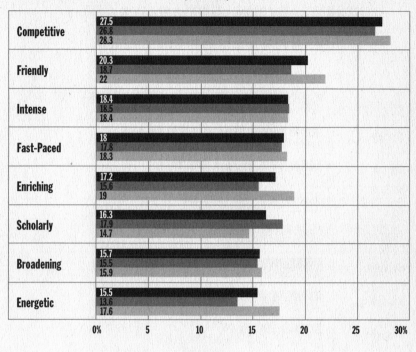

	Total Respondents	Male	Female
Competitive	27.5	26.8	28.3
Friendly	20.3	18.7	22
Intense	18.4	18.5	18.4
Fast-Paced	18	17.8	18.3
Enriching	17.2	15.6	19
Scholarly	16.3	17.9	14.7
Broadening	15.7	15.5	15.9
Energetic	15.5	13.6	17.6

(PART TWO)

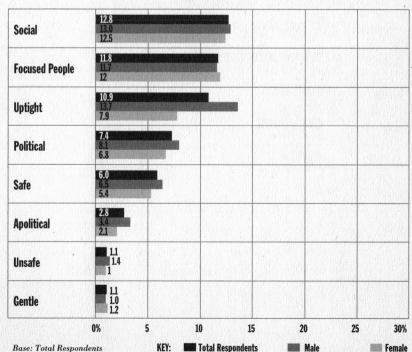

	Total Respondents	Male	Female
Social	12.8	13.0	12.5
Focused People	11.8	11.7	12
Uptight	10.9	13.7	7.9
Political	7.4	8.1	6.8
Safe	6.0	6.5	5.4
Apolitical	2.8	3.4	2.1
Unsafe	1.1	1.4	1
Gentle	1.1	1.0	1.2

Base: Total Respondents
College and University Study
Target Management, Inc.

KEY: ■ Total Respondents ■ Male ■ Female

Two Words/Phrases That Best Describe the Overall Campus Environment

(Total Private Universities vs. Duke)

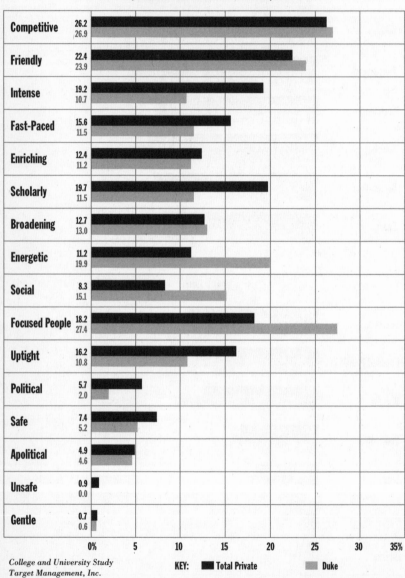

Word/Phrase	Total Private	Duke
Competitive	26.2	26.9
Friendly	22.4	23.9
Intense	19.2	10.7
Fast-Paced	15.6	11.5
Enriching	12.4	11.2
Scholarly	19.7	11.5
Broadening	12.7	13.0
Energetic	11.2	19.9
Social	8.3	15.1
Focused People	18.2	27.4
Uptight	16.2	10.8
Political	5.7	2.0
Safe	7.4	5.2
Apolitical	4.9	4.6
Unsafe	0.9	0.0
Gentle	0.7	0.6

0%   5   10   15   20   25   30   35%

*College and University Study
Target Management, Inc.*

KEY: ■ Total Private   ▨ Duke

Two Words/Phrases That Best Describe the Overall Campus Environment

(Duke—Split by Gender)

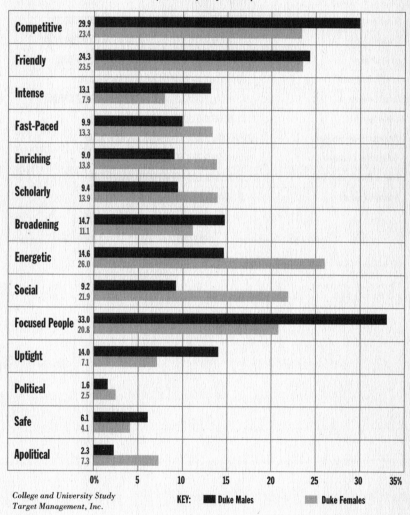

	Duke Males	Duke Females
Competitive	29.9	23.4
Friendly	24.3	23.5
Intense	13.1	7.9
Fast-Paced	9.9	13.3
Enriching	9.0	13.8
Scholarly	9.4	13.9
Broadening	14.7	11.1
Energetic	14.6	26.0
Social	9.2	21.9
Focused People	33.0	20.8
Uptight	14.0	7.1
Political	1.6	2.5
Safe	6.1	4.1
Apolitical	2.3	7.3

*College and University Study
Target Management, Inc.*

KEY: ■ Duke Males ▨ Duke Females

Attributes of Student Body That
Exceeded, Met, or Failed to Meet Expectations

(Total Public Universities)

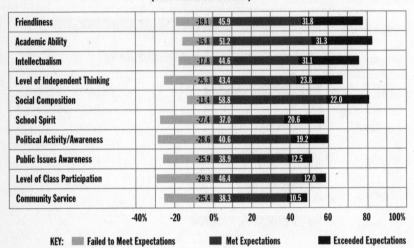

	Failed to Meet	Met	Exceeded
Friendliness	-19.1	45.9	31.8
Academic Ability	-15.8	51.2	31.3
Intellectualism	-17.8	44.6	31.1
Level of Independent Thinking	-25.3	43.4	23.8
Social Composition	-13.4	58.8	22.0
School Spirit	-27.4	37.0	20.6
Political Activity/Awareness	-28.6	40.6	19.2
Public Issues Awareness	-25.9	38.9	12.5
Level of Class Participation	-29.3	46.4	12.0
Community Service	-25.4	38.3	10.5

-40%   -20   0%   20   40   60   80   100%

KEY: ▦ Failed to Meet Expectations   ■ Met Expectations   ■ Exceeded Expectations

Base: Total Public University Respondents
College and University Study
Target Management, Inc.

FIVE
Diversifying the Campus

What is it like to be a minority student in an elite university? The words of a talented, ambitious young woman of color at Stanford represent the situation of many Select minority students who have surmounted a number of obstacles to enroll in one of America's great schools:

> Stanford University has been a very challenging experience for me. When a right-wing publication prints an improperly researched article called "From the Back of the Bus to the Back of the Class" about Stanford's African American students' academic situation, not only does it contradict the supposedly "politically correct" atmosphere of the school, but it also has a detrimental effect on the African American student at Stanford and raises questions about the admissions process. An article of this nature places a huge challenge upon the African Americans here, forcing them to clear their name, justify their presence, and assert their credibility.

It's been three decades since America's elite campuses began to recruit ethnic and racial minority students. As a result, the population and basic nature of the nation's elite universities have changed dramatically. But as this Stanford sophomore knows firsthand, minority undergraduates face distinct and sometimes debilitating challenges as they try to establish a sense of belonging and legitimacy. The multicultural campus has also challenged white students, whose reactions to the presence and attitudes of their minority classmates range from insight and sympathy to anger and resentment. And now, with affirmative action contested in the public arena, diversity and how to achieve it have become "hot-button" issues that directly affect how Select students construct their college lives. Even as the nation debates the terms under which minorities enter mainstream American society, college students live in the laboratory of that controversy.

The Rationale for Diversity

Responding to the impact of the civil rights movement and the social and political upheavals of the 1960s, America's leading colleges and universities developed a radical new policy of recruiting more students of color, particularly African Americans. Today, the majority of elite colleges remain committed to racial diversity on campus. It has become a central tenet of most colleges' missions. Harvard's president Neil Rudenstine views diversity as central to a liberal education:

> [Here is] the most fundamental rationale for student diversity in higher education: its educational value. Students benefit in countless ways from the opportunity to live and learn among peers whose perspectives and experiences differ from their own. A diverse educational environment challenges them to explore ideas and arguments at a deeper level—to see issues from various sides, to rethink their own premises, to achieve the kind of understanding that comes only from testing their own hypotheses against those of people with other views. Such an environment also creates opportunities for people from different backgrounds, with different life experiences, to come to know one another as more than passing acquaintances, and to develop forms of tolerance and mutual respect on which the health of our civic life depends.

In a speech to entering students, Dartmouth President James Oliver Freedman saw diversity as a vital contribution to the overall body politic:

> Effective leadership in this country in the years ahead will require many more national leaders from minority groups—leaders not only in politics

and public policy, but in academia and the sciences, culture and the arts, business and the professions. Indeed, all of our future leaders must understand and be prepared to deal with the increasing diversity of our society. Dartmouth and other select colleges and universities seek diverse student bodies because their obligation today is—as it always has been—the preparation of students for positions of national leadership.

Not all the nation's leaders will come from Select schools, but Freedman and Rudenstine know that elite colleges like theirs can lead the way for the rest of academia and, in many respects, for the society as well. If the most prestigious and selective colleges and universities could see their way to make room for disadvantaged youngsters and maintain their educational status and integrity, then so could any other college.

Using scholarships to broaden the social representation of the student body has a longer history than many might suppose. In 1904, president Charles Eliot of Harvard, the first among equals of the old-line colleges, wrote to his Board of Trustees, that he "wanted the college to be open equally to young men with much money, little money, or no money at all, provided they have brains." Even in the nineteenth century, the nation's oldest colleges, such as Yale, Dartmouth, Brown, Williams, and Bowdoin, extended their limited budgets to bring working-class students into their communities. Only Princeton among the leading institutions saw its mission as serving the gentry of the middle states and the South. It would be decades before African Americans and women were encouraged to participate in the educational feast at Harvard and its peer institutions. Nevertheless, the seed was planted that has blossomed into today's garden of opportunity.

As an admissions officer and a college counselor, I've witnessed the three decades of change in the composition of the Select schools' student bodies, and it has been dramatic. In 1964 I left Harvard for Princeton to work with a handful of other young admissions officers in carrying out the university's new policy of recruiting more African American students to a campus that historically discriminated against minorities. At that time, fewer than ten African American students were enrolled in one of the richest and most visible institutions in the nation. More than any of its sister institutions, Princeton had a long-established attitude that led even Woodrow Wilson, its president in the first decade of the century, consciously to block the admission of African American students. Catholics and Jews received letters indicating they were qualified for admission, but were encouraged to enroll elsewhere, since they were not likely to feel at home at Princeton. Wilson was a leading spokesman for "the old drill, the old memory of time gone by, the old schooling in precedent and tradition, the old keeping of faith with the past."

As an adviser to a group of Princeton undergraduates in the 1960s, I grew aware of how little support existed for students who did not match the traditional social and academic background. There were almost no role models, social organizations, or counselors who were experienced in working with minority students. I listened to several young African American men recount incidents of racial abuse, inflicted both purposefully and unintentionally. Despite that hostility, almost all the early minority students persevered and graduated—testimony to their own strengths and convictions.

Today when the public or academic professionals debate the merits of minority recruitment, they should look at the extraordinary changes an institution like Princeton has undergone. More than a hundred student organizations on the Princeton campus are officially recognized by the university; of them, forty identify themselves as ethnic, racial, or religious. Arab, African American, Native Americans, Asian Pacific, Asian American, Caribbean ancestry, Chicano, Chinese, Jewish, Filipino, Italian, Irish, Ismali, Japanese, Hawaiian, Korean, and Catholic groups represent only a portion of the organizations with specific religious or cultural orientations on Select college campuses today.

The demographic change at Stanford illustrates the dramatic result of an effort to create a community more representative of the larger society. Jean Fetter, the dean of admissions at Stanford from 1984 to 1991, noted in her book *Questions and Answers*—a study of the admissions issues and policies at Stanford—that the university's 1948 yearbook reveals the faces of a small number of minority students—mostly Asian; today, almost half the student body is non-white. The yearbooks of all the top-tier colleges present a similar contrast between their contemporary student bodies and those of earlier generations.

A diverse student body means more diverse academic offerings as well. As at Stanford and all the other elite institutions, the president and the faculty at Princeton are actively creating new curricular offerings in racial, ethnic, and cultural diversity, as well as identifying and recruiting faculty qualified to teach such programs. In 1996, a faculty and student task force on diversity created a pamphlet intended to call to the attention of undergraduates the variety of courses in the curriculum "that explore racial, ethnic, and cultural diversity, or that focus on cross-cultural encounter." As the battle rages in some quarters for ownership of what the university should teach and who should do the teaching, the major institutions are moving forward in refining and expanding their academic programs to reflect the growing diversity of their student bodies.

The Debate Over Affirmative Action

With the 1978 *University of California v. Bakke* legal confrontation—which called into question for the first time the issue of reverse discrimination—recruitment and special consideration of minority students became a hotly contested issue. Previously, protests had come only from pockets of alumni who worried that their alma maters were undergoing radical changes in their social and cultural identities. Some feared their own children would lose out in the increasingly competitive admissions race. A number of the Ivy League colleges witnessed the development of vocal conservative groups who attempt to rally their fellow alumni against the perceived negative ramifications of diversity.

In the *Bakke* case, the Supreme Court determined that affirmative action programs are justifiable. Although the Court explicitly banned the use of ethnic or racial quotas in college admissions, it allowed the use of race and ethnicity as one among many factors in selecting an entering class of students. From this point on, colleges felt comfortable expanding their efforts to recruit "nontraditional students." Sometimes they competed for these students with a vengeance: The

race among the elite institutions to identify and recruit the most outstanding minority students took on a life of its own. Since 1976 the
overall enrollment of minority students in American colleges has
doubled to 3.4 million. Today, 24% of all college students are from
minority backgrounds. In the twenty colleges in this survey, the
minority enrollment is anywhere from 10% to 50% of the total undergraduate population.

As the number of minority students has risen, so has the vehe-
mence of the debate about affirmative action. The shift in political
and civic attitudes in a more conservative direction has resulted in a
number of attacks on minority recruitment policies that have had a
chilling effect on higher education. A 1994 decision of the U.S.
Court of Appeals for the Fourth District, later upheld by the U.S.
Supreme Court, ruled that the University of Maryland could not limit
a special scholarship fund to African Americans. Maryland had
awarded its Banneker Scholarship to recruit outstanding African
Americans with generous subsidies; the Court ruled that this was a
violation of the Fourteenth Amendment's equal protection clause.

In 1995 the University of California's Board of Regents eliminated
racial preferences in admission to the state university system, a policy of aggressive diversity seeking that began in the 1960s. The
admissions director at Berkeley, the flagship campus of the state's
vast public system, stated publicly that if affirmative action was to
end, "Berkeley will become 92% or 93% white and Asian. The lack
of diversity will diminish the education of all students at Berkeley."
According to an article by Ethan Bronner appearing in the *New York
Times* on April 1, 1998, he was correct. Bronner stated that the percentage of minority students—African American, Hispanic, and
American Indian—who were admitted as freshmen in 1998 was
10.4%, down from 23.1% in 1997. The comparable figures for UCLA
were 12.7% in 1998, down from 19.8% in 1997.

In the 1996 case *Hopwood v. State of Texas*, the U.S. Court of
Appeals for the Fifth District ruled that the University of Texas could
not consider race in admitting students. In the 1996 presidential
election year, California voters—residents of a state in which half the
high school graduates belong to racial or ethnic minority groups—
adopted Proposition 209, known as the California Civil Rights

Initiative. This law bars the state from using preferences in hiring or college admission based on race or gender. A number of other states have raised the same issue as an expression of their attitudes toward special preferential treatment. Although Proposition 209 and similar legislation may prove to be unconstitutional, the underlying force to expand opportunities will not go away. These legal decisions have already virtually eliminated racial minority representation in the professional graduate schools at Berkeley, the University of Texas, and other major public universities. The public universities are now seeking new methods and criteria for encouraging minorities to apply and gain admission without violating various state and federal laws.

Most of the elite private universities of America, and certainly all those in this study, are determined to continue to take into account the importance of differences in the backgrounds, talents, and special circumstances of their students and prospective students in their admissions and academic policies. Less restricted in their actions than their peer public institutions, private colleges can determine their own admissions goals and implement them as they see fit. Yet all elite schools, public and private, seemed unnerved and defensive about diversity issues. One hears the term *affirmative action* only infrequently in the elite schools. "A diversity of talents and backgrounds" is the common phrase used to make it known that administrators seek students of minority and disadvantaged backgrounds. The attitude of the dean of admissions at the University of Pennsylvania is typical of the Ivies' viewpoint:

> Our philosophy is that this university should reflect the pluralistic society we live in. And for the past 25 years we have had a significant agenda of recruiting students of color, especially Black students.

If the most selective institutions were to cut back their efforts to create diverse student bodies, the ramifications would be significant. The managing editor of the *Journal of Blacks in Higher Education* recently wrote that without current affirmative action programs "it appears that two-thirds of the approximately 3,000 African-American freshmen now enrolled each year at the nation's 25 highest-ranking universities would be denied admission." This judgment is based on the historically lower scores on entrance tests for many minorities: At all the colleges in the study, the mean scores on the Scholastic Assessment Test (SAT) of students of color tend to fall below those of white students. Social and economic forces are still at work here, in the opinion of most educators.

But historically, the elite colleges have not given preferences only to minority students. Efforts to recruit minority students are merely the newest element of their long-standing practice of giving special consideration to special-interest groups, including athletes and children of alumni.

Talented athletes are a major category of special admissions considerations. Duke, for example, is a highly selective institution that carries on a tradition of keen athletic competition. Recruited athletes who enrolled at Duke in the 1990–94 academic years had a mean high school grade point average of 3.31 and an SAT score of 1073. These two significant criteria for admission are well below the standard for the entering classes. All the colleges in our study have a long history of treating top athletes as a separate admissions group. The major change in recent years has been the advantage women athletes enjoy as a result of Title IX of the Higher Education Amendment.

Every leading college has a firm policy of admitting the talented sons and daughters of alumni at a significantly higher rate than their application pools as a whole. This fact is often cited as a key example of long-standing special consideration in the competitive admissions process.

One generation of active recruitment of minorities has graduated from the select colleges. Now, ironically, many of their children fall into the category of legacy candidates, with all the advantage in admission that this category has represented historically. Growing numbers of African American, Hispanic, and Asian American students who enter the ivied gates of the elite universities are children of educated and professional parents. The full meaning of affirmative action should not be equated automatically with admitting students who are less conventionally qualified or only those who are disadvantaged financially.

Amid the growing antagonism toward any type of program that treats all minority groups with special favor and the determination of leaders in higher education to continue the mission of creating greater access to their universities, I thought it was essential to find out how students of color regard their experience on campus. I also wanted to know how nonminority students feel about the diverse cultural mix of which they become a part when they enter college. Is all the ennobling talk of educational leaders actually building a better community of understanding?

What Matters to Minority Students

One quarter of the students in my twenty-campus survey identified themselves as members of minority groups. In virtually all aspects of their college experiences, they have the same priorities, attitudes, expectations, and goals as their nonminority counterparts. But they also have distinct areas of concern and perspectives about the Select college scene. Their outlook is not monolithic, however, and—as their own comments will show—they often have different ideas about what their challenges are and how to meet them. In many instances, their educational and economic backgrounds reflect their views of the college experience.

In selecting colleges, prestige, the name recognition of the institution, and the colleges' academic programs were as important to minority students as they were to whites. Preparation for admission to graduate school was also a comparably major consideration for them. Yet these students did not want to feel isolated from others of their own races: The importance of racial and ethnic diversity in choosing their colleges was of far greater significance to 41% of the students of color and 35% of the Asian American students versus 14% of the nonminority students. Having a base of people of your own race is important because, as one University of Pennsylvania African American student, a male junior, said:

    ❝White students seem to have little social interaction outside of their race while other students have no choice.❞

An African American woman at Yale—who transferred out after two years—noted how onerous the atmosphere can be for minority students, even if they otherwise like their college:

66 Yale has an excellent academic climate. I did, however, find that the racial environment was somewhat oppressive. New Haven is a predominantly black city, and campus officials often mistake minority students for townspeople. If you have a thick skin, you will prosper. 99

A high percentage of African American and Hispanic students—56%—as well as 45% of Asian American students, feel burdened by the cost of their education and its impact on their lives and prospects after college. They are even more aware than white students of the demands of having to hold a paying job and the stress jobs impose on their academic and social lives. These students clearly find it important to attend elite colleges as a pathway to a secure future. Why else would over half these youngsters take on such heavy financial responsibilities as work-study jobs and governmental and institutional loans?

What do minority students like most about their colleges now that they are enrolled? As do their nonminority peers, they rank the people they live and study with as the best feature. Compared to the majority of the students, students of color did not feel as affected by alcohol consumption, drug use, or the activities of sororities and fraternities. Compared to the total population I surveyed, students of color are more affected by the weather; social life; location; financial aid services; counseling opportunities; and, of course, racial tension. Asian American students are less happy with the food service, class size, and personal safety issue. Both Asian American and students of color share with all their classmates an equally negative view of the administrative bureaucracy on their campuses. Issues of personal safety, the safety of local communities, cheating, and plagiarism appear to concern them more than they do the other students.

However, a significant difference between this group and the total campus population centered on their families' expectations for them and the pressure they felt to succeed. A much larger proportion of Asian American students (40%) than of all students (23%) told me that this dynamic had a direct negative effect on their lives. In my focus sessions and individual interviews with minority students, the Asian American students most often would tell me about what their families expected them to accomplish in college and beyond. Family expectations pervade every element of their lives, especially their worries over grade point averages, quality of the faculty, and plans for graduate school—but also how they constructed their extracurricular lives. In private conversations, many Asian American students revealed their frustration and emotional conflict over how their families have ordered them to avoid such time-consuming activities as athletic teams, debating, and dramatic productions.

Racism on Campus

When I asked the Select students what components of college life had a *direct* negative effect on them, only 10% of the students of color and Asian Americans cited racism. However, when I asked them to identify the factors that had an *indirect* impact—that is, a friend or roommate had been treated unjustly or abusively or had felt excluded from specific organizations—over a third of the minority students said they had been affected negatively by racism. In the words of one sophomore African American man at Duke:

> Racism is probably the biggest reason for social discomfort here. As a member of a minority, I feel the presence of racism all the time, and I am sad that it is so pervasive. But I guess that is the reality of life, both on campuses and in America at large.

Over two-thirds of the minority men and women thought that ethnically or racially based activism has a significant effect on the campus atmosphere. The Asian American students indicated that racism had a negative impact on them, but not as frequently as on African Americans and other students of color.

I learned that many of these students feel constant pressure from their peers to participate in the activities of relevant special-interest groups. If their interests or opinions deviate from those of the dominant minority organization, they may risk public criticism and social ostracism—being made to feel that "you are either with us or against us," that there is no middle ground. A white male senior at Berkeley concurred:

66 Races are polarized. "Multicultural" pride organizations help to build walls that keep the hatred alive, and the level of ignorance remains the same among the drifters—the ones that don't participate. 99

Many students, minority and white, feel that no matter how much universities propound multiculturalism, preconceived notions persist on all sides of the racial and ethnic divides. This white MIT student, a male senior, spoke for many about the limits of multiculturalism on elite campuses:

66 The pervading attitude socially is that "you have to be *like* me if you want to be *with* me!" For as "pc" as everyone pretends to be, racial and ethnic divisions are the norm. 99

Sometimes the minority presence stirs up resentment, as evidenced in this comment from a white male junior at Brown:

66 The Greek system at this school is the saving grace for the "normal" students. Student athletes, student leaders, and reasonably conservative types are to be found there. This school focuses too much on helping extreme concerns or minority concerns and *never* focuses on the mainstream. 99

How Minority Students Manage

My survey found that the Select "nontraditional" students feel significantly greater personal stress than the white students do. When I asked them to list areas of primary concern to them personally, their stress levels became apparent. Here are the issues that preoccupy them most:

- academic workload
- grade point average
- financial costs of attending
- postcollege plans
- graduate school

- job placement
- general stress

In my counseling work both on and off campus, I have found that if minority students are to succeed, the stakes are still higher for them in college. Given how much they have had to surmount, both personally and financially, getting to the top of the job market or into an outstanding graduate school is a strong expectation for both the students and their families.

When asked to rate the quality of support services on their campuses, the minority students displayed a more favorable attitude than the total student population. They expressed a greater respect and appreciation for such programs as academic counseling, tutoring, and career and job placement counseling. A slightly greater number of the minority students actually used the academic skills and tutorial services in their colleges. They also took greater advantage of the science facilities, computer centers, and teaching assistants than did their peers.

An interesting and somewhat unexpected finding was the almost-universal reliance by students of all backgrounds on teaching assistants. Of the students in the survey, 85% relied on their TAs as an information and study resource. Here is a clear message to college administrators that these support programs must be maintained and enhanced to meet the needs of *all* undergraduates on their campuses—but with special attention to minority students.

The stress that nontraditional students feel can burst into anger and protest. It is little surprise to me that spontaneous eruptions by minority student groups occur, often when the administration least expects them and over specific issues that may not matter to the larger student body. The number of recent protests on campus by minority students and their supporters have concerned themselves with

- racial incidents
- increased costs of tuition, room, and board
- expansion of financial aid
- affirmative action policies

- development or expansion of multicultural academic disciplines
- hiring of more minority faculty
- cultural housing facilities and funding
- appropriate food options

In the past several years, students at Columbia, Princeton, Berkeley, and Yale, as well as at many other schools, staged sit-ins on campus to demand more multicultural course offerings and to protest the attacks on affirmative action and recruitment of minority candidates. A group of Asian American students at Stanford mounted a series of political actions to influence the content of courses and the choice of faculty in the university's new Comparative Studies in Race and Ethnicity program. At the University of North Carolina–Chapel Hill, a long and intense debate, with the potential for physical violence, broke out over the site for a new African American cultural center. Asian American, Hispanic, and African American students are all playing increasingly large roles in stirring debates and demonstrations on campus as they grow in number and demand that their voices be heard.

Racial Polarization on Campus

Reflecting the pattern of groups separating themselves by cultural identity on all twenty campuses, Cornell University has instituted eight special-interest houses that students can choose to join. Three are special dorms for racial groups: the Ujama Residential College for African Americans, the Latino Living Center, and the Akwe:kon House for Native Americans. These so-called self-segregating centers have incited a great deal of contention among students and outside commentators. In a case that argued that these special dorms were a form of reverse discrimination, the Appellate Court of New York State declared them legal and nondiscriminatory because students of all backgrounds can apply for membership. Predictably, this rendering did little to quell the anger felt by many traditionalists, both inside and outside the university. In an attempt to find a workable solution, the president of Cornell announced that he will permit the program houses; however, all first-year students will be required to reside in a common campus area. Cornell has found that a form of de facto segregation developed on its large, sprawling campus over time. This new policy is intended to force more interaction among the increasingly diverse student body. A similar pattern of self-selection by race or ethnicity has become evident at all the elite campuses.

As Select students of all races gather in greater number, they come together in controversial ways. Some minority students seek the company of others who share their race or ethnicity; other minority students feel comfortable in the mainstream. Some white students feel resentful of the cliquishness they perceive among minorities and grow defensive when nontraditional students challenge the ways they construct their friendships. The result is a persistent murmuring of debate that can escalate into public anger on all sides. In my survey, one Yale student, a white male junior, vented some of the anger many students feel about what they perceive to be special treatment:

> There is such a double standard, with all these minority groups getting special treatment, from Asian Americans to gay men of color, that if I were to start a group where white male Christians from the upper South were to meet and share values and ideas, I would be accused of holding a KKK meeting. It's not fair.

A white male student at Wesleyan, a famous liberal-minded campus, stated the issue succinctly and with sophistication:

> The myth of diversity works to make campus life stressful. The makeup of the school *is* diverse, but what does this mean when the student body is so segregated?

A male working-class student at Brown addressed a dynamic that affects many collegians who do not identify themselves with special groups based on color, religion, or ethnicity:

> As a nonminority student from an underrepresented state, I have had a difficult time finding a comfortable niche here. However, the struggle to do so has been a difficult but valuable experience.

A sophomore at Northwestern was also bothered by how *his* classmates divide around opposite poles.

> If there's one thing on campus I could fix, it would be the racial/ethnic polarization. The school atmosphere puts so much emphasis on making everyone find his or her own identity that it promotes polarization.

A fourth-year white woman at Berkeley agreed:

> The negative aspect of the social life at Berkeley is the unexpected ethnic polarization so prevalent on campus. Most conspicuous is the division between Asian Americans and Caucasians. Those who do associate with people of the other race are seen as "oddballish," even though such desegregation should be promoted by the student body and not looked down upon.

The minority students, quite naturally, had strong opinions about racial and ethnic fraternization and polarization. An African American sophomore woman at Cornell expressed the attitude and frustration of a great many minority students I interviewed:

> The administration and white kids bicker about program-related housing that they say causes segregation and racism. They neglect to notice that they surround themselves with white people.

An African American male athlete in his third year at Williams articulated the importance for students of all colors to belong to organizations that provide a commonality of interests and friendship:

> I have been very fortunate to attend a great institution and to participate in sports. This has provided me with a sense of identity and many close friendships. I worry about my fellow minority students who need to find that common bond, not an easy thing to do on a small, rural, predominantly white campus.

The attitude of this female sophomore at Princeton is similar to that of many mainstream students on all the elite campuses:

> ❝I like being a member of my sorority, and life on the street (eating club/fraternity row) is fun as long as you hang out with the right group. Overall I really like being young and free!❞

The many students I have talked to on both sides of the racial-cultural divide have one element in common—a feeling of frustration about how to make their closed environments work better. The students at Berkeley, ground zero of the affirmative action debate, seemed to recognize the complexity of the great social laboratory experience they were part of as they communicated the value of diversity on campus—and how difficult it is to achieve. One Berkeley senior, a white woman, told me flatly:

> ❝Cal is a great school. The campus will be robbed greatly if the diversity is not maintained. A great part of what I have learned has come from the diverse people I have encountered.❞

But no student was unaware of the difficulty of so many people with different experiences trying to maintain communication and harmony, as this African American junior woman at Berkeley stated:

> ❝Cal houses many diverse personalities. It is or tries to be a huge melting pot. I wish there was more integration between the different groups. Sometimes the animosity between groups scares me.❞

And this male sophomore at Cal, an Asian American, proclaimed with a measure of realism what was the majority's view:

> ❝Affirmative action has not yet achieved its purpose and yet it is being repealed. This needs to be counteracted!❞

How Minority Students Value Themselves

How nontraditional students regard their intellectual worth is one of my most important concerns. The emotional and often distorted facts surrounding affirmative action, by whatever name, can lead minority students to think they are less valuable members of the student body politic. I have heard more than a few minority undergraduates question whether they should ever have been admitted to their Select colleges. I always act on the belief that individuals succeed in direct relation to how they view themselves. So how do the Select minority students compare themselves to their peers? The news is pretty good on this front. An equal number of minority and white students feel they are as smart as their classmates overall. One-fifth of the African American and Hispanic students and one-quarter of the Asian American students believe they are smarter than the norm. A small number of both groups rate themselves less smart, just as their nonminority peers do.

These students are telling us that they have full confidence in their native abilities. Their self-assurance and determination to succeed free them to use whatever academic assistance they need to become successful. It is a positive sign that young minority men and women—who were, in the majority of cases, admitted to the Select colleges as part of outreach programs—believe they are as inherently talented as the majority of students. It reflects well on them and on the admissions officers who saw good reasons for accepting them. Still, affirmative action has become so entangled in emotion, political grandstanding, and distortions that it's not always easy for minority students to arrive at elite institutions with the same welcome their fellow students receive. They face a real and continuing burden to justify their presence and themselves. In her book *The Measure of Our Success: A Letter to My Children and Yours,* Marian Wright Edelman, the founder and director of the Children's Defense Fund and one of this nation's most active advocates for disadvantaged children of all backgrounds, laid out the terms of their persistent struggle:

> It can be exhausting to be a Black student on a "white" campus or a Black employee in a "white" institution where some assume you are not as smart as comparable whites. The constant burden to "prove" that you are as smart, as honest, as interesting, as wide-engaging and motivated as any other individual wears you out—as does the need to decide repeatedly whether you'll prove to anybody what they have no right to assume or demand.

> I understand the resentment of some young Blacks who have decided "who needs it?" and are opting for Black colleges where their "personess" [stet] is not under constant assault and testing. They are freed (for a short while) from having to decide whether to ignore, think about, or challenge the constant daily insensitivities of some whites who expect every Black to be a general expert on everything Black at breakfast, lunch, and dinner when you'd rather discuss art, gossip, or simply listen, or who assume you are less competent than they are because of "affirmative action."*

Minority students may become discontented with much that they find hurtful and wrong on campus, but they don't appear to become disconsolate. For example, on the topic of what several participants referred to as "the bottom line," I asked the students to gauge the value of their colleges' education for their futures. The minority students had the same positive outlook as the total group; that is, 91% of all the minority students said that the most important gift their college education will give them is credibility and respect in the outside world. Whatever problems and disappointments they may endure, whatever the price they may pay to prevail socially and academically in such a rarefied environment, minority students believe that the number-one benefit is the reflective glow of their institutions' halo.

When they checked off the postcollege goals that were most important to them, the minority students as a group revealed some specific variations. They gave greater weight to making money and being in a position of power—and voiced concern for such social issues as serving the community and correcting social and economic inequalities.

Just like their mainstream peers, a majority of the African American, Hispanic, Native American, and Asian American students endorse the overall experience they have had in Select institutions. A full 80% of the students of color and Asian American students in the study indicated they would choose the same colleges again. This is virtually the same percentage as the total population of students and an encouraging indication that the elite colleges may be on their way to fulfilling their mission of diversity.

*HarperCollins Publishers (New York: 1993).

Racial and ethnic groups are the fastest-growing segment of America's population. The projected high school graduation rate in the year 2004 is 5.6 million young men and women, almost half of whom will be people of color or ethnic minorities. A good portion of these students will aim for college, and all our higher educational institutions will be called upon to give them access. Of course, the elite colleges cannot meet the full demand for places for these students, but they will certainly have a greater number of qualified candidates knocking at their doors. Thus they must be prepared to accommodate an ever more disparate student population.

I find myself alternatively encouraged and dispirited by the experiences and attitudes of students of all backgrounds whom I encountered in this survey. We have a way to go, it would appear, to resolve underlying issues and conflicts on campus—just as we do in the society at large.

In high school an English teacher introduced me to Ralph Ellison's *The Invisible Man*. I was mightily impressed by the writing and the message Ellison presented so poignantly, but, truth to tell, I got it more on an intellectual than an emotional level. You see, I had virtually no contact, in my community or my school, with minority and disadvantaged students. Even my college and graduate school environments were comprised of a homogeneous student body. That is not the case for young men and women who make their way to the outstanding educational institutions today. As our society becomes more culturally and racially diverse and our schools and colleges mirror this pattern, Ellison's concluding words in *The Invisible Man* will be ever more relevant: "America is woven of many strands; I would recognize them and let it so remain. . . . Our fate is to become one, and yet many."

Students Who Feel Direct* Negative Effect of Campus Racism

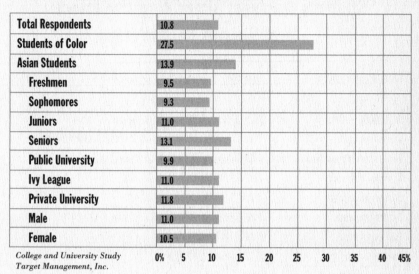

	0%	5	10	15	20	25	30	35	40	45%
Total Respondents	10.8									
Students of Color	27.5									
Asian Students	13.9									
Freshmen	9.5									
Sophomores	9.3									
Juniors	11.0									
Seniors	13.1									
Public University	9.9									
Ivy League	11.0									
Private University	11.8									
Male	11.0									
Female	10.5									

College and University Study
Target Management, Inc.

*Direct = Personal involvement.

Students Who Feel Indirect* Negative Effect of Campus Racism

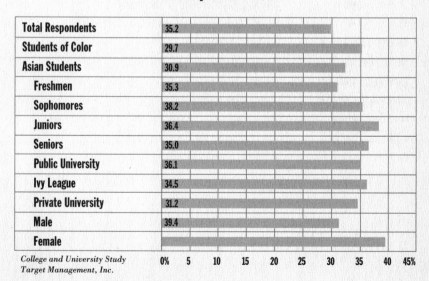

	0%	5	10	15	20	25	30	35	40	45%
Total Respondents	35.2									
Students of Color	29.7									
Asian Students	30.9									
Freshmen	35.3									
Sophomores	38.2									
Juniors	36.4									
Seniors	35.0									
Public University	36.1									
Ivy League	34.5									
Private University	31.2									
Male	39.4									
Female										

College and University Study
Target Management, Inc.

*Indirect = Through a friend, roommate, or classmate; not direct personal involvement.

Students Who Feel Direct* Negative Effect of Campus Racism

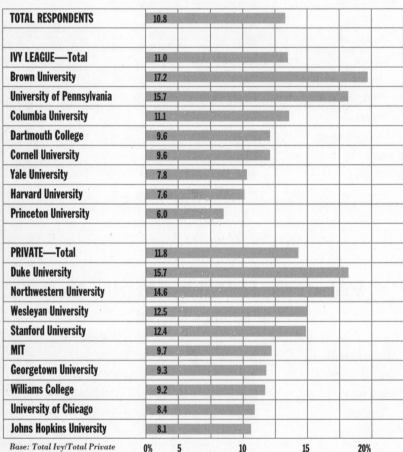

	0%	5	10	15	20%
TOTAL RESPONDENTS	10.8				
IVY LEAGUE—Total	11.0				
Brown University	17.2				
University of Pennsylvania	15.7				
Columbia University	11.1				
Dartmouth College	9.6				
Cornell University	9.6				
Yale University	7.8				
Harvard University	7.6				
Princeton University	6.0				
PRIVATE—Total	11.8				
Duke University	15.7				
Northwestern University	14.6				
Wesleyan University	12.5				
Stanford University	12.4				
MIT	9.7				
Georgetown University	9.3				
Williams College	9.2				
University of Chicago	8.4				
Johns Hopkins University	8.1				

Base: Total Ivy/Total Private College and University Study Target Management, Inc.

*Direct = Personal involvement.

SIX
Alcohol and Drugs on Campus

A Widespread Problem

Alcohol abuse on today's college campuses is a pervasive and deadly serious dilemma. A comprehensive 1995 study by Harvard's School of Public Health revealed some disturbing patterns that affect both students who drink heavily and those around them. Of the more than 14,000 undergraduates surveyed at 115 colleges with fraternities and sororities, 5 out of every 6 drank during the school year. Heavy or "binge" drinking—which is defined as consuming five or more drinks at one sitting within a two-week period—is a common activity of college students today, just as it was in the past—despite stricter rules on campus and the rise in the nationwide legal drinking age. Students at Select colleges are aware of the widespread problem and its ramifications firsthand, as this sophomore woman at Princeton made clear:

> The social life is more like other schools than I expected. Saturday nights find a large portion of the student body stumbling drunk back to their rooms. The dating scene sucks!

The understatement of another sophomore woman, this one at Harvard, made it clear that the situation wasn't limited to one elite school:

> 66 The social life at Harvard is not that great if you are not into drinking all night. 99

The Harvard study showed unequivocally that the use and abuse of alcohol affect everyone:

- Over 80% of the residents of fraternity and sorority houses engaged in binge drinking on a regular basis.
- For non-Greek members, the figures were 45% of the men and 36% of the women.
- For members of fraternities and sororities who did not live in houses, the proportion who binge drank was 71% of the men and 58% of the women.

These statistics do not necessarily include the greater population of students who drink regularly and heavily on campus.

Recently, stories about the effects of drinking and drug use in college have made headlines. Some of the stories are tragic. In 1996, a fire started by a cigarette tossed into a trash can in the basement of a fraternity house at the University of North Carolina killed five students who were asleep upstairs. Autopsies indicated that four of the five had blood alcohol levels above the state's intoxication limit. In the same year, a drug bust by campus police at Harvard resulted in the arrest of two undergraduates who were distributing LSD, ecstasy, hallucinogenics, and marijuana on campus. According to Harvard's chief of police, "There were several students who registered concern for the well-being of fellow students because their use of narcotics directly related to these people who were distributing." Thus these students decided to report the dealers to campus security. Curious, is it not, that students typically will not report friends or roommates for using illegal drugs. The director of the Harvard University Health Services stated that the abuse of alcohol and drugs at Harvard mirrors national trends. In my opinion, he is begging the issue by assuming that the situation is neither better nor worse than anywhere else.

Dr. Henry Wechsler of the Harvard School of Public Health found, in a 1993 study, that more than one out of every seven Harvard undergraduates had used marijuana or hashish within the month before the study began. This rate compares to a similar national rate of use of 14%. Alcohol consumption is still the larger concern on campus, with 41% of Harvard undergraduates classified, in Wechsler's study, as binge drinkers, compared to 47% of the under-graduates at other East Coast private universities. These percentages are stunning when you consider that these students are the most pro-ductive, achievement-oriented young men and women to congregate anywhere in the nation.

A star wrestler at Brown University was arrested on campus in 1996 for possessing bags of cocaine and a weight scale. He was sus-pended from the university pending criminal proceedings. The young man was an outstanding athletic competitor; he was also described as having difficulty adjusting to the academic and social life of the cam-pus. Although his problems may seem like a convenient excuse for dealing drugs, this young offender proves that many drug and alcohol abusers use substances as self-medication for the painful stress and anxiety rampant on elite campuses—as our survey confirms.

On the basis of my experience on four Ivy League campuses and my direct contact with thousands of undergraduates, I was not sur-prised by any of these findings. Alcohol in an earlier time was the magnet for ritualistic bonding among groups of fairly innocent young men. To belong to the cool group and show one's courage meant drinking heavily, always to the point of total drunkenness. To get "blotto" or "smashed" was the sole purpose of a weekend party, espe-cially in the fraternity or club houses. As an employee of Princeton in the 1960s, I had two responsibilities: to help admit a freshman class from a large pool of highly talented candidates and to advise a group of undergraduates as they attempted to adjust to a new envi-ronment that could be both stimulating and overwhelming. What shocked me was observing students I'd seen through the admission process drawn to a heavy party scene—drinking regularly and exces-sively every weekend. Some expressed their concern to me when they recognized the seriousness and habit-forming aspect of their behavior. Others made light of their partying and shot back comments to the effect that this was what college was all about; this is what they had been working so hard to achieve in high school. As a chaperone of a number of dances at several eating clubs, occasions when women were "imported" from the numerous women's colleges then in existence, I observed firsthand the consequences of excessive alcohol consumption. Physical fights would break out, women would get sick from overdrinking, and many women were mauled and left on their own. All these patterns of behavior took place at Harvard, Yale, and Dartmouth. Stories from other elite colleges only confirmed the phenomenon.

Today, the stakes appear to be even higher, as more women join in the heavy abuse of alcohol amid the easy accessibility of narcotics. I am convinced that the greater incidence of life-threatening stupors from overuse, as well as sexual assault and date rape, are due not to the better reporting of such occurrences, but to the greater opportunities and drive of students to blot out the weeklong pressures of academic life and evidence of a desperate desire to belong to a group. I have students relate their concern to me, either over their own drinking or their failure to belong if they do not join in "the party." They even talk about transferring to a campus where drugs and alcohol may be less pervasive. I also hear from many students who have failed out of college because of their drinking or drug problems. The majority got into difficulty either with their grades or with the disciplinary authorities before they were faced with the downward spiral in which they were trapped.

I see a combination of social factors leading to the growing substance abuse among college students. Clearly, students are under greater stress to compete successfully for grades to move onto the next level of training—graduate school. Furthermore, the overall quality of Select students is more impressive than a generation ago. Also, concerns about financing their education affect at least 50% of the students. Moreover, a sense of alienation from their campus peers leads them to seek to belong at any cost or, just the opposite, to escape into their own world with heavy drinking or drug taking. This is not a dynamic that can be easily eliminated by administrative decree.

As I discussed earlier, the elite colleges have determined to diversify their student population dramatically by intentionally admitting more students of various socioeconomic backgrounds. One significant result has been the individual student's drive to find a comfortable group of friends either through extracurricular activities or social clubs. Many less sophisticated students, in an effort to be part of that larger group, quickly fall prey to the sirens of excess with alcohol or drugs. No matter that most students are underage, and no matter the vigor with which a university enforces its alcohol policies; drinking remains a major activity in both the Greek houses and other social units. Fraternities, and increasingly sororities, tend to attract members who see the verb "to party" as a license for heavy drinking.

A first-year female at Berkeley, despite the many opportunities and resources at a large university, has this perception of the environment:

> Berkeley's atmosphere is very academic. There is not a whole lot to do in terms of social activities, unless you are a political or radical activist or, worst of all, a heavy drinker or pot smoker.

One of the thorniest issues that college presidents and trustees grapple with today is the role of fraternities and sororities on their campus. Viewed by the stewards of the college as an obstacle to the intellectual life of the institution and the primary source of on-campus negative social behavior, the Greek institutions are often policed with great rigor. In some cases, including Williams College, they have been banned from the campus. At the same time, one should not overlook the heavy alcohol consumption that takes place outside the fraternity-sorority environment—off campus among students who attend colleges in urban locations or on campuses where the Greeks have been eliminated altogether.

Whatever the social structures that dominate a particular campus, many Select students have decided that if they are going to work hard, then they are going to play hard, too. Yet when I asked the students I surveyed what they would change to improve their colleges, they most frequently mentioned eliminating alcohol consumption. While some elite colleges have more obvious drug and alcohol problems than others, as my survey revealed, the environment at all

Select schools challenges students to come to a personal accommodation with the pervasiveness of drugs and drinking.

The Impact of Alcohol and Drugs on Students

About one-fifth of the Select men and women I surveyed told me that
alcohol on campus had affected their lives directly, and under 10%
indicated the direct, negative effect of drug usage. However, the proportion of students who felt the *indirect* effects of drug and alcohol
use was much higher. More than one-third of the men and women
reported that they had been affected negatively in a secondary way:
24% of the men and 40% of the women. Overall, fewer than half the
students cited no direct or indirect effect on them of alcohol consumption or drug use.

Note the greater effect the use of alcohol and drugs has on women.
It should be obvious why women feel the greater impact of drinking
and drugging and why they have a higher level of vulnerability. Every
study, and certainly every conversation I had with women who have
experienced physical or sexual assault or date rape or engaged in
casual sexual activity, has referred to the influence of alcohol or
drugs. Under the rubric "times change, but they don't really change
all that much," men get drunk and behave badly, usually aggres-
sively, and while men may suffer serious consequences, young
women are at a greater risk on every count.

To put this problem in a larger context, the need to hold down a
paying job had a greater direct negative effect on students than alcohol consumption did. Yet alcohol use is the social factor that had the
most frequent indirect repercussions for the students. The effect may
be as simple yet ubiquitous as the atmosphere a college fosters for
everyone, whether a student drinks or not. A Cornell sophomore, a
woman, explained the situation this way:

> 66 Parties often are not fun for nondrinkers because of such an
> emphasis on alcohol. 99

Far too great a proportion of students are affected by their own or
other individuals' dysfunctional behavior. Many have no choice but

to deal with an environment that is pervaded with the ethos of alcohol, which this female junior at Williams described succinctly and plaintively:

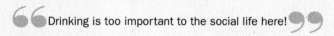 Drinking is too important to the social life here!

A Princeton sophomore remarked on the same phenomenon at her school:

The amount of unchecked drinking that goes on at the eating clubs is amazing. It would be nice if there were a way to join the clubs without paying alcohol fees.

Note that the undergraduates who belong to social clubs and fraternities are required to pay for parties, meaning alcohol, whether or not they drink themselves or are underage.

The critical issue, as the Harvard report stated, is the impact of alcohol abuse not only on the individual user but on other members of the campus community. The "secondhand binge" effects are serious, unnerving, often dangerous, and sometimes criminal. They include

- date rape
- unwanted or unsafe sexual activity
- physical abuse
- disruption of sleep and study time
- baby-sitting sick or alcohol-poisoned friends, dates, or roommates
- property damage and theft
- general fear for one's safety

Students are well aware of these issues, and many would echo the words of this woman, a junior at Cornell:

There is a significant group here that loses all moral qualms about drinking and sex, which really turns me off. These students are exemplified but not limited to the people in the Greek system, which makes me sick.

Drug use is far less prevalent than alcohol consumption on the majority of college campuses. Marijuana appears to be increasing among college students nationwide and is certainly prevalent on elite college campuses. I suspect that this generation of students has a romantic notion of the heavy pot-smoking college culture of the 1960s and 1970s. The harmful fallout from drugs that many of those generations experienced is too remote in time to influence the actions of today's undergraduates. An insight into this college generation's attitude toward marijuana can be seen in the Stanford University Cannabis Re-Education Alliance, a student organization whose "main purpose . . . is to promote an open dialogue about the uses of cannabis and ultimately increase its awareness, acceptance, and use." The findings of my survey did not indicate that drug use has had a major impact on the student body at large—at least not yet. I've spoken to several Ivy League students who confessed their surprise that there were fewer students doing drugs in their colleges than in their high schools. But if more of today's high school students have experienced drugs firsthand, what will happen when it's their turn to go to college?

What Can Be Done?

Discussing social life on campus today, students in virtually all the prestigious institutions commented frequently on the high rate of alcohol and drug use they encountered. The number of individual references to the downside of campus life in the elite colleges that is due to heavy drinking is dismaying. I am afraid that the many negative factors discussed throughout this study are taking a toll on students—directly by the use of drugs or indirectly by being abused as a result of their use.

According to a 1989 Carnegie Foundation report, college presidents regard alcohol abuse as the most serious problem they face on campus. My survey found the same patterns of behavior as did the Harvard study and several other research projects. As my survey shows, there are compelling reasons for college administrators to seek reasonable and realistic solutions to the problem of substance abuse. Some Select students, like this male Columbia senior, have strongly realistic attitudes even though they acknowledge that the university cannot shirk its role:

> ❝ Kids entering college are going to drink, and it is easy for them to get whatever alcohol they want. The university should accept this and realize that if students are going to drink, they ought to do it on campus where they will be close to help if they need it. But turning its back and ignoring the obvious and unavoidable could really come back to hurt the university—not to mention the students who drink and those of us who have to live with them. ❞

Students want the freedom to experiment and express themselves at the same time as they expect the adults on campus to help them through the potential consequences.

Then, too, the prevalence of drugs and alcohol affects not just the users, but those around them who are trying to get an education and live contented social lives. It is not within the purview of this book to set forth all the solutions, but it certainly is appropriate to add to the call for both extensive educational programs for all students—no matter what their relationship to alcohol—and supportive medical and counseling services for those who suffer from substance abuse.

One indicator of the discontent shared by many "straight" students is the growing number of "substance-free" dormitories or designated floors in dormitories. At the least, such facilities offer concerned undergraduates the opportunity to avoid the direct or indirect consequences of drugs, alcohol, and smoking.

Advice to Parents and Students

Students who contemplate going to an elite college, as well as their parents, require a word of caution. I have seen immature and insecure young people ruin their educational careers needlessly: They walked onto an ivied campus without being aware of the risks they would face. Students should not believe that winning admission to an elite college grants them immunity from temptation and human frailty. The Halo Effect of reputation should never blind them to the challenges they will face. The environments of Select colleges offer a universe of promise—complete with black holes.

Prospective students should know, as any seasoned upperclassman will tell them, that it is not necessary to overdrink or escape reality with drugs to fit in. Select students reveal their character not by how they act out around substances; they show what they are made of through good deeds and excelling in their given talents and passions.

Parents also have a responsibility, even after they have written the tuition checks and sent their progeny off to college—especially then, in fact. They must look honestly at their children for any signs of dramatic alteration in personality and behavior. They need to listen to the signals they receive about the stress their children are undergoing and how their children are reacting to it. If they sense resignation or inability to cope, they need to communicate immediately with the appropriate dean, adviser, or on-campus health service. Parents should never allow anyone to tell them that their children are now college men or women and are fully capable of acting on their own. As the Select students I've dealt with have long made clear to me, children venturing into the larger world need the continuing support and care of their elders if they are going to build lives that are filled with genuine pleasures and true balance.

Items of Primary Concern to Student Life

(Split by Race)

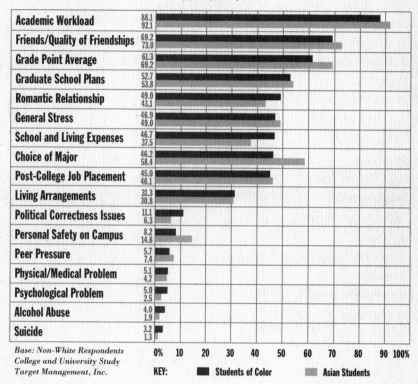

	Students of Color	Asian Students
Academic Workload	88.1	92.1
Friends/Quality of Friendships	69.2	73.0
Grade Point Average	61.3	69.2
Graduate School Plans	52.7	53.8
Romantic Relationship	49.0	43.1
General Stress	46.9	49.0
School and Living Expenses	46.7	37.5
Choice of Major	46.2	58.4
Post-College Job Placement	45.0	46.1
Living Arrangements	31.3	30.8
Political Correctness Issues	11.1	6.3
Personal Safety on Campus	8.2	14.6
Peer Pressure	5.7	7.4
Physical/Medical Problem	5.1	4.7
Psychological Problem	5.0	2.5
Alcohol Abuse	4.0	1.9
Suicide	3.2	1.3

0%   10   20   30   40   50   60   70   80   90 100%

Base: Non-White Respondents
College and University Study
Target Management, Inc.

KEY: ■ Students of Color   ■ Asian Students

Items of Primary Concern to Student Life

(Split by Gender)

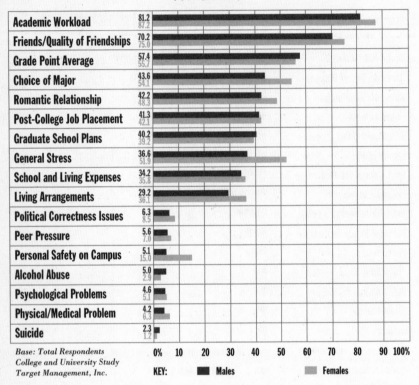

	Males	Females
Academic Workload	81.2	87.2
Friends/Quality of Friendships	70.2	75.0
Grade Point Average	57.4	55.7
Choice of Major	43.6	54.1
Romantic Relationship	42.2	48.3
Post-College Job Placement	41.3	42.1
Graduate School Plans	40.2	39.2
General Stress	36.6	51.9
School and Living Expenses	34.2	35.8
Living Arrangements	29.2	36.1
Political Correctness Issues	6.3	8.5
Peer Pressure	5.6	7.0
Personal Safety on Campus	5.1	15.0
Alcohol Abuse	5.0	2.9
Psychological Problems	4.6	5.1
Physical/Medical Problem	4.2	6.3
Suicide	2.3	1.2

Base: Total Respondents
College and University Study
Target Management, Inc.

0%   10   20   30   40   50   60   70   80   90   100%

KEY:　　■ Males　　　　　▨ Females

Students Who Feel Direct* Negative Effect of Campus Alcohol Consumption

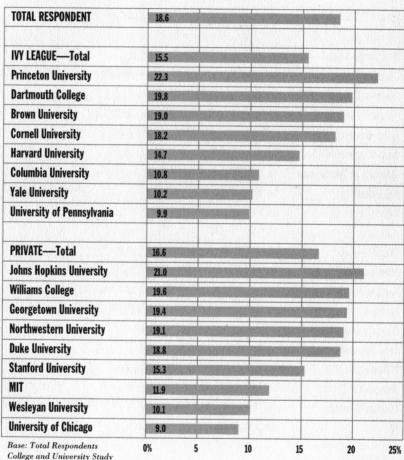

	0%	5	10	15	20	25%
TOTAL RESPONDENT	18.6					
IVY LEAGUE—Total	15.5					
Princeton University	22.3					
Dartmouth College	19.8					
Brown University	19.0					
Cornell University	18.2					
Harvard University	14.7					
Columbia University	10.8					
Yale University	10.2					
University of Pennsylvania	9.9					
PRIVATE—Total	16.6					
Johns Hopkins University	21.0					
Williams College	19.6					
Georgetown University	19.4					
Northwestern University	19.1					
Duke University	18.8					
Stanford University	15.3					
MIT	11.9					
Wesleyan University	10.1					
University of Chicago	9.0					

Base: Total Respondents
College and University Study
Target Management, Inc.

*Direct = Personal involvement.

Students Who Feel Direct* Negative Effect of Campus Drug Usage

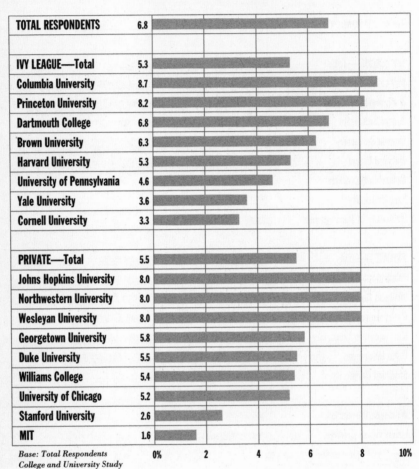

TOTAL RESPONDENTS	6.8	
IVY LEAGUE—Total	5.3	
Columbia University	8.7	
Princeton University	8.2	
Dartmouth College	6.8	
Brown University	6.3	
Harvard University	5.3	
University of Pennsylvania	4.6	
Yale University	3.6	
Cornell University	3.3	
PRIVATE—Total	5.5	
Johns Hopkins University	8.0	
Northwestern University	8.0	
Wesleyan University	8.0	
Georgetown University	5.8	
Duke University	5.5	
Williams College	5.4	
University of Chicago	5.2	
Stanford University	2.6	
MIT	1.6	

0%   2   4   6   8   10%

Base: Total Respondents
College and University Study
Target Management, Inc.

*Direct = Personal involvement.

SEVEN
Danger in the Ivory Tower:
SAFETY ON CAMPUS

The State of Crime on Elite Campuses

An ivy-walled campus does not guarantee a secure living environment, as many Select students have learned through bitter experience. As all of us who have survived the high school and college years may remember, young adults feel physically invincible and thus can be particularly vulnerable to crimes of all kinds. I regard it as a primary responsibility of anyone involved with students to make them aware that college campuses are not immune to the perils that plague the rest of America. And a concentration of young people in a circumscribed physical setting is a natural breeding ground for all sorts of antisocial behavior. As Chapter 6 showed, the abuse of alcohol and of drugs are major contributors to physical and sexual offenses. The relative innocence of college students about protecting themselves and their expensive property makes them sitting ducks for thievery and assault.

In response to the rising incidence of criminal activity on campus, from petty theft to sexual assault and murder—and the accompanying consternation among parents and students—the federal government enacted the Federal Crime Awareness and Campus Security Act in 1990. The law requires all higher educational institutions that receive federal funding to report annual crime statistics to the U.S. Department of Education in ten categories defined by the FBI, from petty to violent crime. This information must be made available upon request to present and prospective students. The act also calls for colleges to detail their safety policies and procedures. A provision that was added to the law two years later requires colleges to have active programs that promote awareness of date rape and other categories of sexual offenses.

There have been many criticisms of the Federal Crime Awareness and Campus Security Act because of irregular, often self-serving, reporting by individual institutions; poor compliance enforcement by the U.S. Department of Education; and the omission of statistics for crimes that occur off campus. Several advocacy groups are working at the state level to broaden the range of information that colleges maintain and report, particularly for off-campus crimes and rapes—incidents that most often are not reported. Nevertheless, the act has helped to raise the public's awareness that serious crimes can and do occur on campus.

Many parents assume that somehow all elite schools are safe, as if the presence of ivy magically precludes crime. So it is that the Halo Effect of the elite institutions frequently obscures the presence of criminal acts that are committed on these seemingly unassailable campuses. I urge students to ask for the information published by the colleges that interest them and to seek further data if they think that the impact of the off-campus community on the campus itself has not been thoroughly addressed. A first-year student at Columbia had this response to attending college in a large city:

> New York City has a huge influence on life at Columbia. It is not a college town. It is the real, big, unfriendly, uncaring, exciting, amazing, intense, hostile world. Be prepared and be aware!

Although the Federal Crime Awareness and Campus Security Act is a welcome source of information, there is a good deal of inconsistency in the data that colleges report. Just as not all institutions list every criminal act on and off campus, many schools do not report offenses dealt with by their own judicial systems or crimes that occur off campus. A recent national study of compliance with the act revealed that nearly 50% of the colleges in the sample did not make information on campus and neighborhood security available to prospective students. For the institutions that did, noncompliance within the stated requirements was frequent. The public outcry to this rising incidence of campus-related crimes has led Congress to propose legislation that would require colleges and universities to make their campus police logs accessible to the public and extend the categories of crimes that must be reported. In a great many instances, colleges refuse to release such information, claiming that doing so would violate the privacy and confidentiality required under the terms of the Family Educational Rights and Privacy Act. In fact, Congress amended this act in 1992 to ensure that such information is made available upon request. All this public relations subterfuge makes it hard for outside analysts to compare precisely crime at different colleges.

Colleges tend to deal internally with disciplinary issues and complaints through their own standing committees. Often these meetings and deliberations are held in secret. It is difficult to imagine that the interests of the institutions are not weighed in the balance as these tribunals arrive at decisions of guilt or innocence and mete out punishments. Whether dealing with a string of burglaries or a date rape between students, colleges have a vested interest in dispensing justice in a way that will not reflect ill on the reputation of the schools themselves. The demands of justice and the desire to preserve an institution's good name can sometimes be clashing interests.

How serious have on-campus acts of violence and sexual assault become? Here are a few sobering incidents to consider:

- After a contentious debate, campus police at the University of Pennsylvania are now issued semiautomatic weapons, as a response to a rise in serious crimes that resulted in one death. A recent string of robberies at gunpoint reinforced the university's decision to arm its campus police with more powerful weapons. Following the shooting of a student, the university president felt it necessary to write directly to the parents of all students, reassuring them that the university was doing all that was necessary to make its urban campus safe from such crimes. The University of Pennsylvania spends over $15 million a year for on-campus law enforcement and plans to increase its security measures still further.

- In April 1996, a student at Johns Hopkins was killed by a fellow student, a friend and fellow member of a campus political organization, following an argument. Students at this city campus have long complained about campus and neighborhood safety.

- A Harvard undergraduate, an international student from Ethiopia, stabbed and killed her roommate, critically injured another student who tried to stop the assault, and then hanged herself.

- While returning to his dormitory after a party, a popular Yale undergraduate athlete and campus leader was shot to death in front of the university president's house. This was not a robbery of a privileged student, according to the police investigation. It was a random act of violence against a college student by a disadvantaged, angry, local teenager.

These kinds of tragedies have occurred on a number of campuses in the past several years and seem to be on the rise. Crime at colleges is a result of many factors, many of which no campus police force can ever totally control. But in my discussions with a number of deans, I heard a common theme: Crime often results from the naïveté of many students who believe they are immune to major forms of crime—precisely because they are college students. Students are frequently the easy prey of criminals because of their inexperience in living in a new and unfamiliar environment. Because they are perceived as well-to-do and arrogant by the outside community—an attitude that can be shared by their fellow students within their own cloistered campus—they are easy targets for crime. The demise of dormitory parietals, the rise of coed dormitories, and the greater interaction between the campus and surrounding community have all exacerbated the type and level of crimes to which today's students are vulnerable.

As Chapter 6 described in detail, the heavy incidence of campus drinking results in a number of incidents of sexual assault and date rape. Alcohol can loosen inhibitions and blur the line between consent and force. This is a particular anxiety frequently voiced on campus. Most institutions deal with complaints of sexual assault internally and normally do not make the information public. It is up to prospective students and their parents to ask the administration directly for hard facts about sex crimes. Students themselves are often the most reliable sources about incidents of sexual assault and how crimes in general are handled by campus security and the administration

How Select Students View Campus Crime

In my survey, I asked the Select students a series of questions about their awareness of crimes and their concern for personal safety. The responses uncovered a significant difference between the reactions of the men and women. Regarding all the various security and crime concerns I asked about, the women expressed a greater degree of uneasiness. The opinion of a female junior at the University of Chicago is indicative of how many of the women in the survey replied:

> Among both students and administrators, the awareness and handling of sexual and racial issues is simply despicable. We pay $30,000 a year to come here. Why are we not fully protected and informed about on-campus violence and harassment?

When I asked the Select students to rate the importance of a number of factors in choosing their colleges, 44% of the men and 54% of the women indicated that geographic location was extremely important; prospective students took very much into account whether they wanted to spend four years at a relatively bucolic campus or an urban school. Parents are becoming more aware of the crime rates at urban campuses and are weighing this factor into their children's choice of colleges. I am asked by virtually every family I counsel to consider the safety element when I suggest appropriate colleges.

Querying Select students about which components of campus life have affected their own existence and whether they felt directly or indirectly influenced, I found that issues of campus safety had a direct negative effect on only 6% of the men and 12% of the women. By contrast, 30% of the men and 40% of the women in the study indicated that campus safety had an *indirect* negative impact on them. This finding means that although they may not have experienced some criminal act firsthand, a friend has—or that their concern for safety affected their decisions, such as when to be out of the dormitory and where to go in their daily lives. Following the same pattern, 3% of the men and 14% of the women declared they had been directly and negatively affected by sexism and sexual harassment. Yet the proportion of students who experienced some kind of sexism or sexual harassment indirectly jumped to 18% of the men and 26% of the women. Only 1% of the men and 5% of the women said they had a direct experience with date or acquaintance rape. But 12% of the men and 21% of the women indicated some indirect impact: A friend or roommate had endured such a traumatic event.

In another, more general question, I asked the students to tell me what factors on campus are of primary concern to them, meaning that these factors are a constant source of unease or anxiety. The response to any particular factors was insignificant. While the students worry less about crime than about their academic standing, as *secondary* issues a high percentage of Select students do worry about alcohol abuse (22% of the men and 15% of the women) and personal safety (30% of the men and 49% of the women).

An impressive one-half of the female undergraduates in this survey function in their daily lives with a conscious concern for their personal safety. They consider themselves to be at a greater risk than men. The number of both men and women who know someone affected by crimes shows how much safety issues influence Select students today. A sophomore woman at Berkeley expressed her shock at the rate of criminal behavior, both on and off the campus:

> I guess I was pretty naive to expect a crime-free environment when I came to Berkeley. Students complain about theft in their dorms and in the library—calculators, computers, bicycles disappearing frequently. And forget about venturing out into the neighborhood. I feel like a moving target for physical attack. I have learned, sadly, to keep to a straight path from classroom to library to my room.

A Georgetown woman complained about inadequate housing available after her first two years of college, presenting her with a situation she finds undesirable:

> If I had known that I would have to move into private housing after living in the dorms for two years, I might not have enrolled here. I feel insecure every time I leave the campus or social center at night to go home. This is a dangerous area, known for attacks on women. Why couldn't the administrators be more up front about limited housing, and why can't they do something about this concern? I am not alone in this matter.

As a typical indication of how many Select students consider the safety issue in choosing their college, this sophomore female at Dartmouth told me:

> I am really glad I came to Dartmouth for many reasons. One of them is the sense of security I have walking around campus and the town. There is a real feeling of being part of both rather than having to manage town/gown tensions—or worse—that I heard about at some of the other Ivy schools I had considered.

However, one can get a false sense of security on a handsome, ivy-clad, self-contained campus. Many colleges have a history of friction with the surrounding communities. This is, at heart, a socioeconomic issue that can break out unhappily at any time. I know a young man, an outstanding athlete and solid citizen, who is at Duke. One night in 1996, he and two friends entered a local bar just minutes from the main campus. He was confronted by a group of locals who decided to have fun at his expense. The encounter escalated into an all-out brawl with fists and bottles flying. He was smashed on the head with a glass bottle and suffered severe head injuries that may result in permanent damage. Local town hangouts and college students are "an accident waiting to happen." To say the least, this young man regrets his decision to enter the bar in the first place and acknowledges that he should have stayed away from it.

Date and Acquaintance Rape

If the statistics are to be believed, hardly any Select college students are victims of acquaintance rape or date rape. Eighteen colleges in this study reported to the federal government that only three to five forcible sex offenses occurred on their campuses. Two others, Stanford and Wisconsin, reported much higher numbers of such incidents, fourteen and twenty-five respectively. I strongly doubt, however, that these two campuses have a greater number of sex offenders than any of their peer institutions.

I am afraid the reported statistics are not to be believed. Various studies done on individual campuses in the past several years have claimed that 20% to 25% of the women have been date raped. These figures are higher than campus administrators, counselors, and security forces would know about or admit, since many victims, especially targets of date rape or sexual assault, do not report their experiences to security officers. Moreover, the very interpretation of the terms *acquaintance rape* and *date rape* is problematic for many undergraduate women, who can have trouble communicating to men their decisions about sexual activity. What influence does alcohol or drugs have in sexual activity between a couple? Where does assent start and end? According to counselors and deans, confusion and shame keep many victims from coming forward. Some of the most painful counseling sessions I have had over the years are with young women who want to leave college because of a sexual event they did not desire. Either they were raped or consented to sex under the influence of alcohol.

A case at Brown—which could have taken place on any elite campus—points up the complications involved in assaying and punishing possible sex-crime offenders. A female student accused a male acquaintance of raping her while she was under the influence of alcohol—and filed her complaint one month after the alleged incident took place. The male student testified that his accuser knew what she was doing and even gave him her telephone number and address after having sex. The disciplinary council hearing the case declared that the young man should have determined if his partner was drunk and thus was incapable of acting as she really wished to. In her testimony, the woman acknowledged having drunk a great deal of alcohol before the sexual encounter. The male student, who was put on probation, has filed a lawsuit against his accuser for libel and has sued Brown for wrongful punishment. It's easy to understand an individual's reluctance to bring charges when this kind of publicity is likely to occur—and where sexual mores and honor are themselves open questions. For many, the weight of their own behavior is a burden they simply cannot bear publicly.

The majority of colleges have established guidelines for appropriate sexual conduct, complete with attempts to define the terms of mutual consent, which are extremely difficult to delineate. Some schools have embarrassed themselves by setting guidelines that make students fearful of even shaking hands spontaneously with members of the opposite sex.

Inappropriate sexual activity is a serious concern not only among students on any given campus but also between students and faculty. Undergraduates of both genders have had relationships forced on them by their teachers, and sexual harassment or outright manipulation by faculty members is apparently increasing on the elite campuses. Yale University recently acknowledged its concern as a result of several incidents, publishing an edict that bans sexual relationships between faculty and students. Many other campuses have established clear lines of behavior as a response to complaints of sexual harassment. Yale's new policy reads as follows: "Any such relationship jeopardizes the integrity of the educational process by creating a conflict of interest." This is especially the case when a professor or the ubiquitous teaching assistant has direct responsibility or authority over students. Prospective students should inquire about school policies as they make the rounds of the colleges they are interested in attending.

Do college administrators really appreciate the degree of concern students feel as they negotiate the uncharted terrain of contemporary sexual mores? Higher education officials often see themselves as caught between a rock and a hard place. Taking aggressive action to reduce alcohol consumption and the antisocial behavior it causes, tightening campus security, and confronting accusations of sexual assault and date rape all can bring undesirable publicity to their institutions and lead to lawsuits by angry families. The U.S. Department of Education has been criticized for not monitoring colleges more critically for compliance with the crime law, not ensuring that reporting is accurate, and not checking to see that measures to improve security are being taken. As a result of the publicity surrounding the shootings and robberies on the University of Pennsylvania campus, for example, the U.S. Department of Education decided to scrutinize the university's reporting of campus crimes.

I strongly believe that college officials have to be more honest in presenting their institutions to prospective Select students. They should tell these candidates the risks they may encounter; the actual availability of housing; and the campus policies on unwanted sexual activity, drinking, and drugs—and let them make their own honest and informed decisions.

Students Seeking Safety on Campus

Out of concern for the frequency of crimes and the many physical dangers that exist on campus, college students nationwide have formed a national organization, Security on Campus, to increase awareness of safety issues and to put pressure on college officials for greater accountability and anticrime measures. They have developed a list of questions for prospective students to consider as they decide where to apply. I recommend that parents and students use this checklist when they query college administrators about campus safety.

- Does the institution publish campus crime information as required by the Student Right-to-Know and Campus Security Act of 1990? (You can request a copy from the U.S. Department of Education.)

- Do the annual crime statistics include reports to the dean's office of campus crimes and judicial hearings and data from campus women's rape/crisis centers?
- Are security logs open for public inspection?
- Does the school ask applicants if they have been arrested and convicted of a crime? Do they admit applicants with a criminal history?
- Are policies and penalties related to campus crime explicitly addressed during orientation and prominently stipulated in the student handbook?
- Are drinking, drugs, and weapons laws strictly enforced?
- How are bathroom doors locked in coed dorms?
- Are single-sex and "substance-free" dormitories available?
- During the academic year, does the school inform the entire student body about growing problems related to campus crime: date rape and sexual assault, alcohol and drug abuse, and sexually transmitted diseases? When? Who addresses the students?
- According to the dean of student life, how many cases did the school's judicial committees handle last year?
- Does the school provide immediate medical, psychological, and legal aid to victims, as required by the Campus Sexual Assault Victim's Bill of Rights (Federal Law 1992)?

As I said at the start of this chapter, the Halo Effect that insulates the most prestigious institutions from the critical scrutiny of the public does a disservice to students who qualify for entrance. The majority of candidates who gain admission to the Select come from the protected environments of their homes and safe schools. These are the students, after all, who have had the advantages that helped to prepare them for admission. They are usually not street smart and, consequently, can fall easy prey to the worst elements of behavior once they arrive on campus.

Crime Rates at Select Colleges

According to the statistics released by each college or university to the U.S. Department of Education under the Federal Crime

Awareness and Campus Security Act for 1995, there are major differences in criminal activity among the campuses I surveyed for this survey. But as I've already noted, the lack of uniformity in gathering and reporting data makes it difficult to make comparisons. For example, I find it incomprehensible that Georgetown did not report a single incident of sex offense, liquor violation, or motor vehicle theft and listed only fifteen cases of burglary. What kind of reporting system does the school have in place that can present as crime-free a highly visible university in the midst of the nation's capital? I have talked with too many Georgetown undergraduates to have any faith in the figures reported here. In contrast to Georgetown, other urban universities like Yale, Stanford, and Berkeley have reported several hundred burglaries. Berkeley and Wisconsin appear to have the most efficient law enforcement programs and/or record-keeping systems. Both have reported hundreds of liquor-law violations.

The greatest number of crimes reported on all the campuses are burglaries. Although Yale had the highest number of such crimes, no one should assume that a college-town setting necessarily means lower crime rates. Cornell, Wisconsin, Duke, and North Carolina, for instance, reported a considerable number of burglaries.

Which colleges provide the safest environment overall? On the basis of my own experience and my conversations with Select students, I would say that Dartmouth and Princeton are the most secure because of their small-town locations and contained physical campuses. Dartmouth has reported few cases of burglary, robbery, or car theft. Princeton had a higher number of burglaries but little criminal activity in all the other categories.

Until there is greater uniformity of reporting criminal activities at elite institutions, I would remain skeptical about using comparative data as part of a decision on where to go to college. Parents and students must take the initiative to get straight answers from the colleges they are considering. Their own common sense will be their best guide in determining just how safe and sound a Select school may be.

Students Who Feel Direct* Negative Effect of Campus Safety Issues

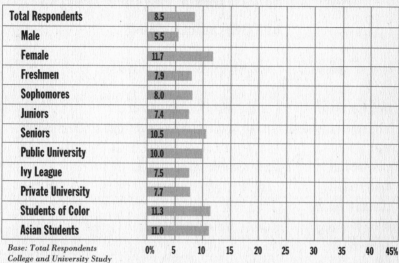

	0%	5	10	15	20	25	30	35	40	45%
Total Respondents	8.5									
Male	5.5									
Female	11.7									
Freshmen	7.9									
Sophomores	8.0									
Juniors	7.4									
Seniors	10.5									
Public University	10.0									
Ivy League	7.5									
Private University	7.7									
Students of Color	11.3									
Asian Students	11.0									

Base: Total Respondents
College and University Study
Target Management, Inc.

*Direct = Personal involvement.

Students Who Feel Indirect* Negative Effect of Campus Safety Issues

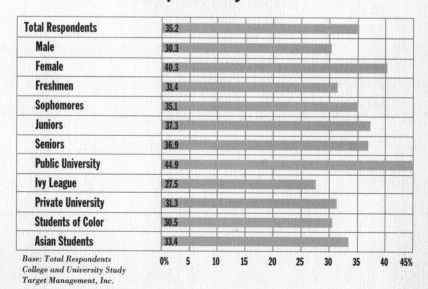

	0%	5	10	15	20	25	30	35	40	45%
Total Respondents	35.2									
Male	30.3									
Female	40.3									
Freshmen	31.4									
Sophomores	35.1									
Juniors	37.3									
Seniors	36.9									
Public University	44.9									
Ivy League	27.5									
Private University	31.3									
Students of Color	30.5									
Asian Students	33.4									

Base: Total Respondents
College and University Study
Target Management, Inc.

*Indirect = Through a friend, roommate, or classmate; not direct personal involvement.

Students Who Feel Direct* Negative Effect of Campus Safety Issues

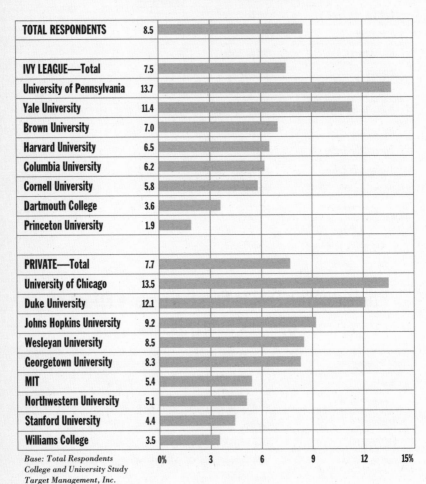

		0%	3	6	9	12	15%
TOTAL RESPONDENTS	8.5						
IVY LEAGUE—Total	7.5						
University of Pennsylvania	13.7						
Yale University	11.4						
Brown University	7.0						
Harvard University	6.5						
Columbia University	6.2						
Cornell University	5.8						
Dartmouth College	3.6						
Princeton University	1.9						
PRIVATE—Total	7.7						
University of Chicago	13.5						
Duke University	12.1						
Johns Hopkins University	9.2						
Wesleyan University	8.5						
Georgetown University	8.3						
MIT	5.4						
Northwestern University	5.1						
Stanford University	4.4						
Williams College	3.5						

*Base: Total Respondents
College and University Study
Target Management, Inc.*

*Direct = Personal involvement.

Students Who Feel Direct* Negative Effect of Campus Sexism/Sexual Harassment

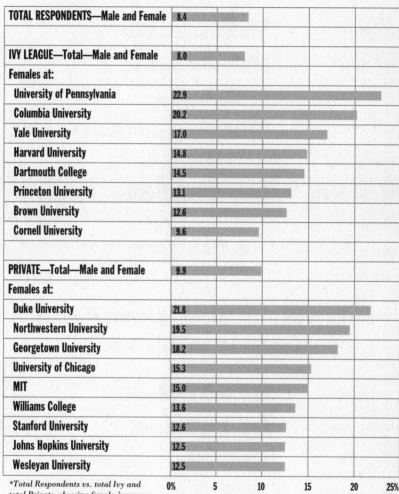

	0%	5	10	15	20	25%
TOTAL RESPONDENTS—Male and Female	8.4					
IVY LEAGUE—Total—Male and Female	8.0					
Females at:						
University of Pennsylvania	22.9					
Columbia University	20.2					
Yale University	17.0					
Harvard University	14.8					
Dartmouth College	14.5					
Princeton University	13.1					
Brown University	12.6					
Cornell University	9.6					
PRIVATE—Total—Male and Female	9.9					
Females at:						
Duke University	21.8					
Northwestern University	19.5					
Georgetown University	18.2					
University of Chicago	15.3					
MIT	15.0					
Williams College	13.6					
Stanford University	12.6					
Johns Hopkins University	12.5					
Wesleyan University	12.5					

*Total Respondents vs. total Ivy and total Private, showing females' response rate from each school.
College and University Study
Target Management, Inc.

Students Who Feel Direct* Negative Effect of Campus Sexism/Date Rape

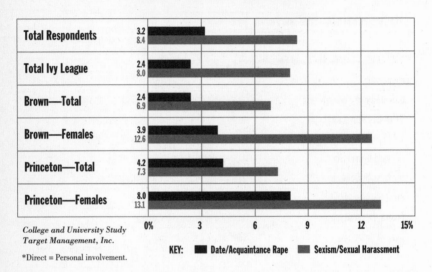

	Date/Acquaintance Rape	Sexism/Sexual Harassment
Total Respondents	3.2	8.4
Total Ivy League	2.4	8.0
Brown—Total	2.4	6.9
Brown—Females	3.9	12.6
Princeton—Total	4.2	7.3
Princeton—Females	8.0	13.1

College and University Study Target Management, Inc.

KEY: ■ Date/Acquaintance Rape   ■ Sexism/Sexual Harassment

*Direct = Personal involvement.

Students Who Feel Indirect* Negative Effect of Campus Sexism/Date Rape

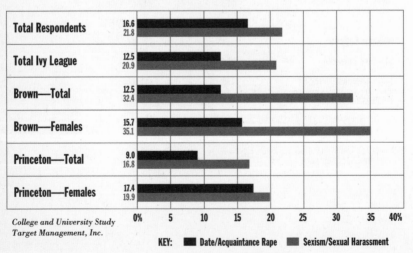

	Date/Acquaintance Rape	Sexism/Sexual Harassment
Total Respondents	16.6	21.8
Total Ivy League	12.5	20.9
Brown—Total	12.5	32.4
Brown—Females	15.7	35.1
Princeton—Total	9.0	16.8
Princeton—Females	17.4	19.9

College and University Study Target Management, Inc.

KEY: ■ Date/Acquaintance Rape   ■ Sexism/Sexual Harassment

*Indirect = Through a friend, roommate, or classmate; not direct personal involvement.

Students Who Feel Direct* Negative Effect of Campus Sexism/Date Rape

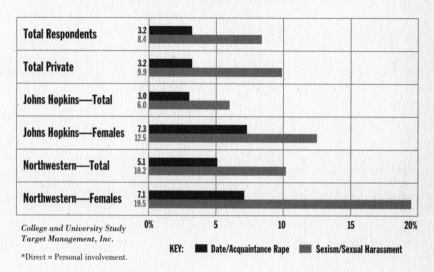

	Date/Acquaintance Rape	Sexism/Sexual Harassment
Total Respondents	3.2	8.4
Total Private	3.2	9.9
Johns Hopkins—Total	3.0	6.0
Johns Hopkins—Females	7.3	12.5
Northwestern—Total	5.1	10.2
Northwestern—Females	7.1	19.5

College and University Study Target Management, Inc.

KEY: ■ Date/Acquaintance Rape ■ Sexism/Sexual Harassment

*Direct = Personal involvement.

Students Who Feel Indirect* Negative Effect of Campus Sexism/Date Rape

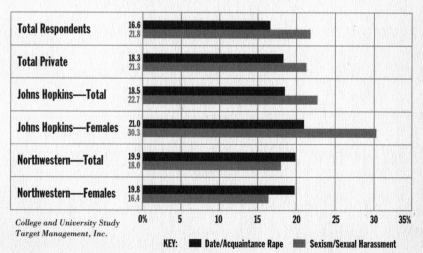

	Date/Acquaintance Rape	Sexism/Sexual Harassment
Total Respondents	16.6	21.8
Total Private	18.3	21.3
Johns Hopkins—Total	18.5	22.7
Johns Hopkins—Females	21.0	30.3
Northwestern—Total	19.9	18.0
Northwestern—Females	19.8	16.4

College and University Study Target Management, Inc.

KEY: ■ Date/Acquaintance Rape ■ Sexism/Sexual Harassment

*Indirect = Through a friend, roommate, or classmate; not direct personal involvement.

EIGHT
Political Activism on Campus

The Battle Around "Political Correctness"

The clash over America's higher education agenda has been growing more and more raucous for several years. The campaign against "political correctness"—a term once used ironically by liberal minds to describe their own attitudes toward sociopolitical diversity—has become the rallying cry for special-interest groups who are seeking to combat what they see as the liberal or leftist agenda that dominates virtually all campuses. The new curricula and standards of behavior being foisted on all members of the collegiate community have triggered a conservative national backlash.

On the academic front lines of the battle, one side contends that the supremacy of a white, male, Euro-centered curriculum—with its purportedly conventional and exclusionary points of view—must give way to greater breadth and multiculturalism, In a democratic system open to all individuals and points of view, they insist, new readings and new ethnic, cultural, and gender subject matter and disciplines must be available to students. The other side resists this movement with ever more heated defiance, believing that the potential demise of a common grounding in Western civilization, one that created the most successful democracy in history, is at stake.

Now that all the selective colleges and universities have acquired more diverse student bodies, the pressure for heightened awareness of new sensitivities, both within and outside the classroom, has become more intense. Such sociopolitical joustings have not been seen on campuses since the uproariousness of the 1960s, when the liberal philosophy presently under attack was first espoused by students who have become teachers and administrators in our leading universities.

There are many examples of the sociopolitical concerns now being played out on elite college campuses nationwide. What follows are but a few:

One of Yale's wealthiest alumni, Lee Bass, a millionaire oilman from Texas, rescinded his gift of $20 million for the development of an extensive course of study of Western civilization. He thought that Yale was dragging its feet, reacting to complaints that Yale already had plenty of Western civilization courses and that adding more would only further entrench Yale's conservative position on cultural diversity. For the same reason, many older alumni threatened to forego any future gift giving to the university. One generous donor asked why, if there were African American and women's studies programs in the curriculum, it was wrong to have a Western civilization department. Even more recently at Yale, the alumnus and gay activist Larry Kramer withdrew his offer of a large donation when the university refused to use the money to start a gay studies program; Kramer argued that since Yale already had a number of established special-interest studies programs, it should have a gay studies program, too.

In 1996, the National Association of Scholars, an independent group of university professors, issued a report assailing the top liberal arts colleges for "purging from the curriculum . . . many of the required basic survey courses that used to familiarize students with the historical, cultural, political and scientific foundations of their society." The report contended that the traditionally required survey courses in literature, foreign languages, history, literature, mathematics, and sciences have either disappeared or have been redesigned with watered-down or politically driven content. It also argued that faculty are interested solely in pursuing their own academic interests and refuse to direct students through the educational experience. Opponents of the study have written it off as the biased interpretation of a conservative cohort of academics who are hostile to special-interest studies and affirmative action in college admissions. The rationale for major changes in the standard curricula, these critics contend, is the explosion of knowledge in all fields.

Jeffrey Hart is a longtime professor of English at Dartmouth, an outspoken critic of multicultural programs, and a senior editor of the conservative magazine *National Review*. In his article "Back to School," in the September 1996 issue of the magazine, he maintained that today's Ivy League students are exposed to too many faddish courses. He urged a return to traditional subjects like American and European history, literature, classical philosophy, the Old and New Testaments, modern languages, Shakespeare, and art and music theory. According to Hart, who is known for his acerbic point of view, colleges should "avoid things like Nicaraguan Lesbian Poets." He further contended that any course that contains the word *studies* should be bypassed at all costs.

Hart would find many courses to bypass: Women's studies programs have been proliferating rapidly on campuses across the country. The debate rages between the more traditional faculty and feminist scholars over the purpose of these programs: Are they intellectually objective and academic in scope and nature, or are they concerned more with a political action agenda? The creation of multicultural and gender courses and the requirement that all students must be exposed to such ideas are two major examples of the topics heatedly debated at the elite colleges. Here are several recent Select course descriptions that rile traditionalists:

Cornell University—The Sociology of Reproduction: "Women's biological potential to bear children and their childbearing experiences are socially constructed and within this realm exists the potential to control women through the control of reproduction and childbirth."

Columbia University—The Invisible Woman in Literature: The Lesbian Literary Tradition.

Dartmouth College—Women and Religion: New Explorations: "Study will be given to the documentation of sexism and Euro-centrism in the canonical writings and institutional forms of Judaism and Christianity."

The National Alumni Forum was created in 1996 by alumni of elite colleges who were disturbed by the direction their alma maters had taken. They claim that campus speech codes and required cultural sensitivity courses, along with the power of the liberal voices on campus, have shut them out of any role in determining their colleges' position on issues. As chief executive of the forum, members chose the former chairperson of the National Endowment for the Humanities, Lynn Cheney. Cheney defends the teaching of Western literature, philosophy, and history and is a critic of many new special-interest studies and what she perceives as the left-wing agenda of many college faculty members.

The Intercollegiate Studies Institute—a growing organization that is comprised of a national network of conservative campus newspapers and student organizations—sponsors conservative speakers and forums and engages in political watchdog activities on campuses. It views its mission as ousting "the pervasive forces of multi-culturalism" from colleges. The institute has publicly targeted elite colleges like Princeton, Stanford, and Duke, which it believes have become victims of liberal excess. It publicized Lee Bass's $20 million gift to Yale by publishing articles on the failure of the university's administration to act on the gift. Mass mailings to alumni exhorting them to withhold donations from their alma mater had a huge impact at Yale and threaten to do so at other schools ISI has targeted. Several years ago, ISI's Stanford campus group led a successful lawsuit against the university's antihate speech code on the grounds that it violated the First Amendment. Certain Select students, like this sophomore male at Williams, definitely agree with their complaints:

> Some of the liberal groups on this campus make life uncomfortable for the majority of the campus. They are constantly pushing radical

causes which only serve to silence opposition by calling any opponents racist, sexist, discriminatory. They just frighten people into obedience because people are afraid to be labeled. 99

This young man, a senior at Brown, had even angrier feelings:

66 Too many damn liberals running around crying about ethnic studies. No one cares about fun or social life. Too many potheads smoking too much dope. Too damn politically correct. 99

Outside the classroom, activism occurs around everything from labor issues to sexism, sexual identity, and racism. At Columbia in 1996, 150 students occupied the main administration building to demand the creation of an ethnic studies department. New York City police arrested 22 of the students, which set off a campuswide demonstration in support of their cause.

Student demonstrations at Columbia and Yale took place during the 1996 academic year to support the demands of union workers on campus who were striking for higher pay and benefits. It's surprising that the undergraduates identified with the union workers, rather than with their college administrators—the people responsible for controlling wages and other operational costs, which, in turn, affect tuition increases. Remember the Yale students who spent the better part of a term finding ways to feed themselves and cleaning their dorms when the union closed down campus services? I spoke with a Yale junior who confessed that the strike was more than just a nuisance. He found that the absence of the best part of Yale, social interaction with his peers in the dining halls, resulted in a dismal term for him.

66 I have lost all respect for the university's administration due to their behavior in the contract negotiations with labor unions and graduate student teaching assistants, and I am losing respect for the student body's overwhelming ignorance of the issue. I worry that so many graduating seniors have gone into investment banking or consulting or to law school. 99

Another Yale junior male agreed with his classmate:

❝ Yale should be more involved in public debate about important issues and should encourage students to become involved as well. ❞

At the University of Pennsylvania, a group of students demonstrated outside the campus bookstore to protest the installation of a new cosmetics counter. The protesters argued that the display signaled women that they must appear attractive physically, and that this message is a form of male social control. They also objected to the size of the makeup department, which was much larger than the shelf space for the literature on women's studies—an indication of insensitivity to the real women's issues on campus.

The following are excerpts from a self-description of the Gay and Lesbian Caucus at Harvard as an example of the goals of one of the most active special-interest groups on the elite campuses:

Our Purposes and Major Initiatives

—Building a sense of community among Harvard and Radcliffe gays, lesbians, and bisexuals
—Maintaining and expanding a network of gay alumni/ae
—Pressing for a non-discriminatory, diverse academic, living and working environment at Harvard
—Urging the College to make gay, lesbian and bisexual Proctors and Tutors available in the freshman Yard and in each upper class House, with particular emphasis on same-sex couples
—Encouraging academic study at Harvard of gay, lesbian and bisexual life, including establishing a visiting professorship and/or gay studies program

The development of special theme houses for students of color and various other ethnic and racial groups is another major focus of debate. Some students, like this young woman, a junior at Brown, feel isolated among identity groups, even though they embrace what diversity represents:

❝I wish there was less drinking and more social and political activism on campus. I hang out with many social groups: the rich conservative white businessmen, the Asian pre-meds, and the high school drinkers on my dormitory floor. But I don't fit in anywhere and don't have a group of friends. The living unit counselors are filled with an artificial political correctness.❞

Rules of behavior that deal more assertively with sexual and racial discrimination and acceptable codes of behavior have proliferated significantly in America's colleges; all the elite colleges in my survey are experiencing the dynamics of these demands for change to a lesser or greater degree. While the *National Review* publishes an annual directory that identifies and extols the leading conservative colleges, a liberal, grassroots magazine, *Mother Jones,* ranks the twenty most politically active colleges. These two widely divergent organizations have recognized some of the same institutions, including these that were part of this study: Brown, Columbia, Stanford, Yale, the University of North Carolina, and the University of Wisconsin.

What has given rise to this war of words and emotions in the groves of academe? To a great extent, higher educational institutions have always mirrored the social, political, and demographic patterns of the society at large. In the past three decades, more people of increasingly diverse backgrounds want to participate as teachers, students, administrators, trustees, and legislators in setting the agenda for higher education. Colleges have found ways to insulate themselves somewhat from the political agenda of any particular period—the most specific example being the time-honored practice of tenure—but are now under scrutiny by the very people who provide financial and political support to state university systems and independent institutions.

The demographic alteration of both the faculty and the student body in higher education over the past several decades has been extraordinary. The U.S. Department of Education reported that 43% of the faculty hired in 1995 were white, male, and American by birth. By contrast, 59% of the older, tenured faculty reflect this traditional profile. Most colleges have worked with deliberation to increase

women and minorities on their faculties, as well as in their student
bodies. Even boards of trustees and state legislators are diverse
today and will become more so in the future. I'm reminded of an
African American student I encouraged to apply to Princeton when I
was an admissions officer there in the 1960s; he eventually became a
trustee of the university.

Quite naturally, as time goes by, there will be increasingly different points of view on what a college should teach and how it should
be run. In 1996 a conference of humanities and social science scholars met to debate the role and responsibility of teachers who advo-
cate their personal points of view in the classroom. A professor emeritus of cultural anthropology at Duke had this to say: "Why has
advocacy, the life-blood of the intellectual world, been labeled political and a threat? Because new voices have come into scholarship,
and some white men can no longer take for granted that what they
teach is standard." (No consensus was ultimately reached by the
group.) Like their teachers and alumni, students have joined the
debate on both sides of the issues, as this senior at Columbia noted:

> 66 Columbia's atmosphere matches its student diversity: There is a
> cause for every person. 99

The top-tier colleges have historically celebrated their communities' intellectual discourse and debate, in which a broad mix of dif-
fering persuasions and conflicting ideas meet to advance the cause of
a rational citizenry and democratic society. The elite colleges are
able, more than most institutions, to attract talented faculties and
diverse student bodies because of their resources and their fame.
This advantage guarantees a contentious atmosphere and contentious
changes in the intellectual and social tones of their schools.

Political Correctness, Activism, and Students' Reactions

The purpose of this study was never to come down on one side or the
other of this ongoing debate. Rather, I set out to determine the impact
of continuing sociopolitical controversy on Select students themselves. To what extent are the students personally affected by the

pressures for change and accommodation, and how do they feel about it? What are they learning and what opinions are they forming as they experience activism firsthand? What will its effect on them be when they assume their future roles as citizens and leaders?

Here are some findings regarding a series of questions I asked about the current political-cultural dynamics on campuses:

- When they were choosing their colleges, the political atmosphere and style of the colleges was extremely or very important to one-quarter of the students.
- Presented with the opportunity to indicate the two factors they like best about their colleges, less than a tenth selected the liberal atmosphere or political activity.
- Asked what two things they like least about their colleges, less than 4% cited the lack of political activity or awareness.
- Under 10% of the respondents indicated that they would describe their campuses to prospective students as political or apolitical.

The vast majority of high school students I speak with do not articulate a great interest in attending highly politicized colleges. The responses of the Select college students in the survey reveal that political activism is not a high priority for the greatest number of them, either in choosing their school or in becoming involved once they are on campus. From numerous discussions with students at the elite colleges, I was aware of a difference between an interest on their part and the impact of political activity or activism initiated by others.

I went on to ask the students to tell me particular forms of activism that had a significant or noticeable impact on the atmosphere of their colleges. The choices were ones I had developed as a result of earlier focus groups and interviews I had conducted with a large number of Select undergraduates. As it turned out, a great number of respondents indeed felt influenced by the political activity swirling around them. These are their answers regarding particular political factors that are dominant on campus:

liberal political attitudes	62%
conservative political attitudes	46%

ethnic or racially based attitudes	69%
gay/lesbian attitudes	64%
feminist attitudes	61%
environmental attitudes	60%
religious attitudes	46%
don't know/no answer	11%

Next, I asked the students to identify the issues that are of *primary or secondary concern* to them. As I discussed in an earlier chapter, academic workload, grades, and financial obligations far outweigh all other student concerns. Having identified a number of activist groups that affect campus life to a significant degree, undergraduates do not, at the same time, attach a significant level of personal concern to issues of political correctness. Only 7% of the total population cited them as being a primary concern. However, they are a secondary concern for 34% of the men and 45% of the women.

How do I interpret this set of responses? I suggest that a majority of students acknowledge the existence of a good deal of political activity on their campuses and choose to focus their energies on their own interests and needs. There is no gainsaying the existence of "in-your-face" activism—of all sorts—on these elite campuses, which requires each student to choose his or her own "brand" of response and action. And students' reactions are as varied as the students themselves. Some resent the contentiousness of activism, like this sophomore woman at Stanford:

> I love the weather, but the people are awful. So many students are immature and socially inept and cruel. Some people force their political opinions on you. It is such an "I have a cause" place. I think there needs to be more focus on studying and less on protest.

This junior at Stanford had a similar complaint, which did not keep him from valuing what the school had to offer students:

> Despite some of its flaws (political correctness/public issues awareness), I would never want to attend a different school. Both the quality of life and intellectual opportunities place it far ahead of Yale, Harvard, Columbia.

And this African American sophomore at Brown felt real anger about what he saw as continuing white male hegemony on campus:

> Student political organizations suck. It's a bunch of white men (or wannabes) electing themselves.

Other students, like this senior man, also at Brown, embrace the value of the causes themselves even though they challenge the tactics used by activists for social change:

> I would like to see activism more geared to finding solutions rather than just yelling, "Unfair!" The amount of activism here shows awareness and concern, but I think there is too much arguing of "causes and their negative effects" instead of focusing on "causes and possible solutions." I kind of wish these interest groups would get over their self-pity and work on self-betterment.

Social Action After College

When I asked the students to reflect on their lives after college by rating the importance of a roster of different goals and aspirations, they showed a high frequency of concern for their future communities—and told me of their plans to engage actively in social action. At the start of their college time, these students generally were not socially engaged. I take their evolution over four years as a strong statement of the values these future graduates have internalized.

Some distinct differences in this category did show up between men and women and between minorities and nonminorities, consistent with the differences revealed in many other issues and concerns throughout the study. The women and students of color expressed a greater stake in political action and concern for their communities while in college and afterward:

- Serving their immediate or larger communities was extremely or very important to 55% of the men and 66% of the women.

- Correcting social and economic inequalities was of great importance to 38% of the men and 47% of the women

Given students' preoccupation with academic success and personal contentment, it may seem surprising that they are affected by the very fact of living among controversy and being in such diverse environments—from classrooms to dining halls. For this first-year woman at Stanford, the political became personal at her own front door:

> College has been great because it has opened my eyes to a lot of different cultural and social issues. I feel I have probably gotten the most out of my interactions with other students, dormmates in particular.

Students in elite institutions today are aware of the interest graduate schools display in candidates' community service or action programs. With a combination of pragmatism and altruism, more undergraduates are participating in a multitude of volunteer programs on and off their campuses. It is not uncommon for prospective graduate students to ask me if particular service programs are viewed with special favor by business, law, medical, and other professional graduate schools. So the game of creating the best possible profile, begun in high school to reach the next rung on the ladder, continues unabated.

Conclusion

In the responses of these Select students, I find a distinction between "political correctness"—which the students perceive as an insistence on thinking and learning according to someone else's ideas and ideals—and engagement in political and social truths. A large percentage of Select students have been negatively affected by pressure to accept the socially approved attitudes they feel are handed to them, as this junior man at Cornell told me:

> There is too much close-minded liberalism here. Being a liberal means having an open mind to ALL opinions, not just the ones you like.

Many claim they're not interested in political issues, which they interpret as politics per se. Yet on the whole, they are open on their own terms to new social ideas. And they are inevitably affected by the debate on what should be taught, who will do the teaching, and which interest groups will most influence the social and political environment—both on campus and nationwide. That debate will continue at a brisk pace into the millennium.

Prospective Select students should make sure that they're aware of the general sociopolitical issues affecting the colleges to which they apply. Along these lines, there are several key factors for students to keep in mind when they are considering schools. First, few campuses among the elite are immune to the pressures for change made by increasingly sophisticated, concerned, and diverse streams of students. Traditional education today is vastly different from what a prospective college student's parents experienced a generation ago. Second, savvy student investigators of the college scene quickly ascertain which schools have more politically and socially activist environments. If such a milieu is important to them, they will enroll in an activist institution, thereby reinforcing the campus ethos. I refer to this phenomenon as the "self-selecting dynamic," which influences a college environment enormously. Once again, I encourage all prospective Select students to ward off the Halo Effect and view each school critically to ensure which schools genuinely feel right for them.

Forms of Activism Having Significant Impact on College Atmosphere

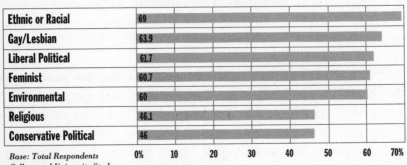

Ethnic or Racial	69
Gay/Lesbian	63.9
Liberal Political	61.7
Feminist	60.7
Environmental	60
Religious	46.1
Conservative Political	46

Base: Total Respondents
College and University Study
Target Management, Inc.

Forms of Activism Having Significant Impact on Campus Atmosphere

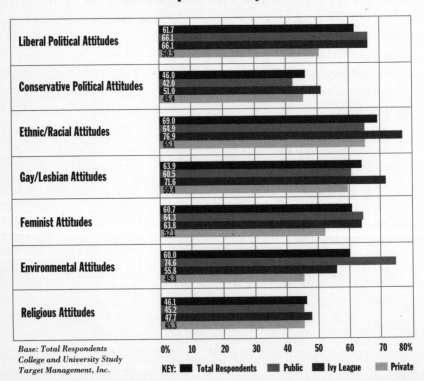

	Total Respondents	Public	Ivy League	Private
Liberal Political Attitudes	61.7	66.1	66.1	50.5
Conservative Political Attitudes	46.0	42.0	51.0	45.4
Ethnic/Racial Attitudes	69.0	64.9	76.9	65.1
Gay/Lesbian Attitudes	63.9	60.5	71.6	59.4
Feminist Attitudes	60.7	64.3	63.8	52.1
Environmental Attitudes	60.0	74.6	55.8	45.3
Religious Attitudes	46.1	45.2	47.7	45.3

Base: Total Respondents
College and University Study
Target Management, Inc.

KEY: ■ Total Respondents   ■ Public   ■ Ivy League   ■ Private

NINE
An Opportunity for Achievement: THE PUBLIC IVIES

Elite and Public

State universities of outstanding academic stature have been labeled the "public Ivies"—a compliment to their excellence and selectivity. There are large differences between the top public and elite private universities in such categories as the size of their undergraduate student bodies, the scope and often the fields of graduate research and faculties, the commitment to serving in-state residents first and foremost, the degree of competition for admission, and the tuition fees. The three state institutions in my survey, the University of California at Berkeley, the University of Wisconsin at Madison, and the University of North Carolina at Chapel Hill, are undisputedly ranked in the top tier of all universities in America.

More and more top high school candidates are heading to the public Ivies every year, which are gaining more and more of the reputation to compete for prospective Select students. I frequently encourage top-achieving high school students to consider the public Ivies as a complement to the elite private institutions they are considering. I suggest the public Ivies especially when a student is seriously concerned about the cost of his or her education; wants the experience of a large, diverse environment; or has special academic interests that the traditional private institutions cannot fulfill. Many aspiring young scholars have a strong enthusiasm for big-time sports and marching bands—so where better to enroll than a top state university? These universities can be great places of enrichment—especially for motivated students like this woman, a Berkeley sophomore:

> Berkeley is a great school; it is amazing in its academic excellence as well as social opportunities. Sometimes academic life can be demanding and stressful, but the challenge is exciting, and I like the intellectual level as well as the opportunities for self-expression. My fellow students have made my experience here great, and so has the faculty.

This Wisconsin junior, a woman, praised her school in similar language:

> Wisconsin is a great school. It is very competitive, so if you want a challenge—it's a great school. The social life is incredible! There are many types of people, and you can definitely make some of the best friends you will ever have.

As noted in Chapter 3, on financial issues, the difference in tuition between the public and private Ivies is large, indeed. A year's tuition for an in-state resident in the 1996–97 academic year was $4,354 at Berkeley, $3,040 at Wisconsin, and only $2,161 at North Carolina. By comparison, the average tuition for the private universities in the study was more than $20,000. Even with the additional tuition fees for nonstate residents, the public Ivies were relative bargains, averaging a $10,000 savings per academic year; thus they are a sensible alternative for students like this junior man at Wisconsin:

> ❝I might have chosen somewhere smaller, but only private schools are smaller and have as good an academic reputation as Wisconsin, and they cost too much. ❞

Presidents of Ivy League institutions have stated publicly that the greatest competition for the most outstanding students comes from the most prestigious state universities. They are right. As the costs of tuition and room and board continue their rise at a pace beyond cost-of-living indexes and real family income, the choice of public universities of stature becomes appealing to more families. Many ask me pointedly if it's worth spending $20,000 to $30,000 for a lackluster private institution when they can consider a more prestigious public university. I have no hesitation in recommending that they do just this because so many public university students can be as delighted with their education as this first-year woman at Wisconsin:

> ❝My experiences at Madison have been absolutely wonderful. I've met so many amazing people and made some great, close friendships. I have grown and changed in many ways by experiencing "college life." As for the academic side, I have learned to prioritize and schedule my time accordingly. I have learned good and bad study habits. Overall, my learning experience so far has been great! ❞

However, a serious cost concern looms on the horizon. From a historical perspective, state universities as a group raised their tuitions by 256% between 1980 and 1995, while the cost-of-living index rose only by 85% and average family income increased by 93% in the same period. This extraordinary rise has put a college education out of the reach of a great many families who have traditionally relied on state universities to educate their children. Public education may be a good value, but many people still cannot afford it.

The benefits of public Ivies for some superlative applicants can be even greater than just a good education and a good deal. Every year, more than 40% of the National Merit Scholars—those who are singled out as the strongest 7,000 academic high school students—matriculate at the top-tier state universities. Many of the state universities use their own funds to award generous scholarships to attract Merit Scholars away from the private Ivies—which years ago agreed among themselves to avoid the "free-agent" syndrome in admission by not granting merit awards. Only proved financial need will win highly talented individuals scholarships to Ivy schools. However, after Harvard, a state school—the University of Texas at Austin—has the nation's largest enrollment of National Merit Scholars and has offered scholarships to some 175 of those who matriculate. UCLA, the University of Minnesota, and Georgia Tech are also generous to these outstanding students. Some of the other state universities that enroll a large number of Merit Scholars include Berkeley, California at San Diego, Chapel Hill, Florida, Georgia, Illinois, Iowa State, Kentucky, Michigan, Michigan State, Missouri, Ohio State, Purdue, and Washington.

Public universities are big, and that can be intimidating to certain kinds of Select students, requiring them to take charge of their own education, as this junior man at North Carolina has realized:

> It's very hard to get things done at this university because of its size—it's simply too big—but persistence will pay off. No one will hold your hand here.

This four-year male student at Berkeley found his own niche, but he still was attracted by the idea of a smaller school:

> Being on Cal crew helps the adjustment both socially and academically, providing a healthy environment in both worlds. However, a smaller-sized campus would enhance the quality of teaching and socializing, making it a better place to be.

To counteract the effects of their bigness and to lure outstanding high school scholars, the state universities have developed the concept of the Honors College. Although they may vary in structure and curricula, Honors Colleges provide exceptional students with special courses, smaller classes, access to top faculty, and fewer basic course requirements. The most prestigious of these special programs is the Morehead Scholars Program at Chapel Hill. In many respects, it is similar to the Rhodes scholarship for graduate students at Oxford

University. The ideal candidate in both cases is a combination scholar, athlete, and student leader. It's difficult to argue against choosing one of the most beautiful college campuses in America, free tuition, and a guarantee of access to the top faculty and programs this richly resourced university offers. I have often encouraged a strongly motivated student to take advantage of such an opportunity. Why not receive a more personalized, high-quality education at a cheaper price with the great resources available in a large institution?

The Select Public Student Experience

I thought it was essential to my study to include several major public institutions because more and more Select students attend them. I wanted to explore the similarities and differences these students experience in their educational and social lives compared to their peers in the elite private colleges. Of the total population of 3,711 students in the study, there were 506 respondents from state universities, 262 men and 244 women.

The overall picture of the students at the Select public schools is remarkably similar to that of the students at the Select private schools. Both groups share virtually all the same goals, interests, and academic and social concerns. The differences are only a matter of degree in some categories, mostly regarding class size, the vastness of the physical university, the geographic spread of the student body, and the pressures for politicalization and social action.

Why did these Select students choose public universities? Like students at private elite colleges, they were initially motivated by the institutions' prestige and name recognition in the outside world. Receiving financial assistance or scholarships was a slightly greater consideration than for those in private colleges. Compared to the students in private colleges, the public college students assigned greater weight to:

- the costs of tuition and room and board
- social atmosphere
- geographic location
- political atmosphere

Students at public colleges have also found they like the climate or atmosphere and the social life more than their private college peers. This junior woman at Wisconsin spoke like an advertisement for the public university:

> This school offers an excellent environment for all aspects of the ideal experience. The workload is challenging, yet interesting and enriching. The social life is diverse, present, fun, and a break from academic pressures.

This Berkeley junior felt she had achieved as much beyond the classroom as within it:

> My greatest learning has come outside of books. I consider myself to have learned the most from the relationships I have formed here, the organizations I have been a part of, and the experience of handling everything from midterms to mending my socks by myself.

There were some differences in academic factors as well between the private and public Select. The public university students differed in that they:

- less frequently referred to the intellectual opportunities available to them
- more frequently cited class size as the least attractive feature of their education
- less frequently described their campus as rigorous
- were less aware of support services on campus except for programs for learning disabilities
- did not rate the majority of the available support services "excellent"—although half regarded the academic counseling and tutorial services as being good

Yet most were impressed with the academic seriousness and mix among their classmates, like this freshman at Berkeley:

> It's amazing how much people are willing to study. I am sure most students want to learn, but most importantly they want to graduate to go

onto another step. There is plenty to do here—too many options! I like the individuality. Each person has his own style and is really focused. 99

Many students thought that their campuses were profoundly competitive and even contentious, like this fourth-year man at Berkeley:

66 I would warn incoming students about the following: The college is very competitive. It seems that all we do is complain all day about everything—administrators, housing, competition, course space availability, etc. If you are not ready for that, then go to a junior college. 99

Even with the honors programs, class size is a major issue for many Select students at all three of the public universities in the survey. Even as she complained about dormitory costs, another first-year student at Berkeley saw problems in getting the introductory support she sought:

66 I think this school should do more to look at a person as an individual, rather than a number, especially when registering for classes or trying to meet on a personal level with a professor or administrative staff. Tuition costs are reasonable but rooming costs are too high. 99

Public students have a more favorable attitude toward all support services on campus than their private school counterparts. These include counseling on:

- depression
- career and job placement
- eating disorders
- religious concerns
- sexual abuse
- mental health
- campus mediation/conflict resolution
- medical problems

Like their private college contemporaries, public university students feel that their expectations of the faculty have basically been met in all categories except academic counseling. Over two-thirds to four-fifths looked favorably on their teachers for these reasons:

- expertise in their disciplines
- quality of teaching
- accessibility to students
- intellectual objectivity
- fairness
- relationships with students
- course offerings meet their expectations

The academic faculty was viewed as the greatest resource for academic assistance and advancement by over half the public and private college students. Teaching assistants were also rated of great value by over half the public college students and a slightly smaller proportion of the private college students. The larger size of the state institutions probably accounts for the differences assigned to the value of faculty vis-à-vis teaching assistants, who are, by necessity, a more substantial presence. Yet some of the public university students like this woman, a junior at Wisconsin, were concerned about the quality of teaching they provide:

> Things are competitive here. At least in my major, mechanical engineering, there is a lot of stress. The TAs I have are inadequate instructors. I end up having to teach myself the material.

This comment offers further testimony to the importance of the faculty and the role they play in determining both the strength of a college or university and the satisfaction of its students. A significant factor that draws top students to all the great universities is, in large measure, the academic resources available to them, which really means the outstanding teachers, who, in turn, are attracted by the quality of their students and the facilities available to them. But for many students, what they learned from professors was only a part of the overall education they were receiving on campus. They also learned a lot from each other, as this woman, a junior at Wisconsin, enthusiastically explained:

> Madison has given me a new outlook on education. I have learned that learning and fulfilling your potential is very important aca-

demically, but I have also learned that only a small portion of learning takes place in the actual classroom. I've learned so much from the political and social activism I've been a part of here on campus. It has changed my life and given me new goals and dreams. The learning that takes place outside of class is just as valuable as class lectures, and Madison offers so many opportunities that I would never change my decision to be here as an undergrad. 99

This senior at North Carolina had basically the same response to academic life on her campus—but with a familiar caveat:

66 The campus is diverse and open to all opinions and ways of life. If only the classes were more personal, the school would be excellent. 99

Her concerns about class size were echoed by students at the two other public universities in the study. This junior woman at Berkeley had a balanced critique of the values and limits of education on a campus of many thousands of students:

66 Berkeley is an amazing school, and I would certainly not want to be anywhere else. Its most positive aspects include its academic integrity, teacher caliber, diversity, and political activism. Negative aspects include a lack of professors who are really good teachers, rather than just reputable in their field. Further, the classes and programs are geared to mass production. I don't want to be a cog in the wheel but a functional unit in making the most of my experience. 99

Another Berkeley student, a freshman, agreed:

66 Life as an undergrad is fun and exciting, but also stressful and intense. The school should have smaller classes, to allow for more one-on-one dialogue and better understanding of the subject material. 99

A junior at Berkeley figured out that she needed to be assertive to make the most of a public-university education:

66 I have really had to work hard at getting the most out of things at Cal. No one really tells you or shows you the way. One must take a great deal of initiative to enjoy what you're doing and get the most out of it. 99

And a third-year male at Wisconsin spoke of the problem succinctly:

66 More of a classroom atmosphere would be nice, instead of 300- to 400-person lectures. 99

Some Select students felt even more frustrated about their attempts to get personal attention in their course work, like this male senior at Wisconsin:

66 Most of my classes were far too large; even though size restrictions were in place, professors still allowed additional students in, thus my upper-level classes always had at least 60 people. I am sorry, but as an out-of-state student I pay roughly $80 per 50 minutes of class time. It's a sham; my money for tuition in no way trickles down to me for my education. 99

In an increasingly polarized era, when critics claim that professors have a liberal agenda to propound, it is interesting to note that 81% of the public university students perceived the faculty to be intellectually objective. This finding could belie the view of faculty as the leading force for political debate and changes in the classroom and on the campus. Can it then be inferred that campus activism and the urge for "political correctness" are generated primarily by the students and administrators?

On the topic of activism and its significant impact on the atmosphere of their campuses, the public students were influenced more by concerns about ecology and the environment (75% versus 60%), but regarding other forms of activism, they varied little from their private college peers. More than half of the total population of students viewed all forms of student activism that are prevalent on campuses today as having an effect on their college environment, as shown in the comments of this woman, a junior at Wisconsin:

> Madison is an extremely open-minded place. You can do anything you want here; you can find any kind of friends you want. It is a place of endless opportunities, but you have to be driven to look for opportunities.

Her fellow Wisconsin student, a male sophomore, found the campus even more stimulating:

> I learn something new every day, just by walking to class. The sidewalks are always chalked with messages about abortion, religion, sexual preferences. I love the education I get from my peers, let alone the faculty.

But on these public campuses, as at the private elite schools, battles continue to rage about the means of achieving and meaning of social action and political activism. This senior at Wisconsin, a woman, saw segregation issues similarly to the students at Cornell and other private colleges:

> Students from different backgrounds (race, religion, and geography) live in different/separate housing from everyone else. This is an obstruction to having a diversified university.

A freshman at Berkeley had the same opinion on the role of minority groups on campus:

> Race is also a big deal here, and it seriously gets old, fast! Every minority seems so splintered into its own interest group. There doesn't have to be, for example, a gay/lesbian organization and then an Asian and Chicano gay/lesbian group. Everyone has to have a label. Why? Get over it, Cal. The '60s and '70s are long gone!

Another Berkeley freshman had come to an accommodation about the political climate that surrounds him:

> I really like the school and I am glad that I moved here from Los Angeles. Although some areas are polarized and sometimes too ethni-

cally/culturally sensitive to students' needs, once you become focused on your own life, most of this "pc" stuff no longer concerns you. Basically, get a life and you won't care about what anyone else is doing. 99

And this Wisconsin male senior saw student apathy in a place where others saw debate and discord:

66 I was looking for a socially aware and politically active campus. Much to my dismay, most of the students I know are overflowing with apathy. They have no greater regard for humanity as a whole than they do about what kind of cigarettes they smoke. The students are absorbed by a selfish need for immediate gratification. Instead of opening my eyes to other views, they reinforced my initial sentiments about their over-whelming ignorance. 99

The state university students have largely the same primary concerns as do private students, with only a slight degree of variation. While they worry slightly less about the academic workload, they are more concerned than private college students with the following:

- grade point average
- living arrangements
- academic workload
- physical and medical problems
- personal safety
- political correctness

Perceptions of the campus environment differ in small ways as well. A degree of difference between the two kinds of institutions showed up in the students' choice of adjectives to describe the campus atmosphere. The public students more frequently chose "full of choices," "diverse," and "exciting." Under the heading of the words that best describe the overall atmosphere, they more frequently cited "energetic" and "social," like this contented sophomore woman at Berkeley:

> 66 I love Cal! It was my first choice for college and I am very happy here. It is very big, and sometimes it is easy to get lost in the crowd, but I feel very sure of myself here. Student groups and clubs, sororities and fraternities, and religious groups are available to those who wish to belong to part of a smaller group. I'm glad I attend one of the top 25 universities in the nation. 99

Some students see the campus divided into identity groups to the detriment of immediate human connections, as this freshman at Berkeley discovered:

> 66 The people here are separated into distinctly different camps—racially, politically. There are also certain types—the idiotic idealistic neo-hippies, the socially awkward people-fearing engineers, the drunken frat boys. Lots of different types, but finding real people is hard. 99

In general, being at a big state school, with its varied student body, can be a social challenge for many students, like this Wisconsin freshman:

> 66 It took me nine months to get accustomed to the way the Midwest works socially. This school is not diverse enough, and there is a lack of intellectual curiosity. Being dumb is cool; it's like a big high school. But it is like a lot of colleges, not just Wisconsin. There are cool people here, but finding them is hard if you don't want to join a fraternity or a sorority. 99

With regard to the factors that have a direct negative effect on campus life, the state students felt the same as their private college counterparts about alcohol consumption, cohabitation of others in their rooms, dating, and sororities and fraternities. The indirect negative effect on their lives in some serious areas is more intense for the state students, who are concerned with the following:

- campus safety
- family expectations/pressures

- campus causes
- having to hold a paying job

Other areas in which the public college students expressed slightly more emphatic concern are:

- financial responsibilities
- drug usage
- local community safety

Substance abuse worried a number of students as well, like this young woman, a junior at Berkeley:

> I did not think so many students drank, smoked, did drugs so much. Even though there is a lot of diversity in the student body, it doesn't really matter since similar groups of people hang out with each other.

This freshman at North Carolina sounded almost plaintive about issues of drug abuse and residential living in general:

> I wish my dorm was less social, cliquish, and more diverse. I wish the drug use was less lethal and less rampant.

Asked what features of their university exceeded their expectations now that they were matriculated, a third of the public students cited friendliness, the only feature that differed from the total population of students whom I surveyed. As to those areas that failed to meet their expectations, the only variances were in school spirit and social composition of the student body. The public students were less disappointed than the private students by each.

Now we come to an important dynamic that reveals a marked difference between the public and private sectors. Only half the public students described the atmosphere of their campuses as intense, compared to more than two-thirds of the private students. Yet both groups seemed to agree on the level of social and academic stress they personally experience. The demand for academic performance certainly exists on public campuses; this freshman at North Carolina felt it:

> 66 The stress of getting good grades is really frightening, and it totally contradicts the notion that "grades are not everything." Grades feel like everything. 99

A senior woman at Berkeley knew the potential cost of ambition in the classroom:

> 66 We are too occupied with academic competition sometimes to bother to really bond with friends. 99

Given a large menu of campus organizations and activities to which all students could assign levels of importance, the public students differed to a significant degree only on one item; that is, 41% of them regarded the marching band as a very important campus activity. The tradition of big-time collegiate sports and opportunities to participate actively on a large campus explains why so many of the public university students were enthusiastic about marching bands.

The public and private students also largely agreed that their education has superb value for their futures. Only two factors show a small variance: More private students believed they will be aided in admission to graduate school, while more public students felt they have gained in personal or social confidence. The overall ratings are positive in all categories of value, meaning that the majority of the students who attend either state or private institutions are pleased with the perceived value of their education.

Even though there is a significant cost differential between the public and private institutions, both groups of students had the same opinion of the value of education for the money they and their parents spent on their institutions. In terms of the money spent on tuition, 69% of the public students and 61% of the private students thought they have received excellent to very good value. For the money spent on room and board, only 24% of the public and 26% of the private students thought they have received excellent to very good value. A third of all the students regarded the money spent on housing and food on campus less than satisfactory or a poor value. This discrepancy between students' views of the return on their money for academics and food and housing is a serious issue for many undergraduates—one that must be confronted by college administrators and trustees. The number of written descriptions of the students' unhappiness with the quality of living accommodations and/or food attests to how crucial this area is to a sense of personal well-being; it can be the one impediment to feeling comfortable at college. Listen to this young man, a Berkeley sophomore:

> I love this place. Classes are interesting and students are very smart. I even love the dorms. I have met many people because of this. Of course the food sucks, but there is really nothing else to complain about.

I found little difference between the public and private school students' goals for the future. All were concerned with:

- making a good deal of money
- being in a position of personal power
- marrying the right person
- having good friends
- using the educational advantages they received

Conclusion

If they had to do it over again, would they choose to attend their state institutions? An overwhelming 85% of the students in these three public universities said yes—exactly the same percentage as those in the private colleges. This is a resounding affirmation of their higher education experience. For the right students—those with a strong sense of themselves, who can find their way in a complex and sometimes impersonal environment, who can garner for themselves the attention they need, and who can choose among myriad social and academic options—the great public universities can definitely be the right places to get a great education.

Future Value of School's Education

(Summary of Top Two Ratings, "Extremely High"/"Very Good Value")

(Split by School Type)

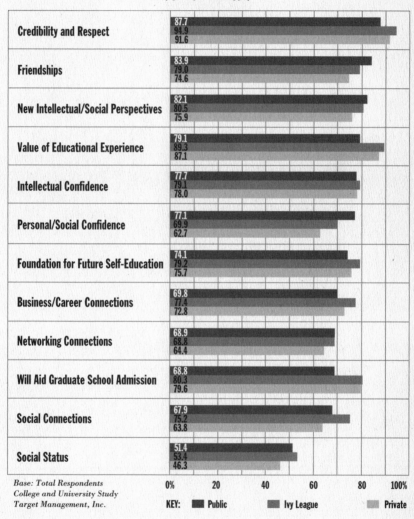

	Public	Ivy League	Private
Credibility and Respect	87.7	94.9	91.6
Friendships	83.9	79.0	74.6
New Intellectual/Social Perspectives	82.1	80.5	75.9
Value of Educational Experience	79.1	89.3	87.1
Intellectual Confidence	77.7	79.1	78.0
Personal/Social Confidence	77.1	69.9	62.7
Foundation for Future Self-Education	74.1	79.2	75.7
Business/Career Connections	69.8	77.4	72.8
Networking Connections	68.9	68.8	64.4
Will Aid Graduate School Admission	68.8	80.3	79.6
Social Connections	67.9	75.2	63.8
Social Status	51.4	53.4	46.3

Base: Total Respondents
College and University Study
Target Management, Inc.

KEY: ■ Public   ■ Ivy League   ■ Private

TEN
Coping with College

Students Under Stress

After the fierce competition for admission, assuming a heavy financial burden and often undergoing a painful emotional separation from their homes and communities, Select students venture into a world with the potential for severe emotional uproar. Though most Select students feel positive about their college experiences, even the most mature and well balanced among them face daunting challenges: the heavy academic workload, making friends, the choice of a major, sustaining an intimate relationship with another individual, general stress, financial anxiety, holding a job, living arrangements, cohabitation in dormitory rooms, negative peer pressures, admission to graduate school, the impact of alcohol and drugs, and hounding by various activist groups. Most students have told me that they can maintain the sense of balance needed to manage their lives. At the same time, they have much to say about what I refer to as "the dark side" of college life: the emotional stress and severe level of psychological problems many undergraduates undergo at elite institutions. This woman, a senior at Harvard, made it clear how alone in their struggle some students feel:

66 What any potential Harvard undergrad needs to understand is that Harvard prides itself on being Spartan. Students receive little attention and pity from the administration and professors. A lot is wrong with Harvard, and the administration prides itself on not changing. It is a sink-or-swim atmosphere. You must know exactly what you want to study and actively seek open-minded professors to help you. People are pretty stressed out here! 99

You'll recall that 90% of the respondents described their campus atmosphere as intense, competitive, or cutthroat. On a scale of one to ten, with one being the highest, the academic stress level had a mean stress factor of between three and four. The item of primary concern to students is their academic workload. This is a fact of life for 81% of the men and 87% of the women, holding consistent over the four undergraduate classes.

How do students typically respond to a severe level of stress, anger, or depression? By escaping into drugs, alcohol, promiscuous behavior, or crime.

I have seen time and again in my work with adolescents and young adults that many of them arrive at college with significant emotional problems. Typically, they harbor hope that their troubles will disappear by virtue of leaving the source of their difficulties. Many are honestly unaware that this is what they're doing. Others are cognizant of the dynamic; they see college as an escape from all they dislike or could not cope with at home. As primary examples, we know there is a high frequency of addiction to alcohol and drugs in the teenage population. It follows that the select colleges will have in each entering class a share of students who bring their addictive "habits" with them.

The responses to my survey revealed that the first-year students had the highest level of distress. This should come as no surprise, considering the extraordinary changes and challenges these highly successful, young people must confront. First-year students are generally prone to self-doubt, a highly critical appraisal of their intellectual ability, and concerns about their social status. Many question whether they're even worthy of attending such esteemed institutions. Was a mistake made in my case? What if I fail out? How can I return home when everyone expects me to excel? Was it worth the money it's costing my family to come here? What if I don't do well enough to get into grad school? These are the questions that many Select students frequently ask themselves. As this female sophomore at Princeton made clear, they need a fair amount of guidance if they are to put these doubts to rest:

> 66 I think that a better academic advising system would have helped me to have had a less difficult freshman year. I took some classes that were way too difficult for me, and my grades certainly show it. 99

Considering what it took to gain that precious place in the elite college—ahead of thousands of comparably competitive candidates—it should come as no surprise that most students will go all out to demonstrate their capabilities to themselves. Again and again, I encounter students who come to talk with me about being overworked, emotionally and physically exhausted, and fearful of crashing both in studies and grades. This angst is commonly abetted by first-year students' determination to demonstrate their abilities and intellectual drive by signing up for too many advanced-level courses. The great majority of Select freshmen enroll with a curricular background replete with three, four, or even five advanced placement courses. To earn advanced credits, they opt for an overly demanding combination of second- and third-year courses for which they are not necessarily prepared. The potential for disaster is all too obvious, yet most students will lay the blame on poor advice from deans and faculty members.

I witnessed this pattern firsthand as a faculty adviser to Princeton undergraduates, and I continue to counsel highly intelligent students who simply burn out or—when the anxiety and emotional turmoil become unbearable—panic and leave college. Far too often I've been in the situation of encouraging students not to drop out or attempt to transfer to other schools. They need to hear from an experienced, supportive adult that it is wiser and saner to drop one course from a hyperambitious schedule or move to lower levels in the same subject.

From the moment they enter college, many undergraduates demonstrate an immediate and intense concern for getting good grades as a gateway to graduate school. Add the first taste of failure, and you have students who are convinced they've ruined their chances of getting into any graduate school at all. It takes a good deal of counseling to convince these young men and women that they really will be all right in the long run if they don't get hysterical.

Two severe conditions that are frequently manifested among women on the elite campuses are anorexia nervosa and bulimia. These life-threatening diseases center on an obsession with food, which can be used as a form of control over oneself and one's environment. Starving or overeating are both ways of responding to extreme levels of stress, anger, depression, and low achievement and a desperate need to be attractive to one's peers. My survey showed that a large number of young women were worried about anorexia and bulimia, in either themselves or their friends. In fact, the personal characteristics of someone with an eating disorder can include a high level of achievement, which makes her a top candidate for a selective college.

Anorexia nervosa is a form of self-imposed starvation in which affected individuals are obsessed with becoming overweight. The syndrome usually begins in junior high school, when girls become highly conscious of the changes in their bodies and their physical image. An anorexic needs to control her environment and other people, to accomplish every task perfectly, to achieve high grades in school, and to please everyone. She is typically highly disciplined, intelligent, and manipulative—but also prone to low self-esteem, depression, fear of independence, and problems dealing with her emerging sexuality. For a person with anorexia, a stressful, competitive, free-form college environment can be lethal.

Bulimia is characterized by an intense fear of becoming fat, coupled with obsessive overeating or bingeing, which is followed by induced vomiting or the use of laxatives to eliminate food from the body. Bulimia tends to develop in older adolescents and is often referred to as "the college disease." People who suffer from bulimia are usually impulsive personalities who are prone to depression, low self-esteem, and the abuse of chemicals like alcohol and drugs. At the same time, they are often socially adept, leaders among their peers, and good students—which again can make them ideal candidates for admission to the elite colleges.

I have encountered a number of young women who suffer from eating disorders. They often come for counseling after their conditions have forced them to leave college. Anorexics are more easily identified because of their physical deterioration. It is often a roommate or close friend, fearing for the young woman's well-being, who reports the disorder to a counselor or the campus health center.

Bulimics describe themselves as surreptitious or sneaky in their behavioral patterns. Only when they find bingeing intolerable or physical illness debilitates them do they get the help they need. Their grades may not have suffered because they are "performers" in public and manage to keep doing what is required of them.

I recently counseled two young women who were formerly enrolled in two of the elite colleges included in this survey. Both had been required by their colleges to withdraw for medical reasons as their struggle with eating disorders escalated; yet both still exhibited an obsessive drive to remain in academia, rather than deal with their underlying problems. I had to urge them to avoid formal studies and enter therapeutic hospitals.

Excellent facilities are available that can help young adults with eating disorders focus on their needs and behavior, rather than their lifelong pursuit of academic success, personal popularity, or perfection in all activities they undertake. After a year of professional support—along with understanding from their families—these two young women were able, with my advisement, to choose new colleges where they would be challenged intellectually and feel greater rewards and achievement. Sad to say, too many Select students have problems like these that go untreated and can eventually cause irreparable physical and emotional damage.

Suicide, the ultimate human tragedy, is a fact of life on all the prestigious campuses. In 1996, the same year that an international student at Harvard College killed her roommate and then committed suicide, two other Harvard undergraduates also took their own lives. Two Dartmouth students did the same—one had just graduated with honors from the college and was a three-sport athlete who had attained all-Ivy and national recognition for her talent and the other was a Native American undergraduate on leave from the college.

The director of the University of Virginia's counseling center has stated that one or more suicides occur on campus each year. The Harvard case, which I mentioned earlier, received national attention because it involved both a murder and a suicide. A university psychiatrist acknowledged that the resources of the health center allowed only for short-term counseling and that the young woman who committed these horrendous acts needed much more intensive therapy. Each year as many as twenty-five undergraduates at the elite colleges are referred, some involuntarily, to psychiatric hospitals. Fewer than 2% of the respondents in my Select survey indicated that suicide is a primary concern in their college lives. However, 11% of both the men and the women viewed suicide as a secondary concern in their lives, which means that they have been affected by the fearsome depression and despair of other students around them; many also acknowledged recurring thoughts of suicide when they are extraordinarily stressed and exhausted.

No major college is immune to the tragedy of suicide. While the national suicide rate for people aged 15 to 24 is 13 in every 100,000 individuals, the estimate for college students is half this rate. This statistical difference shouldn't diminish the concern administrators must have for the many students who come to college with a history of personal and/or family problems, expectations of academic success that exacerbate students' normal levels of stress, or the inability to function in the demanding social hothouse of the college campus. For some minority students, a feeling of alienation and emotional depression because of their different ethnic, racial, or economic backgrounds presents the potential for serious repercussions. I have found that many troubled minority students will not seek help from professionals on campus out of a sense of shame, failure, or a culturally bound prejudice against psychological help. Appropriate role models are crucial to encourage these students to seek personal support.

Still, for all the possible psychic costs of attending elite colleges, most students do make the emotional adjustments and become happy, successful students and adults. Most manage to arrive at a balanced view of the college experience, like this sophomore woman at Cornell:

" I love Cornell. I love the campus. I have met great people, the best friends of my life. The academics are incredibly challenging, but I am constantly amazed at how much I've learned here. There are great athletic teams to watch and lots of school spirit, with great intramural programs to participate in. Student groups exist for any interest you might have, and there are lots of performing groups to watch. I know I've got the opportunity to do anything I want to do, to make college a wonderful experience. "

Confidence, Esteem, Failure, and Survival

As I reported earlier in *The Select*, I found several marked patterns in the way the students compared themselves to their classmates. Both the men and the women gained a better sense of themselves as they progressed through their undergraduate years. The women, however, tended to think less of themselves than did the men. The following statistics are helpful in exploring either the confidence or uncertainty that students feel about their place on campus:

- 33% of the men and 17% of the women rated themselves smarter than their classmates.
- 28% of the first-year men, compared to 40% of the senior men, rated themselves smarter than their classmates.
- 13% of the first-year women versus 25% of the senior women rated themselves smarter than their classmates.
- 51% of the men and 63% of the women perceived themselves to be as smart as their classmates.
- Women in all four classes responded at the same rate in the previous category, whereas the proportion of men who considered themselves as smart dropped to 44% by the senior year.
- 11% of the men and 17% of the women rated themselves not as smart as their classmates

Although only a tenth to a sixth of the Select students regarded themselves as less smart than the norm, it's important to acknowledge that some undergraduates feel bad about themselves, as this Princeton freshman learned firsthand:

> ❝I am surprised at individuals' insecurities, sometimes their inwardness. Perhaps this is attributable to the American culture. I am a Latin American. I feel more expressive and friendly than many students. Perhaps this is just my personal effort, and not one that is representative of the student body overall.❞

The good news from my survey is that women gain strongly in confidence over their four years; only a tiny fraction of the senior women harbored feelings of inadequacy. This is a positive signal that women do adapt to their environments over time. Nevertheless, there is a red flag here: Almost a quarter of the freshwomen felt inadequate. Colleges should pay particular attention to this dynamic. We can admire or feel bemused by the hubris of this graduating senior woman at MIT:

> ❝I firmly believe MIT students are the smartest graduates with the highest learning potential. We shall make dramatic improvements in the world socially and intellectually.❞

Again, no matter how confident or unsure they feel about their own intelligence, the great majority of students not only survive the bumpy transition to college but ultimately thrive. The most selective and demanding of all American undergraduate institutions graduate between 90% and 97% of each entering class. This success rate compares to a national graduation average of less than 50%. Are there particular personality traits, skills, and adaptive techniques that make the majority flourish while a minority fails? My professional interaction with thousands of college-bound and present undergraduates over many years, as well as a review of some of the research literature on the undergraduate experience, has led me to synthesize the major elements I believe play a role in determining which students are likely to prosper, undergo a traumatic experience, fail out, or transfer.

Chief among the characteristics of those who have an emotionally painful time in college are these:

- developmental immaturity
- social ineptitude
- deep feelings of insecurity
- inability to adapt to new situations
- lack of independence
- a rebellious or nonconforming personality
- inexperience beyond one's immediate family
- significant financial worries
- a history of physical or sexual abuse
- alcohol or drug dependence
- a dysfunctional family history
- severe emotional problems, such as a psychosis, character disorder, or chronic depression

Many young men and women who meet one or more of these "criteria" arrive at the elite colleges each year. Although their academic and personal attainments were outstanding enough to gain them admission, they carry with them disabling personal problems that can explode—although their levels of academic preparation and motivation are customarily not a causal factor for failure or emotional crash.

What features characterize the Select individual who navigates the college experience successfully? How is it that so many students overcome their negative histories to carve out productive college careers? The following are several features that I see time and again in these individuals:

- an internalized motivation to attend a Select institution for its intellectual and social resources, rather than for externally imposed motives or pressures—especially from parents
- the ability to adapt to new ideas, environments, and people that goes beyond the norm for their age group
- a high level of comfort with their personalities and abilities, enabling them not to measure themselves solely by grades and relative achievement levels
- an imaginative and creative spirit that brings excitement to their exposure to new intellectual and social experiences

- a tolerance for ambiguity in the intellectual sphere, that is, the capability to appreciate that conflicting ideas are of equal merit
- an interest or fascination with a discipline that extends beyond the basic requirements of mastery
- a spirit of adventure, the capacity to relate to other people, and the ability to appreciate differences
- a sense of humor, allowing them to laugh in the face of predicaments that could seem overwhelming if they took themselves too seriously

Thousands of elite students would agree with this insight from a Georgetown male sophomore, describing how he found the right formula for a positive life at college:

" I came here with no concern for social activities and no expectations for them. When I got here, I realized their importance and found it easy to engage in social activities or clubs. Through these clubs, I have enjoyed life at Georgetown much more. I've felt happy, thanks to my friends and the things I do. I also love my teachers, and they have had a fantastic effect on me. Now that I look back on it, even though I focused on academics at first, the need to have fun still came out. I came to Georgetown to learn and grow. G.U. is fulfilling that need. But it is the friends that make it possible for me to want to stay here and continue on my path. "

Finally, most students will admit that a little good luck has made a difference in the quality of their collegiate experience:

- being assigned to a pleasant room and dorm
- rooming with a compatible, understanding individual
- encountering a teacher who becomes a personal mentor
- making an athletic team or gaining a leadership position in an organization
- meeting a special individual and establishing a healthy emotional relationship; falling in love

A testament to the rewards produced by the challenges of college life was offered by this senior woman at Cornell:

66Cornell is an institution that is not for everyone. Only the strong or extremely crafty survive here. Major experiences in my life happened here to broaden my horizons and shape who I am and what I am to become. I have made lasting friends and become more a part of the world around me. 99

Responding to Students' Stress

As the prestigious colleges successfully open their doors to a broader ethnographic and socioeconomic population of students, the demand for more counseling and other supportive services grows. Major colleges have, in recent years, increased these services to respond more energetically to students' academic and personal needs—and virtually all colleges in my study have reported that a greater number of students are taking advantage of them.

Students have many and varied needs. They may require counseling on financial aid and career choices. They may need help in managing a learning disability or developing study skills. They may have a medical problem or a sexually transmitted disease. They may need therapy to resolve their sexual uncertainty or deal with an eating disorder. They may have issues around race or religion—their own or other people's. All these dilemmas demand the attention of appropriate administrators and specialized professional staff.

The challenge is even greater in treating undergraduates who need a deeper level of psychological help. Most campus counseling centers operate, out of necessity, on what is known as the "student developmental model," rather than a clinical or therapeutic model. Psychotherapy requires a commitment of hours by trained professionals over an extensive period to help students analyze their deep-rooted problems and achieve a level of self-awareness. Unfortunately, few institutions can afford to operate in this manner. The student developmental model, in contrast, focuses on students' wellness, crisis management, study skills, psychoeducational balance, and social-interactive faculties. A majority of undergraduates who seek help do, in fact, profit from the developmental model and can eventually gain control of their lives, as this woman, a Princeton senior, attested to:

> ❝❝ I have always felt extremely safe here, and I know that if I ever need support—medical or psychological—it is here. My roommate took advantage of the counseling services when she recognized the beginnings of an eating disorder. ❞❞

The difficulty in counseling college students—who have so much to cope with and so little time to devote to "extra issues"—is ascertaining which problems will be resolved through general counseling and limited support and which can lead to disaster.

There is, of course, a catch in this situation: The competition in each institution, whatever its relative wealth, for a share of limited financial resources makes it difficult to provide the necessary professional resources. The faculty, meanwhile, are quick to express their dismay at the fact that more administrators than teachers have been hired in recent years. The tug and pull within the ivy walls for money and resources is a perennial issue, one that seems to be escalating as more and more demands are put upon academic institutions.

On most of the Select campuses, students have organized peer counseling and support programs in response to the needs of their fellow students. At Harvard College, for example, a program called "Room Thirteen," a confidential peer counseling center, deals as a kind of clearinghouse for students with the problems Select undergraduates must deal with. The program's brochure (opposite) is widely distributed among Harvard students.

Students do feel grateful for the help a university provides. Support can make a pivotal difference, as it did for this senior man at Brown:

> ❝❝ I would not have become as confident in my decisions about my academics, my social life, and my future plans if it hadn't been for the safe spaces Brown creates to keep you centered and get you the advice you need. ❞❞

While traversing the often rocky path of the college experience, Select students develop strong feelings about the one group who most influences their well-being—the college administrators. I've men-

Why Call Room 13?

It's easy to get the impression that Harvard expects us always to be on top of things—independent and self-sufficient. At Room 13, we believe that it's important to seek a little support in dealing with concerns and questions. It's not a sign of weakness to look for help. Sometimes it can be embarrassing or intimidating to call the University Health Service (UHS) or to talk to your roommates. (Maybe your roommates are the problem!) Perhaps you think your question is too trivial and don't want to bother anyone or risk looking foolish.

On any given night we might hear:

I'm a senior and I don't know what I'm doing next year . . .
I can't seem to get down to work . . .
My roommate is driving me crazy . . .
It's cold out. Can I come in and warm up? . . .
I'm worried about AIDS . . .
I have an exam tomorrow and I'm afraid that I'm going to fail . . .
I'm not ready for intimacy, but I keep feeling pressure . . .
I can't sleep. Can we talk? . . .
I feel so depressed . . .
My tutor made a crude pass at me today . . .
A friend of mine just died . . .
Everybody else always has so much fun at parties. I just feel left out . . .
I don't want to go home for break. I feel like a stranger there now . . .
Harvard just sucks . . .

We offer information about many issues, including (but not limited to) drug or alcohol use or abuse, sexual orientation, sexual abuse or assault, suicide, race relations, eating concerns, harassment and depression. If we can't answer your questions, we'll refer you to someone who can. We know professionals at UHS and the Bureau of Study Counsel, so we can refer you to specific people, not just offices. We can also help with questions about life at Harvard and the university's bureaucratic procedures.

tioned that one-fourth of the Select students stated that the thing they like least about their college is the bureaucracy of the administration. All four classes, men and women of all backgrounds, responded in a similar fashion, and the degree of dissatisfaction did not dissipate over the course of a four-year education. Nowhere in the survey did I ask the students to rate their college administration specifically. However, when I gave them the opportunity to write their thoughts on any feature of academic or social life on their campus, positive or negative, many students chose to comment on this subject. For some, like this young man, a Northwestern sophomore, the complaints were global:

> I am extremely disappointed with my undergraduate experience. Over the past three years, I have witnessed time after time in which the ultra-conservative administration failed to take the initiative to meet student needs. The administration refuses to utilize our tuition money for our benefit.

A more representative sampling came from students who appealed for more timely and sensitive assistance from the various administrative agents, as this female Columbia senior urged:

> The administration is rude and completely useless. The employees in financial services and aid don't have the authority to really help the students who need the most help. They are mean in their treatment of students.

Another Columbia senior, a man, saw the issue as going beyond financial aid:

> The administrative personnel has little regard for students and is very disorganized. There is no substantial career counseling to guide students in fields other than business and pre-med.

Whatever a particular student's views or needs may be, the administrators are perceived as the adults in the community—the ones who are supposed to do something about things. Of course, there is a contradiction in all this. Don't students resent interference in their affairs from adults, wanting to be free to be adults themselves? That's what this fourth-year man at Williams seemed to argue:

> 66 Sometimes I feel that the administration just does not care about the students who go here. Life would be better if they would trust us and treat us like adults. 99

Students seem to want to be left alone until they have a problem that requires help from established adults on campus. Undergraduates aim to experiment in all manner of ways—but with the expectation that they will be bailed out and supported when they yell for help.

Conclusion

In her marvelous novel *Picturing Will*, Ann Beattie touches on the emotional impulse of all parents to protect their children from the harmful conditions in this world. She then describes the variables over which we have no control. The college experience is a microcosm of that larger world of people and events, in which each student will play out his or her own drama—without our being able to write the script:

> Do everything right, all the time, and the child will prosper. It's as simple as that, except for fate, luck, heredity, chance, the astrological sign under which the child was born, his order of birth, his first encounter with evil, the girl who jilts him in spite of his excellent qualities, the war that is being fought when he is a young man, the drugs he may try once or too many times, the friends he makes, how he scores on tests, how well he endures kidding about his shortcomings, how ambitious he becomes, how far he falls behind, circumstantial evidence, ironic perspective, danger when it is least expected, difficulty in triumphing over circumstance, people with hidden agendas, and animals with rabies.*

Parents must keep watch for symptoms of undue stress and unacknowledged emotional problems and be aware of how they can steer

*Random House, Vintage Books (New York: 1991).

their children toward professional support. Yet as they send their sons and daughters off into the fearsome world of higher education, they must come to realize that they can control their children's fates only so much.

In romantic literature, the ivory tower symbolizes safety and isolation from worldly pursuits, conflicts, and travails. The modern university is in no way an ivory tower. I doubt that it ever was. It's more like a cauldron aboil with the fractious interest groups and conflicting ideas we have created.

My hope for every individual I counsel and all other students who enter the contemporary ivory tower is that they attain emotional subtlety and toughness—requisites for a successful and enduring educational experience—and that, however challenging the experience, they will feel a version of what this Yale senior discovered for himself:

> 66 Everyone here has a passion about something. People care about the school, learning, the world. Intellectually this place is fascinating, moral, and driven by a sense of searching. 99

In his brilliant study of human evolution, *The Ascent of Man*, Jacob Bronowski comments on man's unique ability to shape his environment: "His imagination, his reason, his emotional subtlety and toughness, make it possible for him not to accept the environment but to change it." Select students generally have the strength of character to respond to their surroundings and adapt to them, all the while growing more mature, masterly, and wise.

ELEVEN
Students Weigh the College Experience and the Future

Would You Do It All Over Again?

Prospective Select students can feel dazzled by the idea of getting that prestigious elite degree—and then daunted by the trials it takes actually to achieve it. Still, no matter what institution they attend, all American college students bear greater burdens and anxieties than ever before. The major points of stress described in this study are not the sole province of students at the highly selective colleges and universities. UCLA's Higher Education Research Institute—which annually takes the emotional pulse of American freshmen at all types of four-year colleges and universities—found the highest degree yet of financial and personal stress in 1997. These first-year students reported increased worries over mounting debts and loans, not enough time to get their work done, and tension about admission to graduate school. The number of frequently depressed freshmen rose for the fourth year in a row.

If the college experience is so rigorous, would Select students undergo it all over again at the same school? Across the twenty institutions in the study, the answer is overwhelmingly yes.

Of the 3,711 students in the study, 83% said, yes, they would make the same choice all over again. The Select undergraduates were positive about their school experience, no matter what their sex, financial obligations, or racial and ethnic backgrounds. The survey does show that some students grew slightly more dissatisfied by the end of their senior year, but this finding comes as no surprise, since they may simply be eager to move on to the next stage of their lives. Others realize there is much more they could learn from their unique environments. A Princeton junior woman said what many other Select students feel about their colleges:

> Princeton is one of the most valuable experiences I will ever have. While it can always be improved, it is an effective, engaging, stimulating, enjoyable, exhilarating experience. I wish I could stay longer than four years.

This Wesleyan sophomore had a similar response to her university:

> This place has inspired me to want to learn about things I had never thought would interest me. The professors' interest and excitement about their subjects has made me realize how much there is to be learned and excited about.

And a Wisconsin junior gave ample evidence of the wisdom to be gained from active engagement in the community:

> Madison has given me a new outlook on education. I have learned that learning and fulfilling your potential is very important academically, but I have also learned that only a small portion of learning takes place in the actual classroom. I've learned so much from the political and social activism I've been a part of here on campus. It has changed my life and given me new goals and dreams. The learning that

takes place outside of class is just as valuable as class lectures, and Madison offers so many opportunities that I would never change my decision to be here as an undergrad. 99

This Cornell sophomore felt real engagement and affection for his school:

66 I love Cornell. The caliber of education here is first-rate. I have learned more about myself and others than I ever imagined. I have grown spiritually; my mind is more open, and I feel I know more about the world. Yes, it is competitive; yes, it is a challenge. But it is a solid preparation for the real world. 99

This Berkeley sophomore discovered that she is taking the values of her school personally:

66 I have, surprising to myself, a self-motivated drive to do my best in school. I feel no real competitiveness except that I have to do fairly well so as not to fall behind. College life at Berkeley has taught me to become a better individual, both due to my personal experiences and to campus influence. I would not have it any other way. 99

There seems to be a particular moment, though, when many Select students have doubts about the wisdom of having chosen an intensive, competitive college. Many seniors who seek my counsel regarding admission to graduate school are concerned that all their hard work is not reflected in their grade point averages; they lose their confidence and feel they would have been better off attending a less competitive college and achieving top grades; and their vulnerability in the face of fierce competition for a place in a law, business, or medical school or other graduate school programs skyrockets.

A Dartmouth senior I was advising on applying to medical school reflected the attitude of the great majority of Select students. As a computer science major and a biochemistry minor, he had a 3.4 grade point average—which he was convinced would keep him from being considered for admission to any medical school:

> ❝I feel I tried incredibly hard at Dartmouth to do the kind of work the faculty demands. My GPA is likely to keep me out of med school, which has been my dream forever and is the reason I went to this college. I should have gone to the state university, which gave me a scholarship; there I would have saved tons of money and gotten A grades and been in a position to pick a good med school.❞

Like most of his peers in the selective colleges, this young man did get accepted to three excellent medical schools. He is thriving in the one he picked—a state university whose tuition is less than half the tuition of the others he applied to—in part because of his excellent training in an elite college.

What Do Select Students Want to Change?

In what would turn out to be one of the most interesting and revealing topics in the entire study, I invited the students to respond to this question:

> ❝Looking ahead, can you name two major aspects you would want your college to change, add, or remove? Your responses can deal with social or academic issues. Please be specific.❞

The suggestions I got from Select students reveal vividly significant differences among the colleges. In outlining their responses below, I have listed the five subjects most frequently referred to by the students in each college. These insider responses penetrate the elite college halo to give a clear picture of how students perceive their elite colleges. Keep in mind that the great majority of Select students indicated their favorable attitudes toward the student body and their resentment of administrators. The focus here is on the elements of campus life that bother them the most. (The number of responses to this question from students at the University of North Carolina was too small to provide a true sampling.)

Brown University
- improve housing
- end campus divisiveness, political correctness; build more cohesion

- improve the quality of the faculty and their interaction with students
- improve the social life, sponsor more social activities
- improve academic and career counseling

Columbia University
- reduce administrative bureaucracy
- improve academic advising
- review and change the core curriculum
- improve the quality of food
- create more school spirit and a sense of community

Cornell University
- reduce the academic stress and pressure
- lessen racial and ethnic segregation
- eliminate or lessen the influence of fraternities and sororities
- reduce the size of classes
- create a better advising system

Dartmouth College
- de-emphasize fraternities
- create more social options
- provide more dormitory options
- offer certain cross-disciplinary majors
- reduce the bureaucracy

Duke University
- improve housing, create more living options
- de-emphasize the Greek system
- provide more social activities
- improve the food
- review the campus alcohol policy

Georgetown University
- diversify the student body and faculty
- provide more money for the arts
- create more school spirit

- provide more financial aid
- recognize the needs students have of the administration, treat students with more respect

Harvard University

- change or remove core curriculum requirements
- provide more and better academic and social counseling
- improve the accessibility and quality of teaching of the professors and teaching assistants
- reduce the bureaucracy, improve administrative responses to students' needs
- offer more social activities

Johns Hopkins University

- provide more social activities
- review the grading system, eliminate the curving of grades
- improve the athletic facilities
- reduce the cutthroat competition
- improve the faculty; make the faculty more diverse and accessible

Massachusetts Institute of Technology

- improve the quality of food
- reduce the pressure and create more free time
- improve the school spirit
- improve the faculty and their accessibility
- eliminate campus segregation and cliques

Northwestern University

- offer more social events
- improve student-administration relations
- eliminate campus polarization
- provide a better meal plan
- provide more and better teachers

Princeton University

- provide better academic counseling and peer advisers
- offer more social options and activities

- improve the quality of food
- provide more funding for club sports, varsity teams, and facilities
- offer specific specialized majors

Stanford University
- improve the quality and reduce the cost of food
- improve the quality and accessibility of the faculty, increase teaching time over research commitments
- provide more and better counseling programs
- reduce the size of classes
- provide more social activities

University of California—Berkeley
- reduce the size of classes
- improve the quality, teaching skills, and accessibility of the faculty
- provide better food services
- provide more and better academic, career, and personal counseling
- reduce campus racism, cliques, segregation

University of Chicago
- review or remove the core curriculum
- improve the social life
- reduce the stress and pressure of the workload
- reduce the size of classes
- improve the quality of food

University of Pennsylvania
- reduce the segregation and cliques, improve the sense of community
- improve the accessibility and teaching skills of the faculty
- lower the tuition
- improve the social life
- improve the food services; make food plans more flexible

University of Wisconsin—Madison
- increase the racial, ethnic, geographic diversity of the student body and faculty
- improve the quality, teaching and communication skills, and accessibility of the faculty and teaching assistants
- provide better academic advising and career counseling
- reduce the size of classes
- review and change course requirements

Wesleyan University
- improve the quality of the food and meal plan
- improve the housing and the lottery system
- do something about racial and ethnic segregation
- do something about the administrative bureaucracy
- offer more specific departmental majors; improve the course-registration process

Williams College
- improve the advising and counseling services
- offer more social activities and fewer alcohol-related events
- increase the diversity of the student body
- improve relations between students and the administration, reduce the bureaucracy
- lessen the emphasis on athletics and the influence of athletes

Yale University
- improve the quality of the food and the meal plan
- renovate the deteriorating housing and change on-campus living requirements
- create a student center
- deal with the union and workers more effectively
- provide better career advising

The Educational Legacy for Select Students

What do these Select young men and women consider important as they weigh their futures? Do their goals fulfill the ideals of the institutions that gave them the opportunity to live and learn within their communities? Do they agree with James Conant, the longtime president of Harvard, that a person "who enters a university walks on hallowed ground"?

When I queried students about their goals and values, I asked them to assign a value rating to a number of qualities that I had identified originally in interviews and focus groups with students at the elite colleges. The ratings show the extent to which the Select students feel that certain expectations have been met regarding the value of education for their future.

What follows are the top ten advantages that undergraduates believe they have gained as a result of their elite education.

1. credibility and respect	91%
2. value of my educational experience	85%
3. friendships	80%
4. new intellectual/social perspectives	80%
5. intellectual confidence	78%
6. foundation for future self-education	76%
7. aid in graduate school admission	76%
8. business/career connections	73%
9. personal/social confidence	71%
10. social connections	69%

The value of social status did not make the top-ten list of advantages of any of the Select students I polled. I shouldn't be surprised anymore, but I confess that I am, when a student or parent who is contemplating a top-tier college, especially an Ivy League institution, asks me about the degree of social snobbery and elitism that prevails on campus. After all, these schools are the ones with the golden halos—and so many of their graduates become well-known leaders. I appreciate the extraordinary change in the social composition of student bodies over the past twenty-five to thirty years, but most families still carry an image of students at elite private colleges as wealthy kids from socially established families.

Students of all backgrounds enthusiastically believe that many advantages accrue from attending elite colleges. However, the data in this study show a four-year developmental growth in particular values to which students assign importance. First- and second-year students assign a higher rating to more pragmatic values. Juniors and seniors give greater weight to educationally related ones. What does this difference suggest? That over four years, students grow from pragmatists to enlightened humanists.

These three factors are of greater importance to first- and second-year students:

- social connections
- business-career connections
- networking

These values decline in significance for third- and fourth-year students, and the following take on greater importance:

- intellectual confidence
- foundation for future self-education
- new intellectual-social perspectives

A Columbia sophomore reflected on her personal development in a positive way:

> ❝I feel that I have experienced much personal growth here. Through the friends I have met and my independence from my parents, I have learned about who I am. This is what I most value from my experience so far. I have been able to become more focused on my future goals and to discern what qualities and lifestyles I deem important. This is because of friends, talks with professors, and conversations with students further along in their education than I am.❞

This Stanford junior developed a similarly broad perspective as her intellectual curiosity expanded.

> ❝Stanford, like any other institution, has its good things and bad things, and the university can always be improved. However, I really am enjoying my college experience thus far. I feel I have grown socially, aca-

demically, and emotionally in a positive manner. I think the social and intellectual atmosphere at Stanford has really played a major role in that growth. 99

Goals for the Future

Select students feel they have developed certain humanist characteristics as they progress through college. How, I asked them, do they personally measure the importance of those same qualities as they look toward the future? Here are their responses:

1. Having good friends   89%
2. Fulfilling my potential   88%
3. Marrying the right person   77%
4. Using educational advantages received 76%
5. Finding a calling   70%
6. Raising a family   69%
7. Serving the immediate or larger community 61%
8. Being in a position of personal power 44%
9. Correcting social/economic inequalities 42%
10. Making a good deal of money   40%

Only a third of the students, however, plan to maintain ties to the colleges they believe have given them so many future advantages. And while the majority aim to be parents, only a minority want their children to attend the same colleges as they did. This attitude, I am assured, will change as they become parents of daughters and sons with high academic aspirations. The legacy factor and connections to their alma mater will, in due time, take on a special meaning to the Select alumni.

A slight gender gap is reflected in the pattern of responses. The women show greater concern for serving their community and finding their proper calling in life. Conversely, they attach less importance to making a good deal of money and attaining personal power. Yet all groups represented in the study share the same primary goals of using their education in a positive manner, having good friends, marrying the right person, and raising a family. Are these not the traditional values that earlier generations of college graduates subscribed to? Several selective colleges included in our study reported that their recent graduates are marrying earlier than graduates of the past decade. There is a sense that the tide may have turned toward an acceptance of traditional marriage, even as both parties are also focused on building their professional careers. The findings in this study would lend support to this trend.

Conclusion

I view the priorities set by this cohort of talented young adults as a rousing affirmation of the positive influences of their college communities. These students focus far less on future power, money, and status in the community than on the quality of their lives in the larger sense. Thus, as undergraduates, they develop and maintain a set of values and goals that bode well for our society.

It takes a shared history to make a people. I wish for all the past, present, and future students at these colleges that, having entered the academic community as strangers, feeling alone and unsure of themselves, they will leave with a sense that they now share in the venerable traditions of their institution. I hope many will want to support their colleges by maintaining their best traditions. At the same time, I see them making sure that their colleges continue to evolve into even better and more hospitable places—both socially and intellectually—for succeeding generations of talented, ambitious young men and women. I feel strongly that the trustees and executives who are the guardians of the colleges and universities should not deprecate alumni opinions while at the same time holding out their hands for donations. Recent and older graduates alike, who care about the experiences they enjoyed and value, are a vital check on those who walk away from it.

Not long ago, a young Dartmouth woman was discussing with me what the college experience allows—a sense of place and opportunity to think, to experiment, and to dream. In the midst of the conversation, she asked me if I was familiar with John Updike's novel *In the*

Beauty of the Lilies. We smiled at each other in mutual appreciation of a special thought Updike offers, one that speaks to the college journey and how we are shaped by what our hearts and minds can open to: "The world is like stones: dreams and thoughts flow over them." Amen.

Future Value of School's Education

(Summary of Top Two Ratings, "Extremely High"/"Very Good Value")

(Split by Gender)

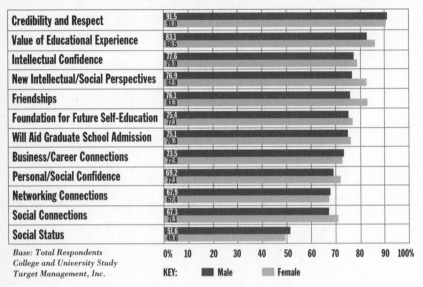

	Male	Female
Credibility and Respect	91.5	91.0
Value of Educational Experience	83.1	86.5
Intellectual Confidence	77.6	79.0
New Intellectual/Social Perspectives	76.9	82.9
Friendships	76.1	83.3
Foundation for Future Self-Education	75.4	77.1
Will Aid Graduate School Admission	75.1	76.3
Business/Career Connections	73.5	72.9
Personal/Social Confidence	69.2	72.1
Networking Connections	67.9	67.4
Social Connections	67.3	71.1
Social Status	51.6	49.6

Base: Total Respondents
College and University Study
Target Management, Inc.

KEY: ■ Male ■ Female

Future Value of School's Education

(Summary of Top Two Ratings, "Extremely High"/"Very Good Value")

(Split by Race)

	Students of Color (Non-Asian)	Asian Students
Credibility and Respect	89.6	92.2
Value of Educational Experience	81.5	87.8
Intellectual Confidence	80.0	77.3
New Intellectual/Social Perspectives	79.4	80.6
Business/Career Connections	78.2	74.2
Will Aid Graduate School Admission	76.5	77.5
Foundation for Future Self-Education	76.1	81.2
Friendships	74.5	81.3
Networking Connections	71.9	65.7
Personal/Social Confidence	68.0	69.8
Social Connections	67.9	67.4
Social Status	51.9	53.2

Base: Non-White Respondents
College and University Study
Target Management, Inc.

KEY: ■ Students of Color (Non-Asian) ■ Asian Students

Future Value of School's Education

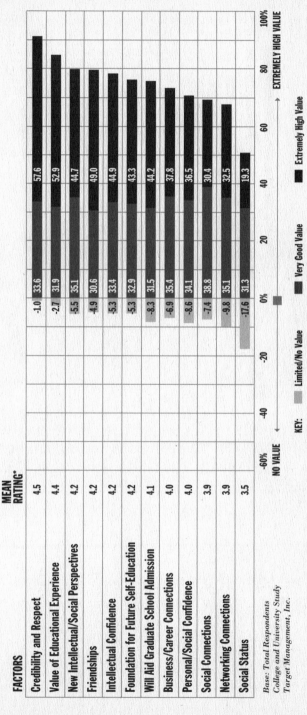

FACTORS	MEAN RATING*
Credibility and Respect	4.5
Value of Educational Experience	4.4
New Intellectual/Social Perspectives	4.2
Friendships	4.2
Intellectual Confidence	4.2
Foundation for Future Self-Education	4.2
Will Aid Graduate School Admission	4.1
Business/Career Connections	4.0
Personal/Social Confidence	4.0
Social Connections	3.9
Networking Connections	3.9
Social Status	3.5

Chart data (Limited/No Value, Very Good Value, Extremely High Value):

Factor	Limited/No Value	Very Good Value	Extremely High Value
Credibility and Respect	-1.0	33.6	57.6
Value of Educational Experience	-2.7	31.9	52.9
New Intellectual/Social Perspectives	-5.5	35.1	44.7
Friendships	-4.9	30.6	49.0
Intellectual Confidence	-5.3	33.4	44.9
Foundation for Future Self-Education	-5.3	32.9	43.3
Will Aid Graduate School Admission	-8.3	31.5	44.2
Business/Career Connections	-6.9	35.4	37.8
Personal/Social Confidence	-8.6	34.1	36.5
Social Connections	-7.4	38.8	30.4
Networking Connections	-9.8	35.1	32.5
Social Status	-17.6	31.3	19.3

-60% NO VALUE   -40   -20   0%   20   40   60   80   100% EXTREMELY HIGH VALUE

KEY: Limited/No Value   Very Good Value   Extremely High Value

Base: Total Respondents
College and University Study
Target Management, Inc.

*Rating Scale: 1 = Of no value, 2 = Of limited value, 3 = Somewhat of value, 4 = Very good value, 5 = Extremely high value.

Importance of Factors for Future

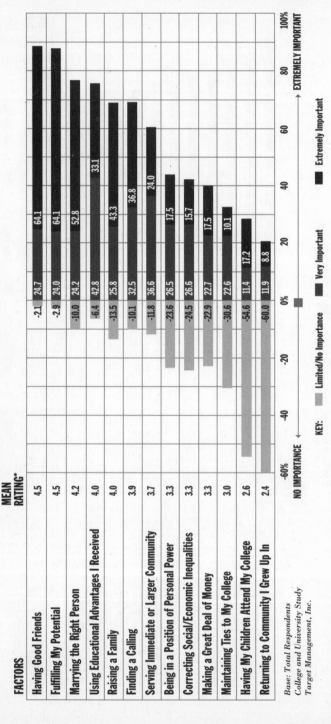

FACTORS	MEAN RATING*
Having Good Friends	4.5
Fulfilling My Potential	4.5
Marrying the Right Person	4.2
Using Educational Advantages I Received	4.0
Raising a Family	4.0
Finding a Calling	3.9
Serving Immediate or Larger Community	3.7
Being in a Position of Personal Power	3.3
Correcting Social/Economic Inequalities	3.3
Making a Great Deal of Money	3.3
Maintaining Ties to My College	3.0
Having My Children Attend My College	2.6
Returning to Community I Grew Up In	2.4

Having Good Friends: -2.1, 24.7, 64.1
Fulfilling My Potential: -2.9, 24.0, 64.1
Marrying the Right Person: -10.0, 24.2, 52.8
Using Educational Advantages I Received: -6.4, 42.8, 33.1
Raising a Family: -13.5, 25.8, 43.3
Finding a Calling: -10.1, 32.5, 36.8
Serving Immediate or Larger Community: -11.8, 36.6, 24.0
Being in a Position of Personal Power: -23.6, 26.5, 17.5
Correcting Social/Economic Inequalities: -24.5, 26.6, 15.7
Making a Great Deal of Money: -22.9, 22.7, 17.5
Maintaining Ties to My College: -30.6, 22.6, 10.1
Having My Children Attend My College: -54.6, 11.4, 17.2
Returning to Community I Grew Up In: -60.0, 11.9, 8.8

-60%   -40   -20   0%   20   40   60   80   100%

NO IMPORTANCE ←   → EXTREMELY IMPORTANT

KEY: ■ Limited/No Importance   ■ Very Important   ■ Extremely Important

Base: Total Respondents
College and University Study
Target Management, Inc.

*Ratings scale: 1= Of no importance, 2= Of limited importance, 3= Somewhat important, 4= Very important, 5= Extremely important

Importance of Factors for Future

(Dartmouth)

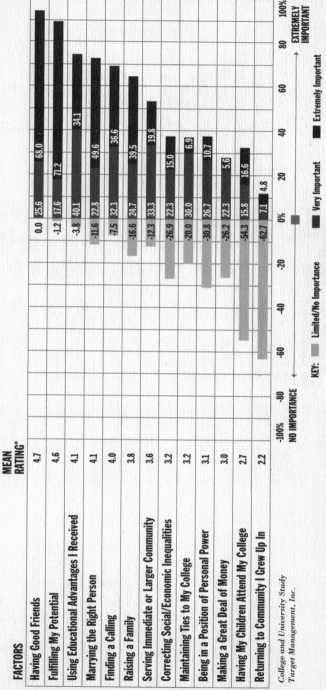

FACTORS	MEAN RATING*
Having Good Friends	4.7
Fulfilling My Potential	4.6
Using Educational Advantages I Received	4.1
Marrying the Right Person	4.1
Finding a Calling	4.0
Raising a Family	3.8
Serving Immediate or Larger Community	3.6
Correcting Social/Economic Inequalities	3.2
Maintaining Ties to My College	3.2
Being in a Position of Personal Power	3.1
Making a Great Deal of Money	3.0
Having My Children Attend My College	2.7
Returning to Community I Grew Up In	2.2

College and University Study
Target Management, Inc.

KEY: ■ Limited/No Importance   ■ Very Important   ■ Extremely Important

NO IMPORTANCE ←——————→ EXTREMELY IMPORTANT

*Ratings scale: 1= Of no importance, 2= Of limited importance, 3= Somewhat important, 4= Very important, 5= Extremely important

Importance of Factors for Future

(Dartmouth—Males)

FACTORS	MEAN RATING*	Limited/No Importance	Very Important	Extremely Important
Having Good Friends	4.6	0.0	29.9	65.7
Fulfilling My Potential	4.5	-2.2	17.6	67.0
Marrying the Right Person	4.1	-9.4	24.6	49.7
Using Educational Advantages I Received	3.9	-4.4	46.3	24.1
Finding a Calling	3.8	-10.3	28.8	32.4
Raising a Family	3.7	-19.3	32.1	33.0
Serving Immediate or Larger Community	3.5	-15.6	30.9	18.1
Being in a Position of Personal Power	3.2	-28.2	35.7	8.2
Correcting Social/Economic Inequalities	3.0	-33.0	24.8	12.0
Making a Great Deal of Money	3.0	-28.6	28.5	5.5
Maintaining Ties to My College	3.0	-20.6	27.6	4.8
Having My Children Attend My College	2.7	-52.1	21.9	14.2
Returning to Community I Grew Up In	2.3	-60.7	11.6	5.5

-100% NO IMPORTANCE   -80   -60   -40   -20   0%   20   40   60   80   100% EXTREMELY IMPORTANT

KEY: ■ Limited/No Importance   ■ Very Important   ■ Extremely Important

College and University Study Target Management, Inc.

*Ratings scale: 1= Of no importance, 2= Of limited importance, 3= Somewhat important, 4= Very important, 5= Extremely important

Importance of Factors for Future

(Dartmouth—Females)

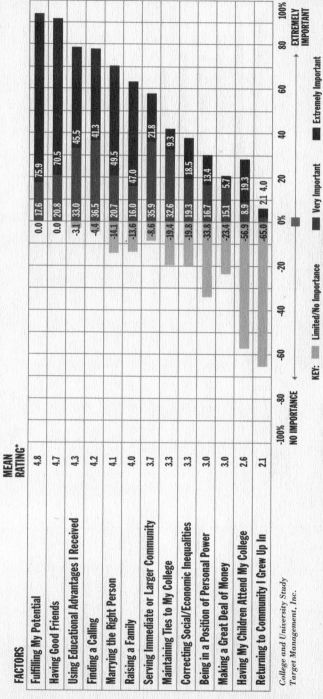

FACTORS	MEAN RATING*
Fulfilling My Potential	4.8
Having Good Friends	4.7
Using Educational Advantages I Received	4.3
Finding a Calling	4.2
Marrying the Right Person	4.1
Raising a Family	4.0
Serving Immediate or Larger Community	3.7
Maintaining Ties to My College	3.3
Correcting Social/Economic Inequalities	3.3
Being in a Position of Personal Power	3.0
Making a Great Deal of Money	3.0
Having My Children Attend My College	2.6
Returning to Community I Grew Up In	2.1

College and University Study
Target Management, Inc.

KEY: ■ Limited/No Importance ■ Very Important ■ Extremely Important

*Ratings scale: 1= Of no importance, 2= Of limited importance, 3= Somewhat important, 4= Very important, 5= Extremely important

Importance of Factors for Future

(Ivy League)

FACTORS	MEAN RATING*	Limited/No Importance	Very Important	Extremely Important
Having Good Friends	4.6	-2.0	23.2	68.5
Fulfilling My Potential	4.5	-3.0	21.4	67.9
Marrying the Right Person	4.3	-8.1	25.4	56.1
Using Educational Advantages I Received	4.0	-6.8	40.5	34.1
Raising a Family	4.1	-10.0	27.8	48.2
Finding a Calling	3.9	-10.4	33.5	34.5
Serving Immediate or Larger Community	3.7	-13.3	35.2	21.9
Being in a Position of Personal Power	3.2	-36.6	25.7	13.9
Correcting Social/Economic Inequalities	3.2	-27.7	24.0	14.9
Making a Great Deal of Money	3.2	-25.6	23.9	12.7
Maintaining Ties to My College	3.1	-28.3	22.4	11.4
Having My Children Attend My College	2.6	-54.8	11.9	16.5
Returning to Community I Grew Up In	2.5	-57.9	12.2	10.0

Axis: -100% NO IMPORTANCE ... -80 -60 -40 -20 0% 20 40 60 80 100% EXTREMELY IMPORTANT

KEY: Limited/No Importance | Very Important | Extremely Important

College and University Study
Target Management, Inc.

*Ratings scale: 1= Of no importance, 2= Of limited importance, 3= Somewhat important, 4= Very important, 5= Extremely important

Importance of Factors for Future

(Students of Color)

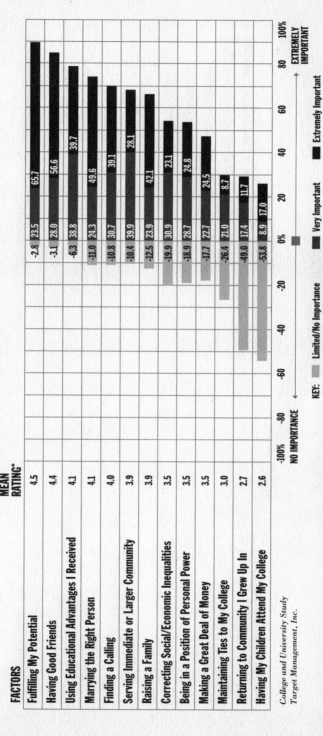

FACTORS	MEAN RATING*	Limited/No Importance	Very Important	Extremely Important
Fulfilling My Potential	4.5	-2.8	23.5	65.7
Having Good Friends	4.4	-3.1	28.0	56.6
Using Educational Advantages I Received	4.1	-6.3	38.8	39.7
Marrying the Right Person	4.1	-11.0	24.3	49.6
Finding a Calling	4.0	-10.8	30.7	39.1
Serving Immediate or Larger Community	3.9	-10.4	39.9	28.1
Raising a Family	3.9	-12.5	23.9	42.1
Correcting Social/Economic Inequalities	3.5	-19.9	30.9	23.1
Being in a Position of Personal Power	3.5	-18.9	28.7	24.8
Making a Great Deal of Money	3.5	-17.7	22.7	24.5
Maintaining Ties to My College	3.0	-26.4	21.0	8.7
Returning to Community I Grew Up In	2.7	-49.0	17.4	11.7
Having My Children Attend My College	2.6	-53.8	8.9	17.0

-100% -80 -60 -40 -20 0% 20 40 60 80 100%
NO IMPORTANCE   EXTREMELY IMPORTANT

KEY: ▨ Limited/No Importance   ■ Very Important   ■ Extremely Important

College and University Study
Target Management, Inc.

*Ratings scale: 1= Of no importance, 2= Of limited importance, 3= Somewhat important, 4= Very important, 5= Extremely important

Importance of Factors for Future

(Brown)

FACTORS	MEAN RATING*	Limited/No Importance	Very Important	Extremely Important
Having Good Friends	4.6	-1.9	25.1	68.4
Fulfilling My Potential	4.6	-1.0	18.0	73.6
Marrying the Right Person	4.3	-8.4	29.5	54.1
Raising a Family	4.2	-6.0	33.7	44.1
Using Educational Advantages I Received	4.1	-4.0	37.0	38.9
Finding a Calling	4.0	-11.6	32.2	37.7
Serving Immediate or Larger Community	3.9	-6.5	38.3	26.8
Correcting Social/Economic Inequalities	3.5	-18.5	29.3	22.1
Maintaining Ties to My College	3.2	-21.5	24.7	9.5
Being in a Position of Personal Power	3.1	-30.0	25.4	9.6
Making a Great Deal of Money	2.9	-29.6	17.9	7.1
Having My Children Attend My College	2.5	-61.8	10.5	16.0
Returning to Community I Grew Up In	2.4	-62.2	11.8	7.8

-100% -80 -60 -40 -20 0% 20 40 60 80 100%

NO IMPORTANCE ←   → EXTREMELY IMPORTANT

KEY: ■ Limited/No Importance   ■ Very Important   ■ Extremely Important

College and University Study
Target Management, Inc.

*Ratings scale: 1= Of no importance, 2= Of limited importance, 3= Somewhat important, 4= Very important, 5= Extremely important

Importance of Factors for Future

(Brown—Males)

FACTORS	MEAN RATING*				
Having Good Friends	4.6	-0.7	35.5	61.2	
Fulfilling My Potential	4.6	-2.1	17.9	72.1	
Marrying the Right Person	4.3	-5.9	32.2	51.9	
Raising a Family	4.2	-4.4	43.8	38.7	
Using Educational Advantages I Received	4.0	-2.8	43.5	27.4	
Finding a Calling	4.0	-12.0	29.8	39.2	
Serving Immediate or Larger Community	3.8	-5.9	36.5	23.5	
Correcting Social/Economic Inequalities	3.3	-20.4	23.2	18.1	
Being in a Position of Personal Power	3.2	-24.8	27.8	12.6	
Making a Great Deal of Money	3.2	-23.4	25.9	12.1	
Maintaining Ties to My College	3.1	-24.2	19.5	10.7	
Having My Children Attend My College	2.4	-64.5	9.9	16.9	
Returning to Community I Grew Up In	2.4	-63.0	14.4	8.2	

-100% -80 -60 -40 -20 0% 20 40 60 80 100%

NO IMPORTANCE ←   → EXTREMELY IMPORTANT

KEY: ▨ Limited/No Importance   ▪ Very Important   ■ Extremely Important

College and University Study Target Management, Inc.

*Ratings scale: 1= Of no importance, 2= Of limited importance, 3= Somewhat important, 4= Very important, 5= Extremely important

Importance of Factors for Future

(Brown—Females)

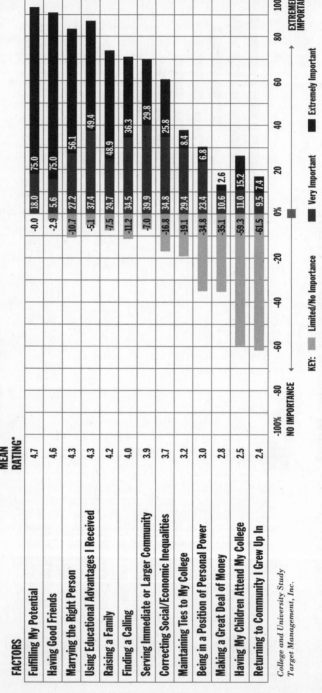

FACTORS	MEAN RATING*				
Fulfilling My Potential	4.7	-0.0	18.0	75.0	
Having Good Friends	4.6	-2.9	5.6	75.0	
Marrying the Right Person	4.3	-10.7	27.2	56.1	
Using Educational Advantages I Received	4.3	-5.1	37.4	49.4	
Raising a Family	4.2	-7.5	24.7	48.9	
Finding a Calling	4.0	-11.2	34.5	36.3	
Serving Immediate or Larger Community	3.9	-7.0	39.9	29.8	
Correcting Social/Economic Inequalities	3.7	-16.8	34.8	25.8	
Maintaining Ties to My College	3.2	-19.1	29.4	8.4	
Being in a Position of Personal Power	3.0	-34.8	23.4	6.8	
Making a Great Deal of Money	2.8	-35.1	10.6	2.6	
Having My Children Attend My College	2.5	-59.3	11.0	15.2	
Returning to Community I Grew Up In	2.4	-61.5	9.5	7.4	

-100% -80 -60 -40 -20 0% 20 40 60 80 100%

NO IMPORTANCE ← → EXTREMELY IMPORTANT

KEY: ▨ Limited/No Importance ■ Very Important ■ Extremely Important

College and University Study Target Management, Inc.

*Ratings scale: 1= Of no importance, 2= Of limited importance, 3= Somewhat important, 4= Very important, 5= Extremely important

Importance of Factors for Future

(Princeton)

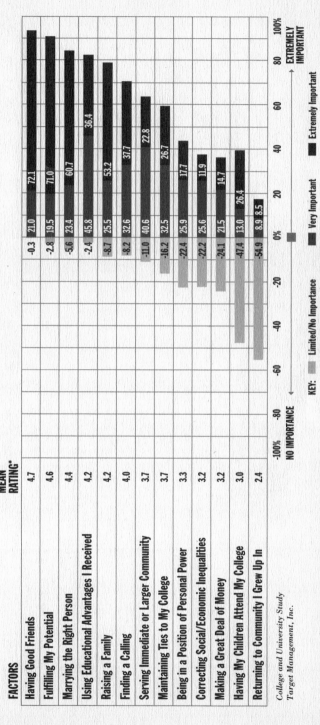

FACTORS	MEAN RATING*
Having Good Friends	4.7
Fulfilling My Potential	4.6
Marrying the Right Person	4.4
Using Educational Advantages I Received	4.2
Raising a Family	4.2
Finding a Calling	4.0
Serving Immediate or Larger Community	3.7
Maintaining Ties to My College	3.7
Being in a Position of Personal Power	3.3
Correcting Social/Economic Inequalities	3.2
Making a Great Deal of Money	3.2
Having My Children Attend My College	3.0
Returning to Community I Grew Up In	2.4

College and University Study Target Management, Inc.

KEY: Limited/No Importance   Very Important   Extremely Important

*Ratings scale: 1= Of no importance, 2= Of limited importance, 3= Somewhat important, 4= Very important, 5= Extremely important

Importance of Factors for Future

(Princeton—Males)

FACTORS	MEAN RATING*	Limited/No Importance	Very Important	Extremely Important
Having Good Friends	4.6	0.0	22.0	69.6
Fulfilling My Potential	4.5	-4.7	19.0	70.2
Marrying the Right Person	4.3	-4.8	25.7	57.6
Using Educational Advantages I Received	4.2	-2.3	48.9	36.0
Raising a Family	4.2	-7.0	28.1	51.8
Finding a Calling	4.0	-6.1	31.7	36.4
Serving Immediate or Larger Community	3.7	-8.0	49.5	16.8
Being in a Position of Personal Power	3.7	-15.2	28.7	27.4
Maintaining Ties to My College	3.6	-15.7	30.9	23.4
Making a Great Deal of Money	3.4	-21.0	26.4	21.1
Correcting Social/Economic Inequalities	3.2	-20.2	27.7	6.9
Having My Children Attend My College	3.1	-44.5	11.1	28.9
Returning to Community I Grew Up In	2.5	-50.2	11.9	9.5

Axis: -100% NO IMPORTANCE ... -80 -60 -40 -20 0% 20 40 60 80 100% EXTREMELY IMPORTANT

KEY: Limited/No Importance — Very Important — Extremely Important

*Ratings scale: 1= Of no importance, 2= Of limited importance, 3= Somewhat important, 4= Very important, 5= Extremely important

College and University Study
Target Management, Inc.

Importance of Factors for Future

(Princeton—Females)

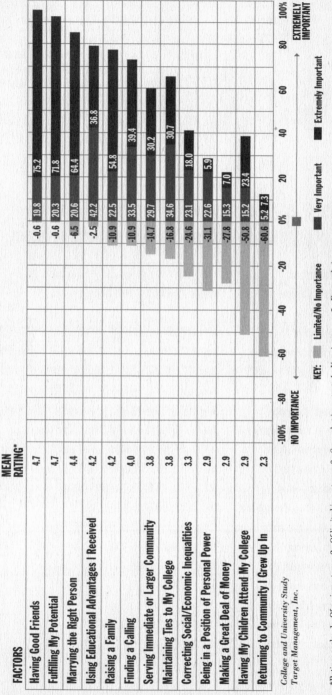

FACTORS	MEAN RATING*
Having Good Friends	4.7
Fulfilling My Potential	4.7
Marrying the Right Person	4.4
Using Educational Advantages I Received	4.2
Raising a Family	4.2
Finding a Calling	4.0
Serving Immediate or Larger Community	3.8
Maintaining Ties to My College	3.8
Correcting Social/Economic Inequalities	3.3
Being in a Position of Personal Power	2.9
Making a Great Deal of Money	2.9
Having My Children Attend My College	2.9
Returning to Community I Grew Up In	2.3

KEY: ■ Limited/No Importance ■ Very Important ■ Extremely Important

Ratings scale: 1= Of no importance, 2= Of limited importance, 3= Somewhat important, 4= Very important, 5= Extremely important

College and University Study Target Management, Inc.

Confidence in School Choice

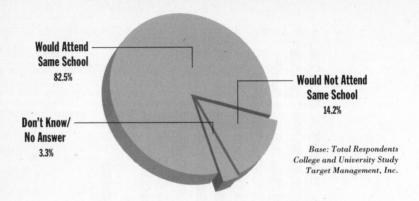

Would Attend
Same School
82.5%

Would Not Attend
Same School
14.2%

Don't Know/
No Answer
3.3%

Base: Total Respondents
College and University Study
Target Management, Inc.

% of Students Who Would Choose
Not to Attend the Same School Again

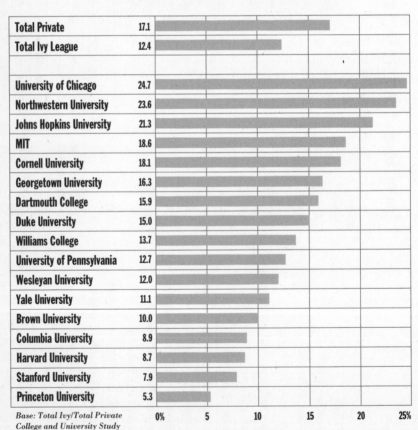

		0%	5	10	15	20	25%
Total Private	17.1						
Total Ivy League	12.4						
University of Chicago	24.7						
Northwestern University	23.6						
Johns Hopkins University	21.3						
MIT	18.6						
Cornell University	18.1						
Georgetown University	16.3						
Dartmouth College	15.9						
Duke University	15.0						
Williams College	13.7						
University of Pennsylvania	12.7						
Wesleyan University	12.0						
Yale University	11.1						
Brown University	10.0						
Columbia University	8.9						
Harvard University	8.7						
Stanford University	7.9						
Princeton University	5.3						

Base: Total Ivy/Total Private
College and University Study
Target Management, Inc.

% of Male Students Who Would Choose Not to Attend the Same School Again

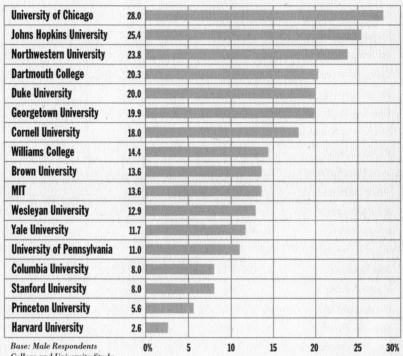

	%							
University of Chicago	28.0							
Johns Hopkins University	25.4							
Northwestern University	23.8							
Dartmouth College	20.3							
Duke University	20.0							
Georgetown University	19.9							
Cornell University	18.0							
Williams College	14.4							
Brown University	13.6							
MIT	13.6							
Wesleyan University	12.9							
Yale University	11.7							
University of Pennsylvania	11.0							
Columbia University	8.0							
Stanford University	8.0							
Princeton University	5.6							
Harvard University	2.6							

0%   5   10   15   20   25   30%

Base: Male Respondents
College and University Study
Target Management, Inc.

% of Female Students Who Would Choose Not to Attend the Same School Again

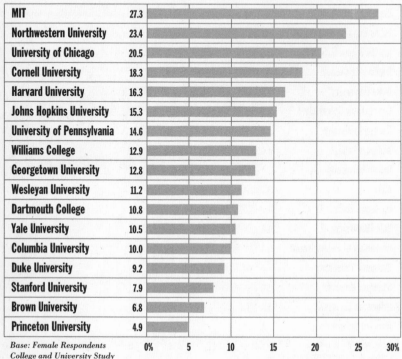

		0%	5	10	15	20	25	30%
MIT	27.3							
Northwestern University	23.4							
University of Chicago	20.5							
Cornell University	18.3							
Harvard University	16.3							
Johns Hopkins University	15.3							
University of Pennsylvania	14.6							
Williams College	12.9							
Georgetown University	12.8							
Wesleyan University	11.2							
Dartmouth College	10.8							
Yale University	10.5							
Columbia University	10.0							
Duke University	9.2							
Stanford University	7.9							
Brown University	6.8							
Princeton University	4.9							

Base: Female Respondents
College and University Study
Target Management, Inc.

TWELVE
Advice for Students and Parents

A Considered Choice for College

In the *Republic*, Plato said that "the direction in which education starts a man will determine his future life." If you are about to join in the admissions game and believe that only one elite college will allow you to realize your dreams, you may have taken this concept much too literally. In our modern world of winner-take-all competitiveness, the truth of Plato's observation can easily be missed: A young man or woman's life will not be entirely a function of the particular college he or she attends; it is education itself—the social, emotional, and intellectual development that starts in elementary school and builds to a crescendo in so many wonderful colleges located all across America—that will establish the direction for your future life.

As I stated at the beginning of *The Select*, my purpose is not to join in the popular pastime of bashing social establishments that smack of selectivity and elitism. Elite colleges are easy targets for potshots. After all, they're a highly visible group of universities that charge far more than the public can pay and accept far too few of those who want to attend. They are outstanding educational enterprises that bring together in a compressed environment extraordinary human and physical resources. Intelligent, curious individuals could spend their entire lives in an effort to take advantage of all the intellectual facilities, human and otherwise, and fail in the attempt. Just about every Select student who has gained the privilege of living and learning for four or five years on any of the elite campuses cannot fail to grow in wisdom and self-knowledge. Nevertheless, there is a long list of negative features that can make college a less-than-idyllic experience for many talented and virtuous young men or women. And developing criteria for choosing the right school—one that promises an abundance of benefits with a minimum of negatives—can be a daunting task.

This chapter is my attempt to give students and parents the confidence they need to deal with the collegiate realities I've explored in this book. I also want to help create a process that will enable them to make a considered college choice.

Developing Criteria for Selecting a College

Faced with a plethora of options, opportunities, considerations, reservations, and questions, you may feel overwhelmed as you attempt to decide on a college. Fortunately, there are a number of resources you can turn to—from consultants like me to the colleges themselves; in time, both students and parents can come to rely on their own judgments, self-analysis, and good sense.

Remember that your education means more than choosing a particular college. I always tell students and parents not to regard any one college or university as absolutely vital to the students' future prospects and happiness. Yes, I tell them, it really is true: There are dozens of first-rate educational establishments that allow young scholars to discover their true talents and interests and instill the skills necessary for them to achieve their goals.

Who in your life can help you structure your choices? First, you can do what I have done in my survey: Talk to graduates and undergraduates from any of the fine colleges; you'll get an immediate grasp of what college has meant for them and how their adult lives were altered, pro or con, by the collegiate decision they made. A student's parents can share their undergraduate experiences—or a favorite teacher or coach, a family doctor, or an older sibling. Whether they tell you that college was the time of their life or four years of pain, ask why. In college, as in life, it's always a matter of "different strokes."

As a student, you need to determine what kind of undergraduate experience will best suit your character, temperament, and aspirations. As a parent, you can assist your child in this process by putting your biases and personal ambitions on hold so that you can be truly helpful. I asked a number of high school seniors who had just completed the stressful process of applying to college what advice they would give to parents of future college applicants. Virtually all of them urged parents to listen to their children. What does it really mean to listen to your children? It means that you pay attention to their fears, desires, needs, and hopes for their college experience, rather than focus only on your own preferences and those of friends and neighbors who may be impressed with the success of their bosses and/or competitors and ascribe their success to the colleges they attended.

Students and parents must get past the Halo Effect; it can keep them from seeing what would be the best of the many academic roads that can be taken. The data assembled here should make you realize that no one college is right for everyone, regardless of how famous and prestigious it may be. Of course, it's terrific to imagine yourself as a student at an elite college or as the bursting-at-the-buttons-with-pride parent of an Ivy Leaguer. But try to imagine how unpleasant it can be to work under the pressures and competition described here by so many Select students. What good is it to get into such a school and undergo four years of frustration, then not do well enough to get into graduate school? I have listened to too many elite college undergraduates and recent graduates express their pain and anger when their mediocre academic performance kept them out of the graduate schools of their choice. I've heard too many others bemoan the passionate personal interests they had to give up to cope with the rigors of academic requirements. Simply attending and graduating from a flagship institution is no longer, if it ever was, a prepaid ticket to whatever destination a student dreams of. Think about it.

As a corollary, many families naively think that attending the undergraduate college of an elite university will put a student first in line for a place in its own graduate school of law, medicine, business, or doctoral studies. You may be shocked to learn that the opposite is closer to the truth; you could actually be putting yourself at a disadvantage. The graduate schools cast their recruitment net as far and wide as possible to attract the superstars who will excel and then spread the name and reputation of their programs. I urge prospective Select students to seek the undergraduate college where they are most likely to be successful; for their own good, they should pay little or no attention to the Olympian graduate schools sitting off on their mountain of self-interest, at least at this critical time when choosing a college can determine a student's personal success.

This leads me to one of my most passionate arguments regarding a college education. I ask all students whom I counsel to consider how they want their education delivered to them. This is the way I phrase it: How would you prefer to have your education delivered? And don't confuse the topic with ordering from the nearest Pizza Hut. By using the term *delivery*, I mean the style of teaching by the majority of professors, the number of students in a typical classroom, and an emphasis on lecturing and exam taking or class discussion and debate.

Consider a few different scenarios. A young man wishes to attend a large university because he loves big-time athletics and lots of campus action. But he has not weighed into his selection formula that he has done well in small high school classes where the teachers are actively engaged with their students. Perhaps his favorite teachers are more Socratic than didactic in their methods of inquiry; that is, they ask students what they think, make them engage in discussions, and query rather than orate for a full class period. The bigger the university, the larger the classes. When he has to answer my question about the educational delivery system, such a student will frequently realize that although he may love to follow sports teams, he cares even more about the way in which he will be taught.

Here is another educational-delivery-system question, this one related to the Halo Effect. As I've shown, the great majority of future collegians state up front that prestige is very important to them. OK, I say to these high school students, I appreciate how your self-esteem would be enhanced by telling yourself and everyone who might care to listen that you go to Ivy U. Now I need to ask you some questions: How hard have you worked in your studies, and do you get pleasure from performing under heavy pressure? Have you extended yourself intellectually by taking advanced-track courses in your high school? A good many students will nod vigorously, primed for the challenge. Just as many will change expression as they realize there is a major difference between donning a status-college T-shirt and working at the level and pace it takes to trade it in four years later for a sheepskin. Then, they ask themselves, where is that social life I looked forward to enjoying in college? In reality, what value is there in graduating in the second half of my class?

The educational-delivery-system question concerns not just academics but environments. I've encountered many a student who insists that she or he will attend only an urban college or university. Enough of this small-town and limited high school social environment, they tell themselves, their parents, and me. I understand the readiness—the raging desire in some instances—of many students to move into a larger, more diverse, action-packed environment. But can we talk about the kind of teaching and community dynamics you're likely to encounter in that large urban university? Some students have mulled over this proposition, like the thoughtful and adventurous high school senior who wrote the following explanation to the University of Pennsylvania of why she was set on enrolling in the university.

> 66 I live in a small town in the southwest corner of Connecticut. Although it is located only a little over an hour from New York City, many of my schoolmates have never visited the city. My peers have typically foregone the stimulation of this bursting metropolis for the quiet sameness of our town. Last year, our English teacher asked us to select three items to place in a time capsule that would capture the flavor of our town. I chose a dollar bill, a bouquet of flowers, and a piece of white bread. The first item symbolized the uniform affluence of the townspeople while the flowers denoted the splendor of the lovely homes and gardens, and its verdant wooded areas. I chose the white bread, however, to represent the demographic composition of its inhabitants: safe, homogeneous, and essentially bland. The University of Pennsylvania

attracts me, therefore, because of its emphasis on recruiting a multi-cultural and ethnically diverse student body. Keeping my metaphor going, I anticipate enjoying some pumpernickel, rye, and raisin bread, and even a bagel or two. Penn's location is also important to me, because the pulse of the city makes me feel alive. Next year will be the time for me to stop being a frequent urban visitor, and become a true resident.

This student is now flourishing at Penn, but not without some sticky adjustments to her dramatically new diet.

As I consult with prospective Select students and their parents, I remind both myself and them that we are talking about the particular needs of a very specific seventeen-year-old individual. Perhaps this is the greatest challenge every high school student must face: to develop the insight, independence of mind, self-awareness, and realistic self-appraisal to decide what educational delivery system—what college—is most likely to ensure success and happiness.

Given some of the social and academic differences among the top-tier colleges, how does a talented high school senior figure out how to undertake the right course of action? Here are some of the major recommendations I can offer from my many years of counseling. First, you can learn a lot about yourself that will help you find the most appropriate college by honestly answering the following questions. Put on some music, relax, and respond spontaneously to them.

- I am most comfortable in a conservative or traditional environment.
- I am most at home in a freewheeling or experimental environment.
- I believe the most important value in life is . . .
- I am most comfortable in a discussion of my personal beliefs and ethics when . . .
- My curiosity is stimulated by . . .
- I am happiest when I . . .
- I love to get dressed and go . . .
- I cannot stand to . . .
- I cannot live without . . .
- My family is . . .

- I do my best when . . .
- I am most fearful about . . .
- I have never had the opportunity to . . .
- The type of person I most admire and would choose to be like is . . .
- My personal strengths are . . .
- My intellectual strengths are in . . .
- I am not very interested in . . .
- I can cope with stress by . . .
- What I most want to do after college is. . . .

Ideally, if you answer these questions from the heart, you will develop insight not only into your strengths but into your weaknesses. Knowing your shortcomings will only make your strengths more accessible to you. This is the best formula for a successful college experience and future that I know of.

Remember that the highly selective colleges choose applicants whom they believe will eventually take positions of leadership and innovation in every arena of our complex social order. Discovering what you are good at and nurturing it will build your self-esteem and help you set your course toward one of those desired positions.

What to Consider in Choosing a College

Now that you have analyzed yourself, how do you analyze a college? Once you discount choosing a college solely on the basis of the Halo Effect, you can evaluate some other primary factors that will help you make a more rationale and appropriate selection. In my counseling work with college-bound students, satisfying the following criteria have proved to correlate directly to the value of the college experience.

- Size of the student body: How large is it, and how happy are you with either an intimate student body or a university in which undergraduate life is one part of a larger campus environment?
- Quality of campus living: Are the dormitories spacious, protected, clean, and livable? Is the campus safe enough? Are

you satisfied with the quality and variety of eating options and the social and academic facilities?

- Endowment per student: How does the financial wealth of a particular college influence the number and quality of faculty and the social and intellectual resources available to students?
- The ratio of financial resources to student services and teaching: How does your group of target colleges fare in comparison? All the leading college guides now publish these statistics.
- Dominant social style: Note the unhappiness or satisfaction among the Select students expressed in this survey. Read your guidebooks and talk to counselors and current students.
- Faculty teaching responsibilities and accessibility.
- Quality of physical resources for learning: the library, laboratories, study rooms, computer center.
- Academic intensity: Will I be comfortable and successful in an environment that demands a particular magnitude of workload?
- Academic requirements to graduate: Is there a required core curriculum with many distribution requirements, or will a student have a great deal of latitude in building an academic program?
- Academic disciplines and fields of study: Will I be able to pursue the academic area I intend to follow? If I change my mind, will I have sufficient acceptable alternatives?
- Tuition and living costs: Can I afford this school without bankrupting my parents or putting an intolerable financial burden on them or on myself?
- Availability of financial aid: Will I be able to accrue sufficient scholarships and loans to make the college affordable?
- Opportunities to work on and off campus: Can I handle a job and go to school full-time?
- Accessibility to home resources: Will I be near enough by public transportation or a car to return home more often than only during vacation breaks?
- Presence and importance of a Greek system: Find out from college authorities what percentage of undergraduates belong to fraternities and sororities. Ask students on campus how

strong a force the Greeks play in determining the college's social life.

- Political activism of students and faculty: Students are the best source of insight into the degree of "politically correct" attitudes and political activity on campus.
- Location (city or country; near home or far away, climate): Here is a critical set of factors a student must determine by first evaluating their personal importance. Visiting a campus is a student's best guide in this regard.
- Composition of the student body: Will I find the appropriate combination of human variety and comfort among my fellow undergraduates?
- Variety of extracurricular programs: How will I be able to explore my interests outside class? Will there be new interests to explore?
- Parietal rules: Every college handbook informs students of the rules and regulations enacted by the college on this point, as well as on the next two.
- Availability of coed and single-sex dormitories.
- Alcohol and drug policy.
- Support services (academic, financial, personal, and medical): If I need help, will I be able to get it quickly and professionally, with a variety of options for assistance?
- Athletic programs for varsity and intramural interests.
- Support groups based on special interests or religious, ethnic, or racial identification: Will this college help me be part of a larger group identity?
- Judicial and governance system and recourse and support of students: Every college publishes in its handbook a description of its judicial system and procedures for dealing with all forms of unacceptable behavior while on campus.

Matching Student and College

Now that you've read *The Select,* you know a lot about life at a number of outstanding colleges and universities. You've seen how minimal are the differences in academic preparation and ability from campus to campus and have learned how several students can perceive a single college environment quite differently, based on their particular interests, strengths, weaknesses, and personal priorities and values. For some students a big school is right, for others it's wrong. Some collegians prefer a rural campus, others the resources of a city. Drinking as a social outlet gives pleasure to many, while it is harmful and disruptive to others. Learning by sitting in a lecture hall for four years appeals to students who absorb information quickly this way and who favor anonymity; yet such a situation distresses others who thrive on faculty-student interaction. Many Select students use college as a dramatic separation from childhood by going far from home; others feel the need to be close to their families. Socially and politically concerned individuals are delighted to be in a charged activist community, but some more traditional or apolitical students are dismayed by their encounters with the forces of social action. Some students who have grown up in a community of people of similar background and values can be made uncomfortable on a highly diverse campus. Others are used to a socially mixed environment and wouldn't want it otherwise.

I cannot tell you what is best for you in considering these campus dynamics. You must perform that difficult but ultimately rewarding exercise of assessing yourself. Plumb the depths. Sound out others on your conclusions. Seek the opinions of the friends who know you best and will offer honest observations. Probe your parents' perceptions; despite their emotional involvement and subjectivity, they often have the greatest insight into who you are and what makes you tick. Your teachers, a coach, adviser, or an employer can also tell you valuable things about yourself. Pull together all your information, sift and sort it, see if it fits with your own assessment, then get on with the search for the best college for you—not for anyone else.

Finally, get off that couch and visit several different kinds of colleges. I refer to this as "prototype shopping." Learn from some of the more reliable guidebooks which campuses potentially match your preferences. Be certain to include several models in your search. Check out large, middle-sized, and smaller schools in urban, suburban, and rural settings. I trust you in this enterprise. In fact, I wish I could bottle the chemistry high school students naturally produce that enables them to walk onto a campus and instinctively know the tenor of the place.

Deciding on the right college and gaining admission is fraught with anxiety, confusion, and stress because of the competition and complexity of the process. I assist students in their search by focusing on five strategies that encompass the key elements in that process. I refer to them as the Five P's.

- Program: The quality of your high school curriculum is the first factor all selective colleges will consider. How many advanced-placement, honors, and unusual intellectual courses have you taken? Have you excelled in those academic areas related to your expressed future interests?
- Passion: The elite colleges are exciting, stimulating environments partly because of the focused talents and involvements of their students. The admissions committee is particularly attracted to candidates who have displayed a superlative level of commitment to a personal activity, whether it is in the athletic, artistic, activist, intellectual, or leadership area. Note how the selective colleges put on their "brag sheet" each year how many team captains, editors-in-chief, class presidents, and national math, science, or arts winners have enrolled in the freshman class.
- Preparation and Planning: Making plans to apply to college is a challenging and time-consuming procedure that must be well thought out. Plan the appropriate curriculum for yourself, take the required admissions tests, research colleges, make appointments to visit campuses for tours and interviews, and ultimately sketch out a schedule for completing the challenging applications. To stay ahead of all the required steps, start early—in the tenth and eleventh grades!
- Presentation: Since elite colleges are faced each year with selecting only one out of every four to six applicants, the personal application and supportive information from your guidance counselors, teachers, activity advisers, and employers is the key to standing out from the pack. Carefully

crafted essays that reveal the special qualities you possess, as well as supporting documents—such as high-quality research papers, an art portfolio, or musical recordings—can make an admissions committee want you in their community. This is a unique opportunity to plead your own case in your own words. Take advantage of it.

Conclusion

The late Charles Revson, founder of Revlon, the world-renowned cosmetics giant, once commented that while his company manufactured beauty products, its real business was providing people with hope. Universities are ostensibly in the business of educating people, but they, too, are in "the hope industry, for the flagship colleges and universities are seen as the gateway to a life of happiness and prosperity. What could be a more powerful motivation for seeking entrance than their seal of approval? I merely suggest that before you buy, check carefully into the product to make sure it can provide you with a full dollop of hope. As you seek the college and the lifestyle that is right for you, please remember that the journey, more than the destination, will ultimately define who you will become.

APPENDIX]

Brown University

(Importance of Factors in Choosing This School)

FACTORS	MEAN RATING*	Limited/No Importance	Very Important	Extremely Important
Academic Programs in Specific Area	3.9	-11.2	41.8	28.5
Prestige/Name Recognition of School	3.8	-7.3	36.0	24.3
Social Atmosphere/Style of School	3.9	-8.1	40.5	31.2
Geographical Location	3.2	-21.2	32.4	9.8
Graduate School Preparation	3.2	-27.6	28.3	13.2
Financial Assistance/Scholarships	2.6	-53.0	12.5	20.3
Racial/Ethnic Diversity of School	3.2	-29.1	25.3	16.5
Political Atmosphere/Style of School	3.1	-37.3	23.6	15.0
Tuition & Room/Board Exclusive of Financial Aid	2.1	-61.5	11.6	3.1
Advice from Peers/Friends	2.4	-55.3	16.4	2.0
Advice from Guidance Counselor/Advisor	2.2	-61.6	9.9	1.7
Parental/Family Pressure	2.0	-70.1	5.9	3.5
Athletic Program	2.1	-68.2	9.4	10.3
Family Legacy	1.3	-92.9	1.3	2.7

NO IMPORTANCE ← -100% -80 -60 -40 -20 0% 20 40 60 80 100% → EXTREMELY IMPORTANT

KEY: ■ Limited/No Importance ■ Very Important ■ Extremely Important

Base: Total Brown Respondents
College and University Study
Target Management, Inc.

*Ratings scale: 1= Of no importance, 2= Of limited importance, 3= Somewhat important, 4= Very important, 5= Extremely important

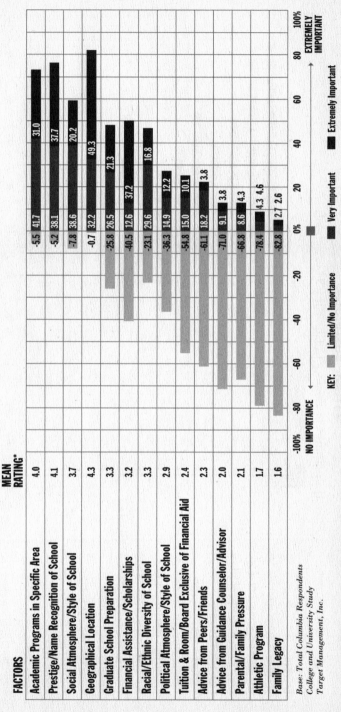

Columbia University

(Importance of Factors in Choosing This School)

FACTORS	MEAN RATING*
Academic Programs in Specific Area	4.0
Prestige/Name Recognition of School	4.1
Social Atmosphere/Style of School	3.7
Geographical Location	4.3
Graduate School Preparation	3.3
Financial Assistance/Scholarships	3.2
Racial/Ethnic Diversity of School	3.3
Political Atmosphere/Style of School	2.9
Tuition & Room/Board Exclusive of Financial Aid	2.4
Advice from Peers/Friends	2.3
Advice from Guidance Counselor/Advisor	2.0
Parental/Family Pressure	2.1
Athletic Program	1.7
Family Legacy	1.6

Chart values (Limited/No Importance | Very Important | Extremely Important):
- Academic Programs in Specific Area: -5.5 | 41.7 | 31.0
- Prestige/Name Recognition of School: -5.2 | 38.1 | 37.7
- Social Atmosphere/Style of School: -7.8 | 38.6 | 20.2
- Geographical Location: -0.7 | 32.2 | 49.3
- Graduate School Preparation: -25.8 | 26.5 | 21.3
- Financial Assistance/Scholarships: -40.5 | 12.6 | 37.2
- Racial/Ethnic Diversity of School: -23.1 | 29.6 | 16.8
- Political Atmosphere/Style of School: -36.3 | 14.9 | 12.2
- Tuition & Room/Board Exclusive of Financial Aid: -54.8 | 15.0 | 10.1
- Advice from Peers/Friends: -61.1 | 18.2 | 3.8
- Advice from Guidance Counselor/Advisor: -71.0 | 9.1 | 3.8
- Parental/Family Pressure: -66.8 | 8.6 | 4.3
- Athletic Program: -78.4 | 4.3 | 4.6
- Family Legacy: -82.8 | 2.7 | 2.6

-100% -80 -60 -40 -20 0% 20 40 60 80 100%
NO IMPORTANCE → EXTREMELY IMPORTANT

KEY: ■ Limited/No Importance   ■ Very Important   ■ Extremely Important

Base: Total Columbia Respondents
College and University Study
Target Management, Inc.

*Ratings scale: 1= Of no importance, 2= Of limited importance, 3= Somewhat important, 4= Very important, 5= Extremely important

Cornell University

(Importance of Factors in Choosing This School)

FACTORS	MEAN RATING*	Limited/No Importance	Very Important	Extremely Important
Academic Programs in Specific Area	4.4	-2.3	31.9	53.3
Prestige/Name Recognition of School	4.2	-2.2	40.3	42.4
Social Atmosphere/Style of School	3.4	-19.9	37.2	13.4
Geographical Location	3.2	-20.4	32.4	6.0
Graduate School Preparation	3.6	-16.4	25.0	28.7
Financial Assistance/Scholarships	2.9	-40.2	17.2	21.4
Racial/Ethnic Diversity of School	2.4	-52.9	11.8	3.3
Political Atmosphere/Style of School	2.3	-59.8	6.1	1.4
Tuition & Room/Board Exclusive of Financial Aid	2.6	-44.6	18.6	7.9
Advice from Peers/Friends	2.6	-45.9	14.8	4.3
Advice from Guidance Counselor/Advisor	2.3	-55.2	15.3	1.0
Parental/Family Pressure	2.2	-61.6	10.0	5.9
Athletic Program	1.9	-74.4	3.5	4.4
Family Legacy	1.4	-88.8	4.4	1.0

-100% -80 -60 -40 -20 0% 20 40 60 80 100%

NO IMPORTANCE ←→ IMPORTANT

KEY: ■ Limited/No Importance ■ Very Important ■ Extremely Important

Base: Total Cornell Respondents
College and University Study
Target Management, Inc.

*Ratings scale: 1= Of no importance, 2= Of limited importance, 3= Somewhat important, 4= Very important, 5= Extremely important

Dartmouth College

(Importance of Factors in Choosing This School)

FACTORS	MEAN RATING*	Limited/No Importance	Very Important	Extremely Important
Academic Programs in Specific Area	3.5	-20.2	36.1	19.6
Prestige/Name Recognition of School	4.0	-5.2	47.2	29.5
Social Atmosphere/Style of School	3.6	-11.9	34.5	22.3
Geographical Location	3.3	-15.3	36.6	7.5
Graduate School Preparation	3.1	-29.9	25.0	15.1
Financial Assistance/Scholarships	2.8	-46.7	12.9	26.2
Racial/Ethnic Diversity of School	2.3	-49.3	8.7	1.8
Political Atmosphere/Style of School	2.5	-55.4	11.8	2.2
Tuition & Room/Board Exclusive of Financial Aid	2.1	-64.4	10.5	5.9
Advice from Peers/Friends	2.4	-55.8	13.5	1.5
Advice from Guidance Counselor/Advisor	2.3	-56.9	11.2	3.5
Parental/Family Pressure	2.1	-65.9	6.5	4.9
Athletic Program	1.9	-72.2	5.5	5.8
Family Legacy	1.3	-89.2	3.0	1.9

-100% NO IMPORTANCE   -80   -60   -40   -20   0%   20   40   60   80   100% EXTREMELY IMPORTANT

KEY: Limited/No Importance   Very Important   Extremely Important

Base: *Total Dartmouth Respondents*
College and University Study
Target Management, Inc.

*Ratings scale: 1= Of no importance, 2= Of limited importance, 3= Somewhat important, 4= Very important, 5= Extremely important

Duke University

(Importance of Factors in Choosing This School)

FACTORS	MEAN RATING*	Limited/No Importance	Very Important	Extremely Important
Academic Programs in Specific Area	4.0	-9.1	35.2	35.1
Prestige/Name Recognition of School	4.2	-1.4	41.4	39.0
Social Atmosphere/Style of School	3.8	-9.7	39.9	24.3
Geographical Location	3.4	-14.0	29.0	14.7
Graduate School Preparation	3.4	-21.6	30.4	20.3
Financial Assistance/Scholarships	3.0	-43.7	13.8	29.5
Racial/Ethnic Diversity of School	2.6	-39.0	16.4	2.3
Political Atmosphere/Style of School	2.7	-40.7	13.8	3.2
Tuition & Room/Board Exclusive of Financial Aid	2.4	-55.9	14.6	8.0
Advice from Peers/Friends	2.4	-49.4	13.0	1.0
Advice from Guidance Counselor/Advisor	2.3	-57.0	15.2	1.0
Parental/Family Pressure	2.1	-65.7	8.8	4.7
Athletic Program	2.6	-48.5	16.3	10.2
Family Legacy	1.5	-86.4	3.9	2.3

Scale: -100% NO IMPORTANCE ← → 100% EXTREMELY IMPORTANT

KEY: Limited/No Importance — Very Important — Extremely Important

Base: Total Duke Respondents
College and University Study
Target Management, Inc.

*Ratings scale: 1= Of no importance, 2= Of limited importance, 3= Somewhat important, 4= Very important, 5= Extremely important

Georgetown University

(Importance of Factors in Choosing This School)

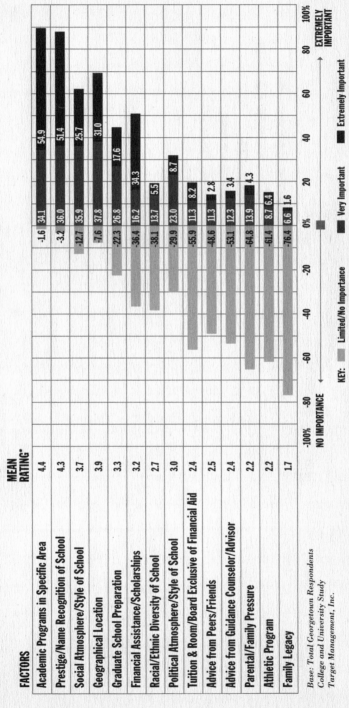

FACTORS	MEAN RATING*
Academic Programs in Specific Area	4.4
Prestige/Name Recognition of School	4.3
Social Atmosphere/Style of School	3.7
Geographical Location	3.9
Graduate School Preparation	3.3
Financial Assistance/Scholarships	3.2
Racial/Ethnic Diversity of School	2.7
Political Atmosphere/Style of School	3.0
Tuition & Room/Board Exclusive of Financial Aid	2.4
Advice from Peers/Friends	2.5
Advice from Guidance Counselor/Advisor	2.4
Parental/Family Pressure	2.2
Athletic Program	2.2
Family Legacy	1.7

KEY: ▨ Limited/No Importance ▪ Very Important ▪ Extremely Important

Base: Total Georgetown Respondents
College and University Study
Target Management, Inc.

*Ratings scale: 1= Of no importance, 2= Of limited importance, 3= Somewhat important, 4= Very important, 5= Extremely important

Harvard University

(Importance of Factors in Choosing This School)

FACTORS	MEAN RATING*	Limited/No Importance	Very Important	Extremely Important
Academic Programs in Specific Area	3.8	-14.5	35.3	32.0
Prestige/Name Recognition of School	4.2	-4.6	41.0	41.6
Social Atmosphere/Style of School	3.1	-29.9	28.0	10.5
Geographical Location	3.4	-22.5	32.4	18.3
Graduate School Preparation	3.2	-33.6	24.8	19.1
Financial Assistance/Scholarships	2.8	-48.8	15.0	23.8
Racial/Ethnic Diversity of School	2.7	-43.4	18.5	9.0
Political Atmosphere/Style of School	2.5	-51.7	14.2	4.7
Tuition & Room/Board Exclusive of Financial Aid	2.0	-69.6	8.9	4.0
Advice from Peers/Friends	2.2	-59.6	10.4	2.9
Advice from Guidance Counselor/Advisor	2.1	-65.5	8.6	3.6
Parental/Family Pressure	2.4	-60.8	14.4	8.6
Athletic Program	1.6	-81.4	3.7	3.3
Family Legacy	1.5	-87.0	2.8	4.4

Chart axis: -100% NO IMPORTANCE — -80 — -60 — -40 — -20 — 0% — 20 — 40 — 60 — 80 — 100% EXTREMELY IMPORTANT

KEY: ▮ Limited/No Importance   ▮ Very Important   ▮ Extremely Important

Base: Total Harvard Respondents
College and University Study
Target Management, Inc.

*Ratings scale: 1= Of no importance, 2= Of limited importance, 3= Somewhat important, 4= Very important, 5= Extremely important

Johns Hopkins University

(Importance of Factors in Choosing This School)

FACTORS	MEAN RATING*	Limited/No Importance	Very Important	Extremely Important
Academic Programs in Specific Area	4.4	-1.3	33.1	56.2
Prestige/Name Recognition of School	4.3	-2.4	33.3	50.7
Social Atmosphere/Style of School	3.2	-19.5	27.1	6.4
Geographical Location	3.1	-24.9	24.4	11.4
Graduate School Preparation	3.8	-16.9	30.1	35.4
Financial Assistance/Scholarships	2.9	-44.2	16.7	19.9
Racial/Ethnic Diversity of School	2.7	-52.3	11.6	5.3
Political Atmosphere/Style of School	2.2	-62.7	8.1	1.0
Tuition & Room/Board Exclusive of Financial Aid	2.4	-55.4	7.5	8.2
Advice from Peers/Friends	2.5	-62.8	7.9	2.4
Advice from Guidance Counselor/Advisor	2.4	-54.5	9.6	7.8
Parental/Family Pressure	2.2	-59.5	14.5	5.1
Athletic Program	2.2	-71.8	11.8	6.1
Family Legacy	1.2	-96.4	0.6	1.0

-100% -80 -60 -40 -20 0% 20 40 60 80 100%

NO IMPORTANCE   EXTREMELY IMPORTANT

KEY: ▮ Limited/No Importance   ▮ Very Important   ▮ Extremely Important

Base: Total Johns Hopkins Respondents
College and University Study
Target Management, Inc.

*Ratings scale: 1= Of no importance, 2= Of limited importance, 3= Somewhat important, 4= Very important, 5= Extremely important

Massachusetts Institute of Technology

(Importance of Factors in Choosing This School)

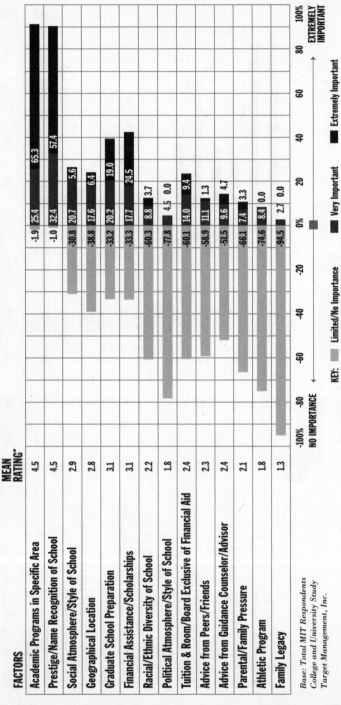

FACTORS	MEAN RATING*
Academic Programs in Specific Area	4.5
Prestige/Name Recognition of School	4.5
Social Atmosphere/Style of School	2.9
Geographical Location	2.8
Graduate School Preparation	3.1
Financial Assistance/Scholarships	3.1
Racial/Ethnic Diversity of School	2.2
Political Atmosphere/Style of School	1.8
Tuition & Room/Board Exclusive of Financial Aid	2.4
Advice from Peers/Friends	2.3
Advice from Guidance Counselor/Advisor	2.4
Parental/Family Pressure	2.1
Athletic Program	1.8
Family Legacy	1.3

KEY: Limited/No Importance   Very Important   Extremely Important

*Base: Total MIT Respondents
College and University Study
Target Management, Inc.*

*Ratings scale: 1= Of no importance, 2= Of limited importance, 3= Somewhat important, 4= Very important, 5= Extremely important

Northwestern University

(Importance of Factors in Choosing This School)

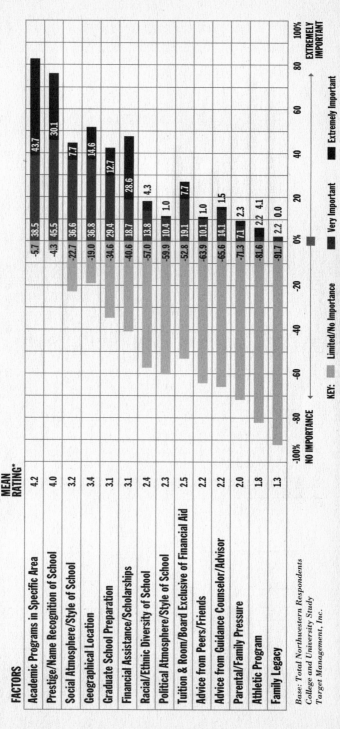

FACTORS	MEAN RATING*	Limited/No Importance	Very Important	Extremely Important
Academic Programs in Specific Area	4.2	-5.7	38.5	43.7
Prestige/Name Recognition of School	4.0	-4.3	45.5	30.1
Social Atmosphere/Style of School	3.2	-22.7	36.6	7.7
Geographical Location	3.4	-19.0	36.8	14.6
Graduate School Preparation	3.1	-34.6	29.4	12.7
Financial Assistance/Scholarships	3.1	-40.6	18.7	28.6
Racial/Ethnic Diversity of School	2.4	-57.0	13.8	4.3
Political Atmosphere/Style of School	2.3	-59.9	10.4	1.0
Tuition & Room/Board Exclusive of Financial Aid	2.5	-52.8	19.1	7.7
Advice from Peers/Friends	2.2	-63.9	10.1	1.0
Advice from Guidance Counselor/Advisor	2.2	-65.6	14.1	1.5
Parental/Family Pressure	2.0	-71.3	7.1	2.3
Athletic Program	1.8	-81.6	2.2	4.1
Family Legacy	1.3	-91.7	2.2	0.0

-100% NO IMPORTANCE   -80   -60   -40   -20   0%   20   40   60   80   100% EXTREMELY IMPORTANT

→ Extremely Important

KEY: ■ Limited/No Importance   ■ Very Important   ■ Extremely Important

Base: Total Northwestern Respondents
College and University Study
Target Management, Inc.

*Ratings scale: 1= Of no importance, 2= Of limited importance, 3= Somewhat important, 4= Very important, 5= Extremely important

Princeton University

(Importance of Factors in Choosing This School)

FACTORS	MEAN RATING*
Academic Programs in Specific Area	3.9
Prestige/Name Recognition of School	4.1
Social Atmosphere/Style of School	3.6
Geographical Location	3.1
Graduate School Preparation	3.1
Financial Assistance/Scholarships	2.9
Racial/Ethnic Diversity of School	2.1
Political Atmosphere/Style of School	2.6
Tuition & Room/Board Exclusive of Financial Aid	2.3
Advice from Peers/Friends	2.5
Advice from Guidance Counselor/Advisor	2.2
Parental/Family Pressure	2.2
Athletic Program	2.5
Family Legacy	1.4

Chart data (Limited/No Importance | Very Important | Extremely Important):

Factor	Limited/No	Very Important	Extremely Important
Academic Programs in Specific Area	-10.6	34.5	34.0
Prestige/Name Recognition of School	-5.7	34.9	39.4
Social Atmosphere/Style of School	-11.1	32.7	20.6
Geographical Location	-30.4	20.7	11.7
Graduate School Preparation	-33.7	26.2	14.4
Financial Assistance/Scholarships	-43.6	21.9	21.3
Racial/Ethnic Diversity of School	-64.5	12.0	0.3
Political Atmosphere/Style of School	-48.7	9.9	2.6
Tuition & Room/Board Exclusive of Financial Aid	-58.4	15.0	6.3
Advice from Peers/Friends	-44.7	12.3	1.4
Advice from Guidance Counselor/Advisor	-61.2	6.9	1.9
Parental/Family Pressure	-65.5	10.7	3.1
Athletic Program	-55.8	14.3	5.4
Family Legacy	-88.5	2.1	1.2

-100% -80 -60 -40 -20 0% 20 40 60 80 100%

NO IMPORTANCE

EXTREMELY IMPORTANT

KEY: ■ Limited/No Importance   ■ Very Important   ■ Extremely Important

Base: Total Princeton Respondents
College and University Study
Target Management, Inc.

*Ratings scale: 1= Of no importance, 2= Of limited importance, 3= Somewhat important, 4= Very important, 5= Extremely important

Stanford University

(Importance of Factors in Choosing This School)

FACTORS	MEAN RATING*	Limited/No Importance	Very Important	Extremely Important
Academic Programs in Specific Area	3.8	-8.7	36.3	26.9
Prestige/Name Recognition of School	4.2	-3.0	46.9	36.4
Social Atmosphere/Style of School	3.8	-9.0	36.8	24.7
Geographical Location	3.5	-16.2	25.4	21.6
Graduate School Preparation	3.3	-21.4	30.7	13.4
Financial Assistance/Scholarships	3.2	-41.7	12.5	31.4
Racial/Ethnic Diversity of School	2.9	-32.4	19.7	8.7
Political Atmosphere/Style of School	2.6	-44.6	13.7	3.2
Tuition & Room/Board Exclusive of Financial Aid	2.4	-57.1	13.1	7.9
Advice from Peers/Friends	2.3	-55.4	8.3	1.7
Advice from Guidance Counselor/Advisor	2.1	-62.2	11.5	3.0
Parental/Family Pressure	2.0	-68.3	5.1	3.0
Athletic Program	2.1	-66.2	9.0	2.5
Family Legacy	1.4	-89.0	2.7	1.0

-100% NO IMPORTANCE -80 -60 -40 -20 0% 20 40 60 80 100% EXTREMELY IMPORTANT

KEY: Limited/No Importance Very Important Extremely Important

Base: Total Stanford Respondents
College and University Study
Target Management, Inc.

*Ratings scale: 1= Of no importance, 2= Of limited importance, 3= Somewhat important, 4= Very important, 5= Extremely important

University of California—Berkeley

(Importance of Factors in Choosing This School)

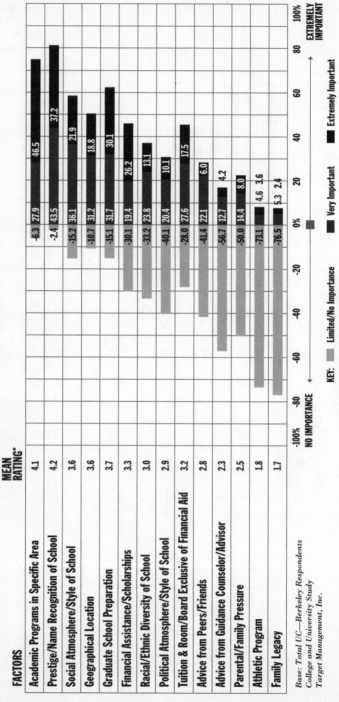

Base: Total UC—Berkeley Respondents
College and University Study
Target Management, Inc.

*Ratings scale: 1= Of no importance, 2= Of limited importance, 3= Somewhat important, 4= Very important, 5= Extremely important

University of Chicago

(Importance of Factors in Choosing This School)

FACTORS	MEAN RATING*										
Academic Programs in Specific Area	4.0	-8.9	29.8	38.6							
Prestige/Name Recognition of School	3.8	-9.8	38.4	28.1							
Social Atmosphere/Style of School	2.9	-32.4	19.5	7.3							
Geographical Location	3.0	-31.0	24.8	12.1							
Graduate School Preparation	3.6	-16.4	28.7	26.0							
Financial Assistance/Scholarships	3.3	-32.4	18.3	32.6							
Racial/Ethnic Diversity of School	2.2	-59.9	14.7	1.3							
Political Atmosphere/Style of School	2.3	-60.6	10.1	3.7							
Tuition & Room/Board Exclusive of Financial Aid	2.2	-62.6	9.0	8.5							
Advice from Peers/Friends	2.1	-65.3	8.2	2.3							
Advice from Guidance Counselor/Advisor	2.2	-66.4	10.9	6.3							
Parental/Family Pressure	1.9	-70.8	6.7	3.9							
Athletic Program	1.7	-76.3	3.6	5.3							
Family Legacy	1.3	-91.5	1.2	1.0							

-100%   -80   -60   -40   -20   0%   20   40   60   80   100%
NO IMPORTANCE   EXTREMELY IMPORTANT

KEY: ■ Limited/No Importance   ■ Very Important   ■ Extremely Important

Base: Total U of Chicago Respondents
College and University Study
Target Management, Inc.

*Ratings scale: 1= Of no importance, 2= Of limited importance, 3= Somewhat important, 4= Very important, 5= Extremely important

University of North Carolina—Chapel Hill

(Importance of Factors in Choosing This School)

FACTORS	MEAN RATING*		
Academic Programs in Specific Area	3.9	-6.3	40.8	28.7
Prestige/Name Recognition of School	3.6	-22.2	38.4	19.5
Social Atmosphere/Style of School	3.8	-9.1	41.8	22.8
Geographical Location	3.5	-25.0	47.7	12.5
Graduate School Preparation	3.1	-26.0	22.3	9.4
Financial Assistance/Scholarships	2.7	-39.7	16.6	9.9
Racial/Ethnic Diversity of School	3.0	-25.9	22.8	3.8
Political Atmosphere/Style of School	3.1	-20.1	26.9	3.3
Tuition & Room/Board Exclusive of Financial Aid	2.6	-41.4	4.2	5.2
Advice from Peers/Friends	2.9	-32.4	21.8	1.1
Advice from Guidance Counselor/Advisor	2.9	-34.2	29.0	0.0
Parental/Family Pressure	2.7	-38.7	10.4	1.0
Athletic Program	3.2	-30.4	29.8	15.5
Family Legacy	2.5	-50.2	19.6	1.0

-100% NO IMPORTANCE   -80   -60   -40   -20   0%   20   40   60   80   100% EXTREMELY IMPORTANT

KEY: Limited/No Importance   Very Important   Extremely Important

Base: Total U of NC—Chapel Hill Respondents
College and University Study
Target Management, Inc.

*Ratings scale: 1= Of no importance, 2= Of limited importance, 3= Somewhat important, 4= Very important, 5= Extremely important

University of Pennsylvania

(Importance of Factors in Choosing This School)

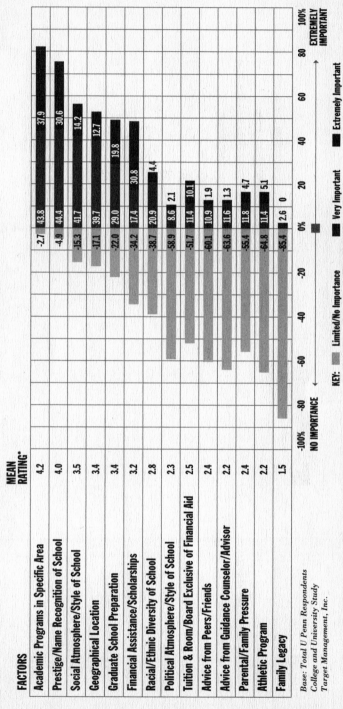

FACTORS	MEAN RATING*
Academic Programs in Specific Area	4.2
Prestige/Name Recognition of School	4.0
Social Atmosphere/Style of School	3.5
Geographical Location	3.4
Graduate School Preparation	3.4
Financial Assistance/Scholarships	3.2
Racial/Ethnic Diversity of School	2.8
Political Atmosphere/Style of School	2.3
Tuition & Room/Board Exclusive of Financial Aid	2.5
Advice from Peers/Friends	2.4
Advice from Guidance Counselor/Advisor	2.2
Parental/Family Pressure	2.4
Athletic Program	2.2
Family Legacy	1.5

KEY: Limited/No Importance   Very Important   Extremely Important

NO IMPORTANCE / EXTREMELY IMPORTANT

*Ratings scale: 1= Of no importance, 2= Of limited importance, 3= Somewhat important, 4= Very important, 5= Extremely important

Base: Total U Penn Respondents
College and University Study
Target Management, Inc.

University of Wisconsin—Madison

(Importance of Factors in Choosing This School)

FACTORS	MEAN RATING*			
Academic Programs in Specific Area	3.9	-10.0	39.2	31.8
Prestige/Name Recognition of School	3.6	-8.7	35.4	18.7
Social Atmosphere/Style of School	4.1	-5.6	41.1	35.3
Geographical Location	3.5	-15.3	34.7	18.2
Graduate School Preparation	3.0	-34.4	23.8	12.3
Financial Assistance/Scholarships	2.5	-51.8	11.9	13.3
Racial/Ethnic Diversity of School	2.9	-35.7	19.4	7.4
Political Atmosphere/Style of School	3.4	-25.4	27.2	19.5
Tuition & Room/Board Exclusive of Financial Aid	3.1	-32.8	25.7	16.6
Advice from Peers/Friends	2.5	-45.7	17.4	1.9
Advice from Guidance Counselor/Advisor	2.3	-59.6	8.8	4.7
Parental/Family Pressure	1.9	-72.1	7.4	2.1
Athletic Program	2.1	-66.1	11.0	2.8
Family Legacy	1.8	-76.9	7.3	3.8

-100%   -80   -60   -40   -20   0%   20   40   60   80   100%

NO IMPORTANCE   EXTREMELY IMPORTANT

KEY: ■ Limited/No Importance   ■ Very Important   ■ Extremely Important

*Base: Total U of W—Madison Respondents
College and University Study
Target Management, Inc.*

*Ratings scale: 1= Of no importance, 2= Of limited importance, 3= Somewhat important, 4= Very important, 5= Extremely important

Wesleyan University

(Importance of Factors in Choosing This School)

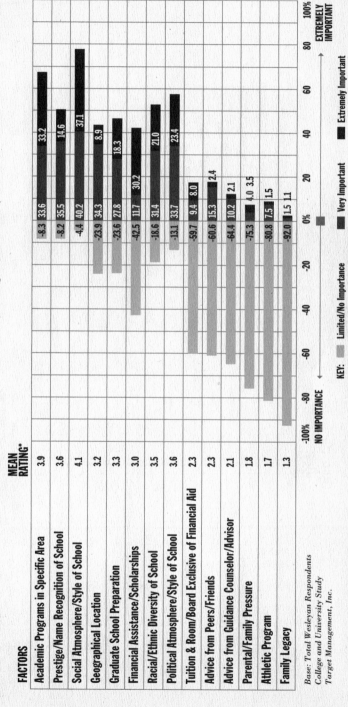

FACTORS	MEAN RATING*	Limited/No Importance	Very Important	Extremely Important
Academic Programs in Specific Area	3.9	-8.3	33.6	33.2
Prestige/Name Recognition of School	3.6	-8.2	35.5	14.6
Social Atmosphere/Style of School	4.1	-4.4	40.2	37.1
Geographical Location	3.2	-23.9	34.3	8.9
Graduate School Preparation	3.3	-23.6	27.8	18.3
Financial Assistance/Scholarships	3.0	-42.5	11.7	30.2
Racial/Ethnic Diversity of School	3.5	-18.6	31.4	21.0
Political Atmosphere/Style of School	3.6	-13.1	33.7	23.4
Tuition & Room/Board Exclusive of Financial Aid	2.3	-59.7	9.4	8.0
Advice from Peers/Friends	2.3	-60.6	15.3	2.4
Advice from Guidance Counselor/Advisor	2.1	-64.4	10.2	2.1
Parental/Family Pressure	1.8	-75.3	4.0	3.5
Athletic Program	1.7	-80.8	7.5	1.5
Family Legacy	1.3	-92.0	1.5	1.1

-100%   -80   -60   -40   -20   0%   20   40   60   80   100%

NO IMPORTANCE ← → EXTREMELY IMPORTANT

KEY: Limited/No Importance   Very Important   Extremely Important

Base: Total Wesleyan Respondents
College and University Study
Target Management, Inc.

*Ratings scale: 1= Of no importance, 2= Of limited importance, 3= Somewhat important, 4= Very important, 5= Extremely important

Williams College

(Importance of Factors in Choosing This School)

FACTORS	MEAN RATING*	Limited/No Importance	Very Important	Extremely Important
Academic Programs in Specific Area	3.7	-13.2	29.9	26.9
Prestige/Name Recognition of School	3.8	-10.0	32.3	30.1
Social Atmosphere/Style of School	3.7	-8.4	38.0	23.3
Geographical Location	3.4	-12.8	33.4	12.0
Graduate School Preparation	3.4	-25.6	28.5	20.1
Financial Assistance/Scholarships	2.6	-55.6	11.8	22.9
Racial/Ethnic Diversity of School	2.8	-40.5	20.5	4.5
Political Atmosphere/Style of School	2.6	-46.1	12.7	5.4
Tuition & Room/Board Exclusive of Financial Aid	2.1	-67.0	8.3	4.7
Advice from Peers/Friends	2.4	-48.8	13.4	2.6
Advice from Guidance Counselor/Advisor	2.4	-52.4	17.6	3.0
Parental/Family Pressure	1.9	-73.9	7.5	2.6
Athletic Program	2.5	-53.7	16.4	11.2
Family Legacy	1.3	-89.1	2.7	2.2

-100%   -80   -60   -40   -20   0%   20   40   60   80   100%

NO IMPORTANCE   EXTREMELY IMPORTANT

KEY: ■ Limited/No Importance   ■ Very Important   ■ Extremely Important

*Ratings scale: 1= Of no importance, 2= Of limited importance, 3= Somewhat important, 4= Very important, 5= Extremely important

Base: Total Williams Respondents
College and University Study
Target Management, Inc.

Yale University

(Importance of Factors in Choosing This School)

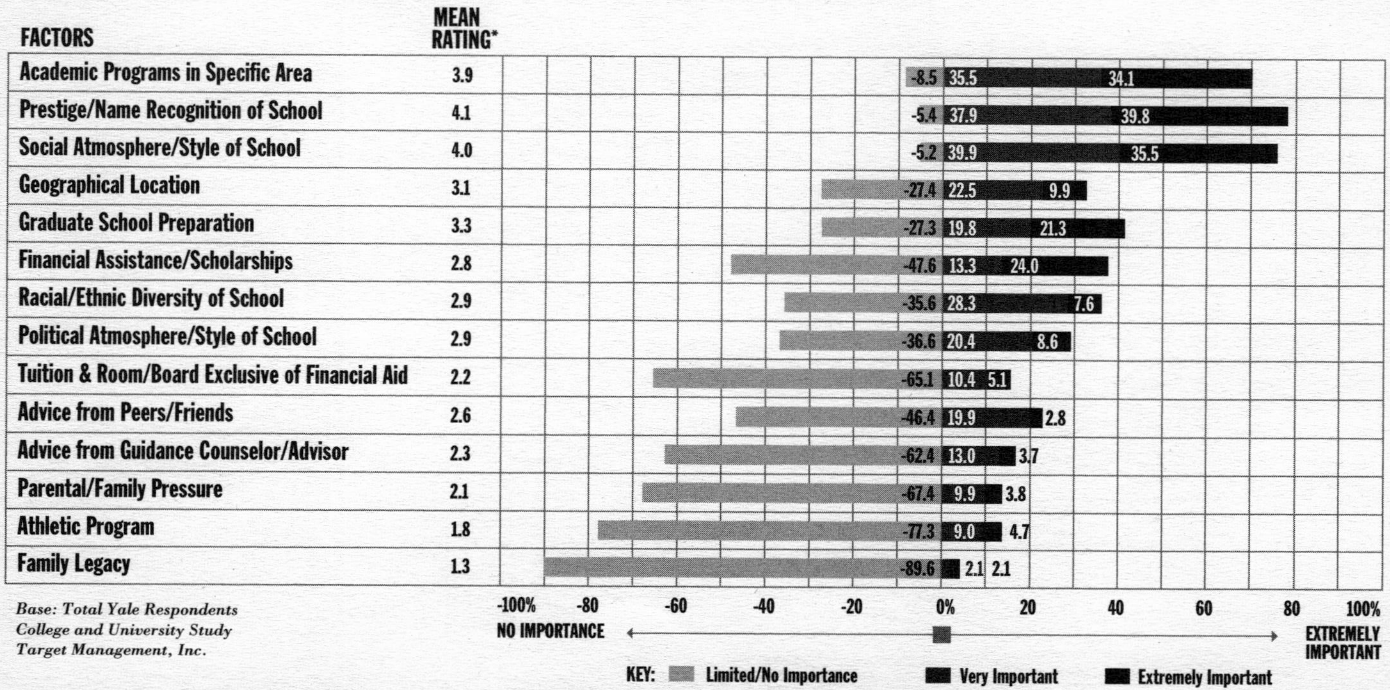
FACTORS
MEAN RATING*
Academic Programs in Specific Area 3.9 -8.5 35.5 34.1
Prestige/Name Recognition of School 4.1 -5.4 37.9 39.8
Social Atmosphere/Style of School 4.0 -5.2 39.9 35.5
Geographical Location 3.1 -27.4 22.5 9.9
Graduate School Preparation 3.3 -27.3 19.8 21.3
Financial Assistance/Scholarships 2.8 -47.6 13.3 24.0
Racial/Ethnic Diversity of School 2.9 -35.6 28.3 7.6
Political Atmosphere/Style of School 2.9 -36.6 20.4 8.6
Tuition & Room/Board Exclusive of Financial Aid 2.2 -65.1 10.4 5.1
Advice from Peers/Friends 2.6 -46.4 19.9 2.8
Advice from Guidance Counselor/Advisor 2.3 -62.4 13.0 3.7
Parental/Family Pressure 2.1 -67.4 9.9 3.8
Athletic Program 1.8 -77.3 9.0 4.7
Family Legacy 1.3 -89.6 2.1 2.1
-100% -80 -60 -40 -20 0% 20 40 60 80 100%
NO IMPORTANCE
EXTREMELY IMPORTANT
KEY: Limited/No Importance
Very Important
Extremely Important

Base: Total Yale Respondents
College and University Study
Target Management, Inc.

*Ratings scale: 1= Of no importance, 2= Of limited importance, 3= Somewhat important, 4= Very important, 5= Extremely important

BIBLIOGRAPHY]

American Association of University Women. *Shortchanging Girls, Shortchanging America*. Washington, D.C.: AAUW, 1991.

Astin, Alexander. *What Matters in College*. San Francisco: Jossey-Bass, 1993.

Astin, A. W., Korn, W. S., Sax, L. J., Mahoney, K. M. *The American Freshman: National Norms for Fall 1995*. Los Angeles: Higher Education Research Institute, UCLA, 1995.

Beattie, Ann. *Picturing Will*. New York: Random House, Vintage Books, 1991.

Boyer, Ernest. *Campus Life: In Search of Community*. Princeton: Princeton University Press, 1990.

Bronowski, Jacob. *The Ascent of Man*. Boston: Little, Brown, 1974.

The Chronicle of Higher Education, August 23, 1996, from the September 1996 issue of *Interview*.

Edelman, Marian Wright. *The Measure of Our Success: A Letter to My Children and Yours*. New York: HarperCollins Publishers, 1993.

Ellison, Ralph. *The Invisible Man*. New York: Random House, 1952.

Fetter, Jean. *Questions and Admissions*. Stanford, Calif.: Stanford University Press, 1995.

Frank, Robert H., and Cook, Philip J. *The Winner Take All Society.* New York: Free Press, 1995.

Freedman, James O. *Idealism and Liberal Education.* Ann Arbor: University of Michigan Press, 1996.

Gilligan, Carol. *In a Different Voice.* Cambridge, MA: Harvard University Press, 1982.

Herrnstein, Richard, and Murray, Charles. *The Bell Curve.* New York: Free Press, 1996.

McCord, David. *What Cheer.* New York: Coward-McCann, 1945.

Massachusetts Institute of Technology. *The Tech,* November 19, 1996, Vol. 116, No. 60.

Navarrette, Ruben, Jr. *A Darker Shade of Crimson.* New York: Bantam Books, 1993.

Peck, M. Scott. *The Road Less Traveled.* New York: Simon and Schuster, 1978.

Pipher, Mary. *Reviving Ophelia.* New York: Random House, 1994.

Updike, John. *In the Beauty of the Lilies.* New York: Alfred A. Knopf, 1996.